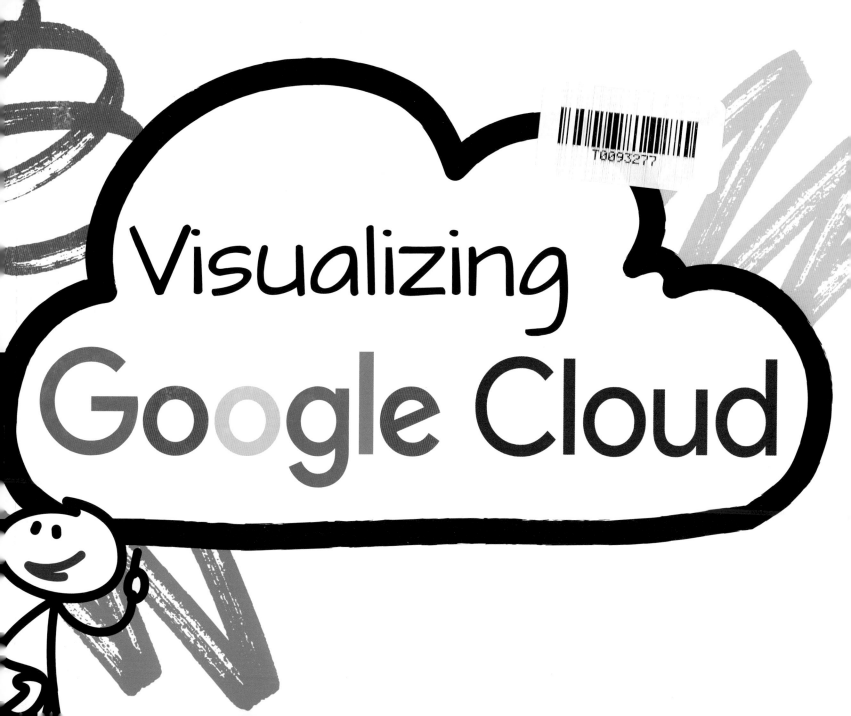

Priyanka Vergadia

Visualizing Google Cloud

101 Illustrated References for Cloud Engineers & Architects

WILEY

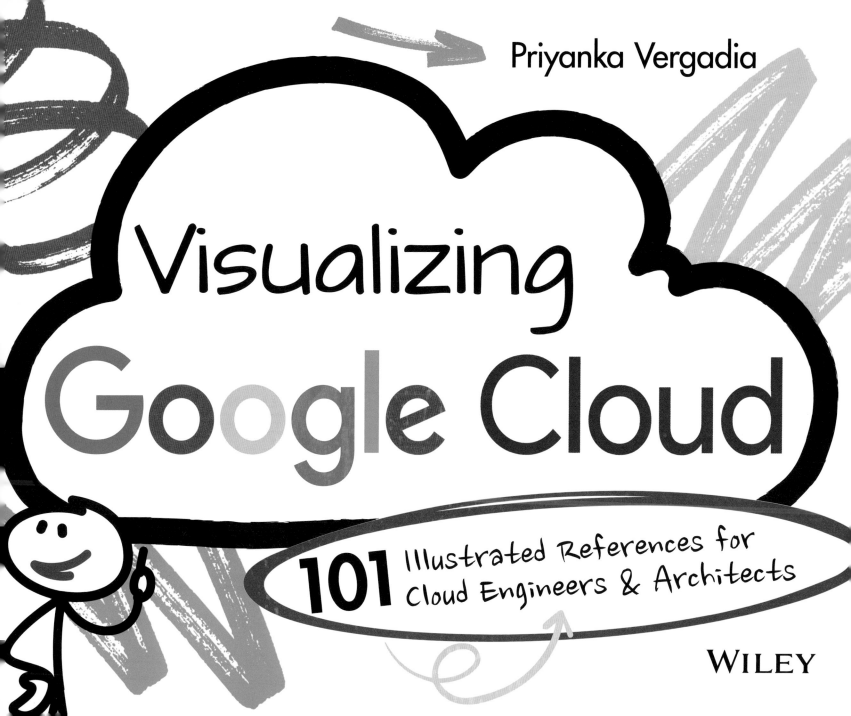

Published by John Wiley & Sons, Inc., Hoboken, New Jersey.
Published simultaneously in Canada.

ISBN: 978-1-119-81632-4
ISBN: 978-1-119-81637-9 (ebk)
ISBN: 978-1-119-81633-1 (ebk)

For general information on our other products and services or for technical support, please contact our Customer Care Department within the United States at (800) 762-2974, outside the United States at (317) 572-3993 or fax (317) 572-4002.

Wiley also publishes its books in a variety of electronic formats. Some content that appears in print may not be available in electronic formats. For more information about Wiley products, visit our web site at www.wiley.com.

Library of Congress Control Number: 2022931550

Cover images: Stick Figures © Google; Cloud © Getty Images/LEOcrafts; Arrows © Adobe Stock/ vectortwins and Adobe Stock/ alex83m
Cover design: Wiley

SKY10035022_063022

For Shashank and Simba, the light of my life
Mom and Dad, who always believed in me
and
Google Cloud users everywhere

ACKNOWLEDGMENTS

This is my first book. I was excited to create something unique, but that goal required a lot of people to put a lot of trust in me and my wacky idea of illustrated explanations for technically complex Google Cloud concepts.

Greg Wilson, Reto Meier, Colt McAnlis, and the entire Google Cloud team believed in the idea and encouraged me to pursue it, and I am very grateful to them for that.

I also want to acknowledge Don Ulinski and Sean Carey from HD Interactive, without whom the illustrations in this book would not have been the same, as well as Jack Wilber, who tirelessly provided edits and recommendations for most of the chapters.

Further, this book would not have been possible without my technical reviewers, including Eric Brewer, who made themselves available to read early versions and those who reviewed the entire book and individual chapters.

Chapter 1: Brian Dorsey, Chelsie Czop (Peterson), Praveen Rajasekar, Steren Giannini, Matt Larkin, Vinod Ramachandran, Ken Drachnik, Kyle Meggs, Jason Polites, Jaisen Mathai, and Drew Bradstock.

Chapter 2: Geoffrey Noer, Ash Ahluwalia, Tad Hunt, Rahul Venkatraj, Lindsay Majane, Sean Derrington, Abhishek Lal, and Ajitesh Abhishek.

Chapter 3: Gabe Weiss, Vaibhav Govil, Minh Nguyen, Ron Pantofaro, Gopal Ashok, Anita Kibunguchy-Grant, and Michael Crutcher.

Chapter 4: Kir Titievsky, Zoltan Arato, Shan Kulandaivel, Susheel Kaushik, Soleil Kelley, Chaitanya (Chai) Pydimukkala, George Verghese, Filip Knapik, Etai Margolin, and Leigha Jarett.

Chapter 5: Richard Seroter, Wade Holmes, Arun Ananthampalayam, Nikhil Kaul, Kris Braun, Shikha Chetal, Lital Levy, David Feuer, and John Day.

Chapter 6: Ryan Przybyl, Adam Michelson, Kerry Takenaka, Tony Sarathchandra, Karthik Balakrishnan, Babi Seal, Tracy Jiang, Irene Abezgauz, Gautam Kulkarni, and Abhijeet Kalyan.

Chapter 7: Sara Robinson, Polong Lin, Karl Weinmeister, Sarah Weldon, Anu Srivastava, Logan Vadivelu, Marc Cohen, Shana Matthews, Shantanu Misra, Josh Porter, Calum Barnes, Lewis Liu, Zack Akil, Lee Boonstra, Arjun Rattan, and Mallika Iyer.

Chapter 8: Robert Sadowski, Max Saltonstall, Scott Ellis, and Jordanna Chord.

I also extend my deepest gratitude to:

- The entire Wiley team, who embraced the challenge of publishing this wacky idea as a book. I remember having my first conversation with Jim Minatel; my own excitement grew when I saw that he was immediately excited about this idea. Then while working further on the editorial process, Pete Gaughan and Kelly Talbot encouraged me constantly to stay on track with a solid deadline plan, without which the entire effort would not be possible. Pete even mentioned that this book is about to become a reference for other authors who want to share their technical thoughts in a visual format, and that really gave me a boost when I needed it!

- Shashank, my husband, for his constant support while I was working on this project over many weekends and evenings.

- Mom and Dad, for their lifelong support and for being understanding when I could not return their calls because I was immersed in the book.

- And. . .YOU for placing your trust in me and providing me with feedback, which ultimately made me pursue the idea of turning these sketches into a reference guide.

Thank you for everything!

—Priyanka Vergadia

ABOUT THE AUTHOR

Priyanka Vergadia has been working with cloud technology for a decade. She holds an M.S. in computer science from the University of Pennsylvania and a B.S. in electronics from Shri Govindram Seksaria Institute of Technology and Science, India. Now a Developer Advocate at Google Cloud, Priyanka works with companies and cloud architects to solve their most pressing business challenges using cloud computing. Her work has helped many cloud enthusiasts get started with the cloud, learn the fundamentals, and achieve cloud certifications.

Priyanka is passionate about making cloud computing approachable and easier to understand by combining her passions for art and technology.

An expert technical visual storyteller, Priyanka has narrated thousands of technical stories that are fun to follow and easy to understand, and that make complex concepts a breeze to grasp. Some of her most popular work includes Build with Google Cloud, Architecting with Google Cloud, google/3g7xAC9, Deconstructing Chatbots, GCP Drawing Board, Cloud Bytes, GCP Comics, Get Cooking in Cloud. You can find all her work on the Google Cloud YouTube channel, her own YouTube channel The Cloud Girl, google/TheCloudGirl, her website thecloudgirl.dev, and her blog posts on Medium. You might also find her speaking at public and private developer events around the world.

CONTENTS

INTRODUCTION

Shortly after I started creating and sharing visual explanations of Google Cloud concepts in 2020, I began receiving overwhelmingly positive feedback. That feedback led me to think about pulling the visual explanations together into a reference guide. So here it is!

This book provides an easy-to-follow visual walkthrough of every important part of Google Cloud, from table stakes — compute, storage, database, security, and networking — to advanced concepts such as data analytics, data science, machine learning, and AI.

Most humans are visual learners; I am definitely one of them. I think it is safe to assume that you are too, since you picked up this book. So, even though it might sound cliché, I am a big believer that a picture is worth (more than) a thousand words. With that in mind, this book is my attempt at making Google Cloud technical concepts fun and interesting. This book covers the essentials of Google Cloud from end to end, with a visual explanation of each concept, how it works, and how you can apply it in your business use-case.

Who is this book for? Google Cloud enthusiasts! It is for anyone who is planning a cloud migration, new cloud deployment, preparing for cloud certification, and for anyone who is looking to make the most of Google Cloud. If you are cloud solutions architects, IT decision-makers, data and machine learning engineers you will find this book a good starting point. In short, this book is for you!

I have read thousands of pages of Google Cloud documentation and experimented with virtually every Google Cloud product and distilled that experience down to this book of accessible, bite-sized visuals. I hope this book helps you on your Google Cloud journey by making it both easier and more fun. Are you ready? Let's go!

Reader Support for This Book

How to Contact the Publisher

If you believe you've found a mistake in this book, please bring it to our attention. At John Wiley & Sons, we understand how important it is to provide our customers with accurate content, but even with our best efforts an error may occur.

In order to submit your possible errata, please email it to our Customer Service Team at wileysupport@wiley.com with the subject line "Possible Book Errata Submission."

CHAPTER ONE

Infrastructure

Cloud computing is the on-demand availability of computing resources—including servers, storage, databases, networking, software, analytics, and intelligence—over the Internet. It eliminates the need for enterprises to procure, configure, or manage these resources themselves, while enabling them to pay only for what they use. The benefits of cloud computing include:

- Flexibility: You can access cloud resources from anywhere and scale services up or down as needed.

- Efficiency: You can develop new applications and rapidly get them into production, without worrying about the underlying infrastructure.

- Strategic value: When you choose a cloud provider that stays on top of the latest innovations and offers them as services, it opens opportunities for you to seize competitive advantages and higher returns on investment.

- Security: The depth and breadth of the security mechanisms provided by cloud providers offer stronger security than many enterprise data centers. Plus, cloud providers also have top security experts working on their offerings.

- Cost-effectiveness: You only pay for the computing resources you use. Because you don't need to overbuild data center capacity to handle unexpected spikes in demand or sudden surges in business growth, you can deploy resources and IT staff on more strategic initiatives.

In this first chapter, you will learn about cloud computing models and dive into the various compute options that Google Cloud offers. The following chapters provide a closer look at specific cloud resources and topics, including storage, databases, data analytics, networking, and more.

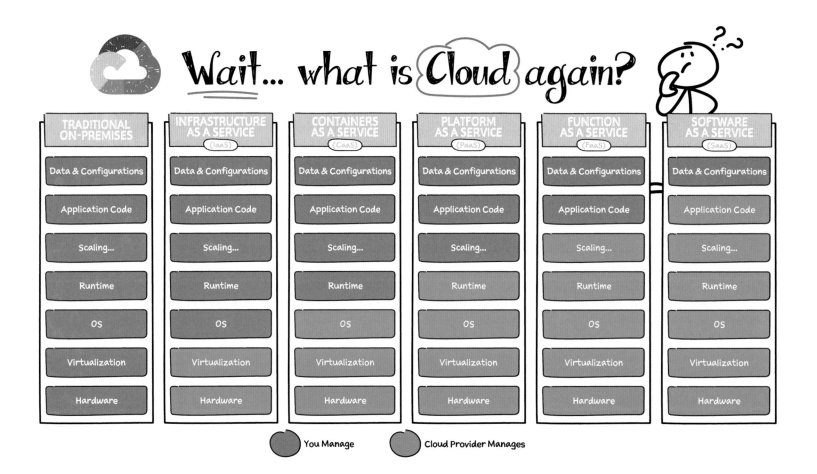

Introduction

To understand the cloud and the different models you can choose from, let's map it with an everyday analogy of housing:

- **On-Premises** — If you decide to make your house from scratch, you do everything yourself: source the raw materials, tools, put them together, and run to the store every time you need anything. That is very close to running your application on-premises, where you own everything from the hardware to your applications and scaling.

- **Infrastructure as a Service** — Now, if you are busy you consider hiring a contractor to build a custom house. You tell them how you want the house to look and how many rooms you want. They take the instructions and make you a house. IaaS is the same for your applications; you rent the hardware to run your application on, but you are responsible for managing the OS, runtime, scale, and the data. Example: GCE.

- **Containers as a Service** — If you know that buying is just too much work due to the maintenance it comes with, then you decide to rent a house. The basic utilities are included, but you bring your own furniture and make the space yours. Containers are the same where you bring a containerized application so that you don't have to worry about the underlying operating system but you still have control over scale and runtime. Example: GKE.

- **Platform as a Service** — If you just want to enjoy the space without having to even worry about furnishing it, then you rent a furnished house. That is what PaaS is for; you can bring your own code and deploy it and leave the scale to the cloud provider. Example: App Engine & Cloud Run.

- **Function as a Service** — If you just need a small dedicated space in which to work that is away from your home, you rent a desk in a workspace. That is close to what FaaS offers; you deploy a piece of code or a function that performs a specific task, and every time a function executes, the cloud provider adds scale if needed. Example: Cloud Functions.

- **Software as a Service** — Now, you move into the house (rented or purchased), but you pay for upkeep such as cleaning or lawn care. SaaS is the same; you pay for the service, you are responsible for your data, but everything else is taken care of by the provider. Example: Google Drive.

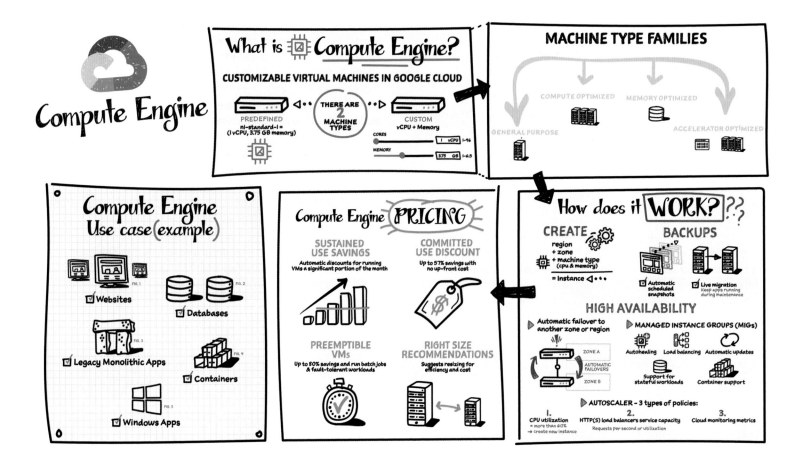

Compute Engine

What is 🖥 Compute Engine?

CUSTOMIZABLE VIRTUAL MACHINES IN GOOGLE CLOUD

THERE ARE **2** MACHINE TYPES

PREDEFINED
n1-standard-1 =
(1 vCPU, 3.75 GB memory)

CUSTOM
vCPU + Memory

CORES — 1 vCPU 1–16

MEMORY — 3.75 GB 1–6.5

MACHINE TYPE FAMILIES

COMPUTE OPTIMIZED

MEMORY OPTIMIZED

GENERAL PURPOSE

ACCELERATOR OPTIMIZED

Compute Engine Use case (example)

☑ Websites *FIG. 1*

☑ Databases *FIG. 2*

☑ Legacy Monolithic Apps *FIG. 3*

☑ Containers *FIG. 4*

☑ Windows Apps *FIG. 5*

Compute Engine PRICING

SUSTAINED USE SAVINGS
Automatic discounts for running VMs a significant portion of the month

COMMITTED USE DISCOUNT
Up to 57% savings with no up-front cost

PREEMPTIBLE VMs
Up to 80% savings and run batch jobs & fault-tolerant workloads

RIGHT SIZE RECOMMENDATIONS
Suggests resizing for efficiency and cost

How does it WORK? ??

CREATE
region + zone + machine type (cpu & memory) = instance

BACKUPS
☑ Automatic scheduled snapshots
☑ Live migration — Keep apps running during maintenance

HIGH AVAILABILITY

▷ Automatic failover to another zone or region
ZONE A
AUTOMATIC FAILOVERS
ZONE B

▷ MANAGED INSTANCE GROUPS (MIGs)
Autohealing   Load balancing   Automatic updates
Support for stateful workloads   Container support

▷ AUTOSCALER – 3 types of policies:
1. CPU utilization = more than 60% → create new instance
2. HTTP(S) load balancers service capacity — Requests per second or utilization
3. Cloud monitoring metrics

What Is Compute Engine?

Compute Engine is a customizable compute service that lets you create and run virtual machines on Google's infrastructure. You can create a virtual machine (VM) that fits your needs. Predefined machine types are prebuilt and ready-to-go configurations of VMs with specific amounts of vCPU and memory to start running apps quickly. With Custom Machine Types, you can create virtual machines with the optimal amount of CPU and memory for your workloads. This allows you to tailor your infrastructure to your workload. If requirements change, using the stop/start feature you can move your workload to a smaller or larger Custom Machine Type instance, or to a predefined configuration.

Machine Types

In Compute Engine, machine types are grouped and curated by families for different workloads. You can choose from general-purpose, memory-optimized, compute-optimized, and accelerator-optimized families.

- **General-purpose** machines are used for day-to-day computing at a lower cost and for balanced price/performance across a wide range of VM shapes. The use cases that best fit here are web serving, app serving, back office applications, databases, cache, media-streaming, microservices, virtual desktops, and development environments.

- **Memory-optimized** machines are recommended for ultra high-memory workloads such as in-memory analytics and large in-memory databases such as SAP HANA.

- **Compute-optimized** machines are recommended for ultra high-performance workloads such as High Performance Computing (HPC), Electronic Design Automation (EDA), gaming, video transcoding, and single-threaded applications.

- **Accelerator-optimized** machines are optimized for high-performance computing workloads such as machine learning (ML), massive parallelized computations, and High Performance Computing (HPC).

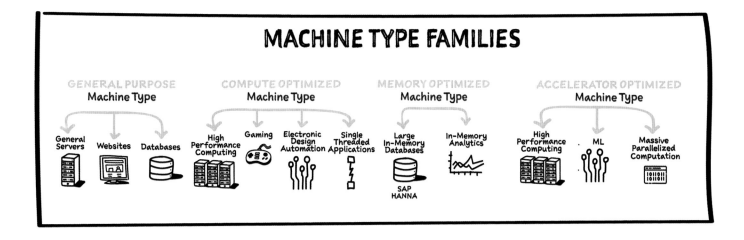

How Does It Work?

You can create a VM instance using a boot disk image, a boot disk snapshot, or a container image. The image can be a public operating system (OS) image or a custom one. Depending on where your users are, you can define the zone you want the virtual machine to be created in. By default all traffic from the Internet is blocked by the firewall, and you can enable the HTTP(s) traffic if needed.

Use snapshot schedules (hourly, daily, or weekly) as a best practice to back up your Compute Engine workloads. Compute Engine offers live migration by default to keep your virtual machine instances running even when software or hardware update occurs. Your running instances are migrated to another host in the same zone instead of requiring your VMs to be rebooted.

Availability

For High Availability (HA), Compute Engine offers automatic failover to other regions or zones in event of a failure. Managed instance groups (MIGs) help keep the instances running by automatically replicating instances from a predefined image. They also provide application-based auto-healing health checks. If an application is not responding on a VM, the auto-healer automatically re-creates that VM for you. Regional MIGs let you spread app load across multiple zones. This replication protects against zonal failures. MIGs work with load-balancing services to distribute traffic across all of the instances in the group.

Compute Engine offers autoscaling to automatically add or remove VM instances from a managed instance group based on increases or decreases in load. Autoscaling lets your apps gracefully handle increases in traffic, and it reduces cost when the need for resources is lower. You define the autoscaling policy for automatic scaling based on the measured load, CPU utilization, requests per second, or other metrics.

Active Assist's new feature, predictive autoscaling, helps improve response times for your applications. When you enable predictive autoscaling, Compute Engine forecasts future load based on your MIG's history and scales it out in advance of predicted load so that new instances are ready to serve when the load arrives. Without predictive autoscaling, an autoscaler can only scale a group reactively, based on observed changes in load in real time. With predictive autoscaling enabled, the autoscaler works with real-time data as well as with historical data to cover both the current and forecasted load. That makes predictive autoscaling ideal for those apps with long initialization times and whose workloads vary predictably with daily or weekly cycles. For more information, see How predictive autoscaling works or check if predictive autoscaling is suitable for your workload, and to learn more about other intelligent features, check out Active Assist.

Pricing

You pay for what you use. But you can save cost by taking advantage of some discounts! Sustained use savings are automatic discounts applied for running instances for a significant portion of the month. If you know your usage upfront, you can take advantage of committed use discounts, which can lead to significant savings without any upfront cost. And by using short-lived preemptive instances, you can save up to 80%; they are great for batch jobs and fault-tolerant workloads. You can also optimize resource utilization with automatic recommendations. For example, if you are using a bigger instance for a workload that can run on a smaller instance, you can save costs by applying these recommendations.

Security

Compute Engine provides you default hardware security. Using Identity and Access Management (IAM) you just have to ensure that proper permissions are given to control access to your VM resources. All the other basic security principles apply; if the resources are not related and don't require network communication among themselves, consider hosting them on different VPC networks. By default, users in a project can create persistent disks or copy images using any of the public images or any images that project members can access through IAM roles. You may want to restrict your project members so that they can create boot disks only from images that contain approved software that meet your policy or security requirements. You can define an organization policy that only allows Compute Engine VMs to be created from approved images. This can be done by using the Trusted Images Policy to enforce images that can be used in your organization.

By default all VM families are Shielded VMs. Shielded VMs are virtual machine instances that are hardened with a set of easily configurable security features to ensure that when your VM boots, it's running a verified bootloader and kernel — it's the default for everyone using Compute Engine, at no additional charge. For more details on Shielded VMs, refer to the documentation at https://cloud.google.com/compute/shielded-vm/docs/shielded-vm.

For additional security, you also have the option to use Confidential VM to encrypt your data in use while it's being processed in Compute Engine. For more details on Confidential VM, refer to the documentation at https://cloud.google.com/compute/confidential-vm/docs/about-cvm.

Use Cases

There are many use cases Compute Engine can serve in addition to running websites and databases. You can also migrate your existing systems onto Google Cloud, with Migrate for Compute Engine, enabling you to run stateful workloads in the cloud within minutes rather than days or weeks. Windows, Oracle, and VMware applications have solution sets, enabling a smooth transition to Google Cloud. To run Windows applications, either bring your own license leveraging sole-tenant nodes or use the included licensed images.

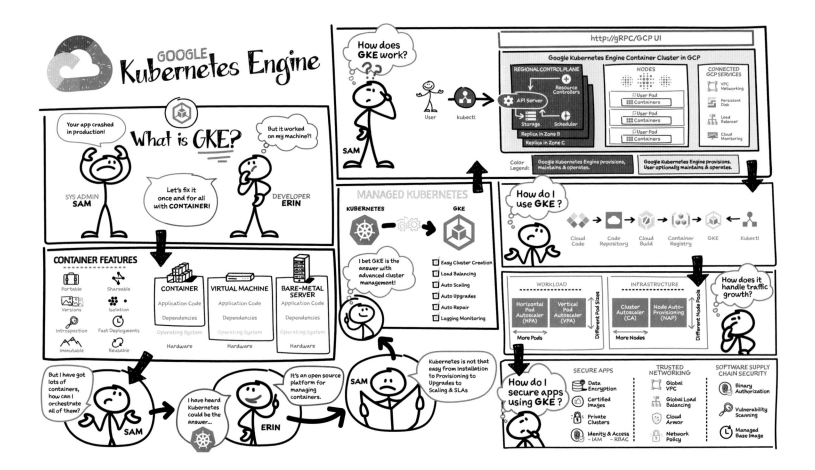

Why Containers?

Containers are often compared with virtual machines (VMs). You might already be familiar with VMs: a guest operating system such as Linux or Windows runs on top of a host operating system with virtualized access to the underlying hardware. Like virtual machines, containers enable you to package your application together with libraries and other dependencies, providing isolated environments for running your software services. As you'll see, however, the similarities end here as containers offer a far more lightweight unit for developers and IT Ops teams to work with, bringing a myriad of benefits.

Instead of virtualizing the hardware stack as with the virtual machines approach, containers virtualize at the operating system level, with multiple containers running atop the OS kernel directly. This means that containers are far more lightweight: They share the OS kernel, start much faster, and use a fraction of the memory compared to booting an entire OS.

Containers help improve portability, shareability, deployment speed, reusability, and more. More importantly to the team, containers made it possible to solve the "*it worked on my machine*" problem.

Why Kubernetes?

The system administrator is usually responsible for more than just one developer. They have several considerations when rolling out software:

- Will it work on all the machines?
- If it doesn't work, then what?
- What happens if traffic spikes? (System admin decides to over-provision just in case…)

With lots of developers containerizing their apps, the system administrator needs a better way to orchestrate all the containers that developers ship. The solution: Kubernetes!

What Is So Cool about Kubernetes?

The Mindful Container team had a bunch of servers and used to make decisions on what ran on each manually based on what they knew would conflict if it were to run on the same machine. If they were lucky, they might have some sort of scripted system for rolling out software, but it usually involved SSHing into each machine. Now with containers — and the isolation they provide — they can trust that in most cases, any two applications can fairly share the resources of the same machine.

With Kubernetes, the team can now introduce a control plane that makes decisions for them on where to run applications. And even better, it doesn't just statically place them; it can continually monitor the state of each machine and make adjustments to the state to ensure that what is happening is what they've actually specified. Kubernetes runs with a control plane, and on a number of nodes. We install a piece of software called the kubelet on each node, which reports the state back to the primary.

Here is how it works:

- The primary controls the cluster.
- The worker nodes run pods.
- A pod holds a set of containers.
- Pods are bin-packed as efficiently as configuration and hardware allows.
- Controllers provide safeguards so that pods run according to specification (reconciliation loops).
- All components can be deployed in high-availability mode and spread across zones or data centers.

Kubernetes orchestrates containers across a fleet of machines, with support for:

- Automated deployment and replication of containers
- Online scale — in and scale — out of container clusters

- Load balancing over groups of containers
- Rolling upgrades of application containers
- Resiliency, with automated rescheduling of failed containers (i.e., self-healing of container instances)
- Controlled exposure of network ports to systems outside the cluster

  A few more things to know about Kubernetes:

- Instead of flying a plane, you program an autopilot: declare a desired state, and Kubernetes will make it true — and continue to keep it true.
- It was inspired by Google's tools for running data centers efficiently.
- It has seen unprecedented community activity and is today one of the largest projects on GitHub. Google remains the top contributor.

The magic of Kubernetes starts happening when we don't require a sysadmin to make the decisions. Instead, we enable a build and deployment pipeline. When a build succeeds, passes all tests, and is signed off, it can automatically be deployed to the cluster gradually, blue/green, or immediately.

Kubernetes the Hard Way

By far, the single biggest obstacle to using Kubernetes (k8s) is learning how to install and manage your own cluster. Check out k8s the Hard Way, a step-by-step guide to install a k8s cluster. You have to think about tasks like:

- Choosing a cloud provider or bare metal
- Provisioning machines
- Picking an OS and container runtime
- Configuring networking (e.g., P ranges for pods, SDNs, LBs)

- Setting up security (e.g., generating certs and configuring encryption)
- Starting up cluster services such as DNS, logging, and monitoring

Once you have all these pieces together, you can finally start to use k8s and deploy your first application. And you're feeling great and happy and k8s is awesome! But then, you have to roll out an update...

Wouldn't it be great if *Mindful Containers* could start clusters with a single click, view all their clusters and workloads in a single pane of glass, and have Google continually manage their cluster to scale it and keep it healthy?

What Is GKE?

GKE is a secured and fully managed Kubernetes service. It provides an easy-to-use environment for deploying, managing, and scaling your containerized applications using Google infrastructure.

Mindful Containers decided to use GKE to enable development self-service by delegating release power to developers and software.

Why GKE?

- Production-ready with autopilot mode of operation for hands-off experience
- Best-in-class developer tooling with consistent support for first- and third-party tools
- Offers container-native networking with a unique BeyondProd security approach
- Most scalable Kubernetes service; only GKE can run 15,000 node clusters, outscaling competition up to 15X
- Industry-first to provide fully managed Kubernetes service that implements full Kubernetes API, 4-way autoscaling, release channels, and multicluster support

How Does GKE Work?

The GKE control plane is fully operated by the Google SRE (Site Reliability Engineering) team with managed availability, security patching, and upgrades. The Google SRE team not only has deep operational knowledge of k8s, but is also uniquely positioned to get early insights on any potential issues by managing a fleet of tens of thousands of clusters. That's something that is simply not possible to achieve with self-managed k8s. GKE also provides comprehensive management for nodes, including autoprovisioning, security patching, opt-in auto-upgrade, repair, and scaling. On top of that, GKE provides end-to-end container security, including private and hybrid networking.

How Does GKE Make Scaling Easy?

As the demand for *Mindful Containers* grows, they now need to scale their services. Manually scaling a Kubernetes cluster for availability and reliability can be complex and time consuming. GKE automatically scales the number of pods and nodes based on the resource consumption of services.

- Vertical Pod Autoscaler (VPA) watches resource utilization of your deployments and adjusts requested CPU and RAM to stabilize the workloads.

- Node Auto Provisioning optimizes cluster resources with an enhanced version of Cluster Autoscaling.

In addition to the fully managed control plane that GKE offers, using the Autopilot mode of operation automatically applies industry best practices and can eliminate all node management operations, maximizing your cluster efficiency and helping to provide a stronger security posture.

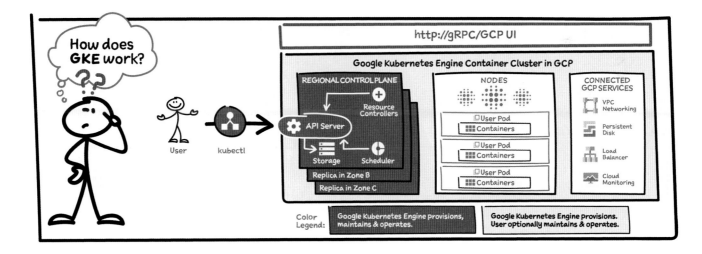

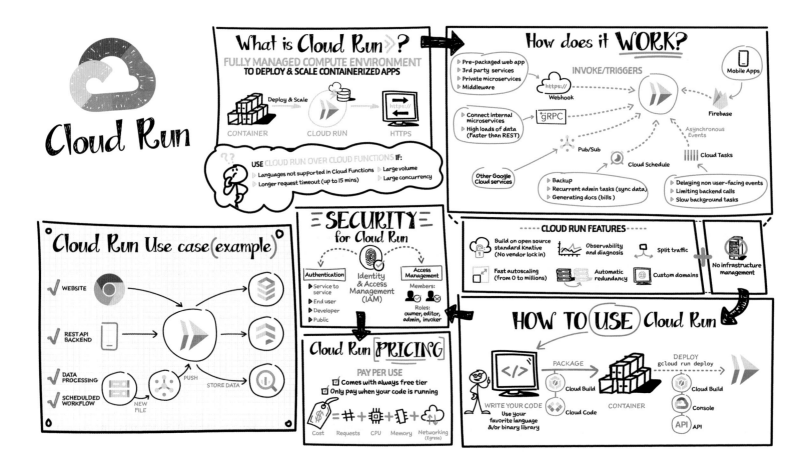

What Is Cloud Run?

Cloud Run is a fully managed compute environment for deploying and scaling serverless HTTP containers without worrying about provisioning machines, configuring clusters, or autoscaling.

- **No vendor lock-in** — Because Cloud Run takes standard OCI containers and implements the standard Knative Serving API, you can easily port over your applications to on-premises or any other cloud environment.
- **Fast autoscaling** — Microservices deployed in Cloud Run scale automatically based on the number of incoming requests, without you having to configure or manage a full-fledged Kubernetes cluster. Cloud Run scales to zero — that is, uses no resources — if there are no requests.
- **Split traffic** — Cloud Run enables you to split traffic between multiple revisions, so you can perform gradual rollouts such as canary deployments or blue/green deployments.
- **Custom domains** — You can set up custom domain mapping in Cloud Run, and it will provision a TLS certificate for your domain.
- **Automatic redundancy** — Cloud Run offers automatic redundancy so you don't have to worry about creating multiple instances for high availability.

How to Use Cloud Run

With Cloud Run, you write your code in your favorite language and/or use a binary library of your choice. Then push it to Cloud Build to create a container build. With a single command — `gcloud run deploy` — you go from a container image to a fully managed web application that runs on a domain with a TLS certificate and autoscales with requests.

How Does Cloud Run Work?

Cloud Run service can be invoked in the following ways:

- **HTTPS:** You can send HTTPS requests to trigger a Cloud Run-hosted service. Note that all Cloud Run services have a stable HTTPS URL. Some use cases include:
  - Custom RESTful web API
  - Private microservice
  - HTTP middleware or reverse proxy for your web applications
  - Prepackaged web application
- **gRPC:** You can use gRPC to connect Cloud Run services with other services — for example, to provide simple, high-performance communication between internal microservices. gRPC is a good option when you:
  - Want to communicate between internal microservices
  - Support high data loads (gRPC uses protocol buffers, which are up to seven times faster than REST calls)
  - Need only a simple service definition and you don't want to write a full client library
  - Use streaming gRPCs in your gRPC server to build more responsive applications and APIs
- **WebSockets:** WebSockets applications are supported on Cloud Run with no additional configuration required. Potential use cases include any application that requires a streaming service, such as a chat application.
- **Trigger from Pub/Sub:** You can use Pub/Sub to push messages to the endpoint of your Cloud Run service, where the messages are subsequently delivered to containers as HTTP requests. Possible use cases include:
  - Transforming data after receiving an event upon a file upload to a Cloud Storage bucket

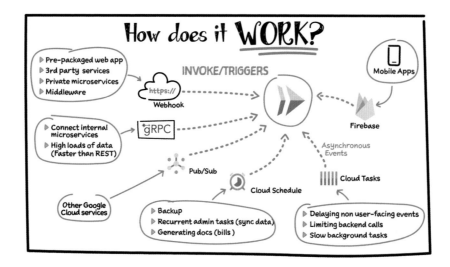

- Processing your Google Cloud operations suite logs with Cloud Run by exporting them to Pub/Sub
- Publishing and processing your own custom events from your Cloud Run services

- **Running services on a schedule:** You can use Cloud Scheduler to securely trigger a Cloud Run service on a schedule. This is similar to using cron jobs. Possible use cases include:

  - Performing backups on a regular basis
  - Performing recurrent administration tasks, such as regenerating a sitemap or deleting old data, content, configurations, synchronizations, or revisions
  - Generating bills or other documents

- **Executing asynchronous tasks:** You can use Cloud Tasks to securely enqueue a task to be asynchronously processed by a Cloud Run service. Typical use cases include:

- Handling requests through unexpected production incidents
- Smoothing traffic spikes by delaying work that is not user-facing
- Reducing user response time by delegating slow background operations, such as database updates or batch processing, to be handled by another service
- Limiting the call rate to backend services like databases and third-party APIs

- **Events from Eventrac:** You can trigger Cloud Run with events from more than 60 Google Cloud sources. For example:

  - Use a Cloud Storage event (via Cloud Audit Logs) to trigger a data processing pipeline
  - Use a BigQuery event (via Cloud Audit Logs) to initiate downstream processing in Cloud Run each time a job is completed

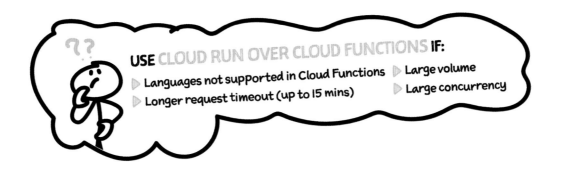

How Is Cloud Run Different from Cloud Functions?

Cloud Run and Cloud Functions are both fully managed services that run on Google Cloud's serverless infrastructure, auto-scale, and handle HTTP requests or events. They do, however, have some important differences:

- Cloud Functions lets you deploy snippets of code (functions) written in a limited set of programming languages, whereas Cloud Run lets you deploy container images using the programming language of your choice.

- Cloud Run also supports the use of any tool or system library from your application; Cloud Functions does not let you use custom executables.

- Cloud Run offers a longer request timeout duration of up to 60 minutes, whereas with Cloud Functions the request timeout can be set as high as 9 minutes.

- Cloud Functions only sends one request at a time to each function instance, whereas by default Cloud Run is configured to send multiple concurrent requests on each container instance. This is helpful to improve latency and reduce costs if you're expecting large volumes.

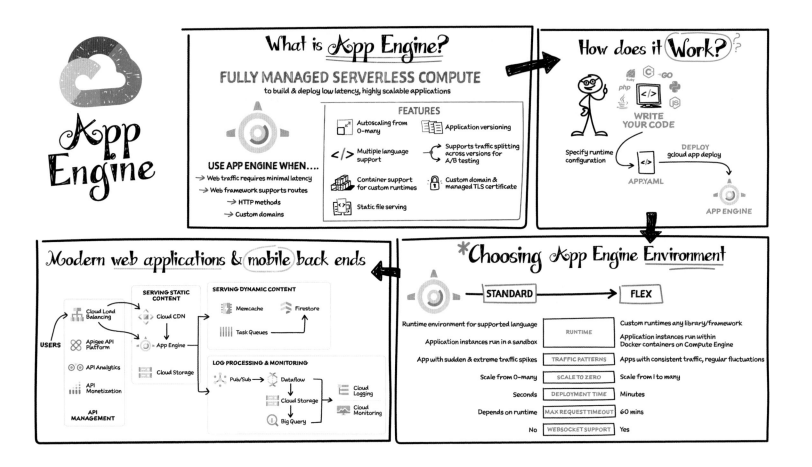

App Engine

What is App Engine?

FULLY MANAGED SERVERLESS COMPUTE
to build & deploy low latency, highly scalable applications

USE APP ENGINE WHEN....
→ Web traffic requires minimal latency
→ Web framework supports routes
  → HTTP methods
  → Custom domains

FEATURES
- Autoscaling from 0-many
- Application versioning
- Multiple language support
- Supports traffic splitting across versions for A/B testing
- Container support for custom runtimes
- Custom domain & managed TLS certificate
- Static file serving

How does it Work?

WRITE YOUR CODE

Specify runtime configuration → APP.YAML

DEPLOY gcloud app deploy → APP ENGINE

Modern web applications & mobile back ends

USERS

API MANAGEMENT
- Cloud Load Balancing
- Apigee API Platform
- API Analytics
- API Monetization

SERVING STATIC CONTENT
- Cloud CDN
- App Engine
- Cloud Storage

SERVING DYNAMIC CONTENT
- Memcache
- Firestore
- Task Queues

LOG PROCESSING & MONITORING
- Pub/Sub → Dataflow → Cloud Storage → Big Query
- Cloud Logging
- Cloud Monitoring

*Choosing App Engine Environment

STANDARD → FLEX

	STANDARD	FLEX
RUNTIME	Runtime environment for supported language	Custom runtimes any library/framework
	Application instances run in a sandbox	Application instances run within Docker containers on Compute Engine
TRAFFIC PATTERNS	App with sudden & extreme traffic spikes	Apps with consistent traffic, regular fluctuations
SCALE TO ZERO	Scale from 0-many	Scale from 1 to many
DEPLOYMENT TIME	Seconds	Minutes
MAX REQUEST TIMEOUT	Depends on runtime	60 mins
WEBSOCKET SUPPORT	No	Yes

What Is App Engine?

App Engine is a fully managed serverless compute option in Google Cloud that you can use to build and deploy low-latency, highly scalable applications. App Engine makes it easy to host and run your applications. It scales them from zero to planet scale without you having to manage infrastructure. App Engine is recommended for a wide variety of applications, including web traffic that requires low-latency responses, web frameworks that support routes, HTTP methods, and APIs.

Environments

App Engine offers two environments; here's how to choose one for your application:

- App Engine Standard — Supports specific runtime environments where applications run in a sandbox. It is ideal for apps with sudden and extreme traffic spikes because it can scale from zero to many requests as needed. Applications deploy in a matter of seconds. If your required runtime is supported and it's an HTTP application, then App Engine Standard is the way to go.

- App Engine Flex — Is open and flexible and supports custom runtimes because the application instances run within Docker containers on Compute Engine. It is ideal for apps with consistent traffic and regular fluctuations because the instances scale from one to many. Along with HTTP applications, it supports applications requiring WebSockets. The max request timeout is 60 minutes.

How Does It Work?

No matter which App Engine environment you choose, the app creation and deployment process is the same. First write your code, next specify the **app.yaml** file with runtime configuration, and finally deploy the app on App Engine using a single command: `gcloud app deploy`.

Notable Features

- **Developer friendly** — A fully managed environment lets you focus on code while App Engine manages infrastructure.

- **Fast responses** — App Engine integrates seamlessly with Memorystore for Redis, enabling distributed in-memory data cache for your apps.

- **Powerful application diagnostics** — Cloud Monitoring and Cloud Logging help monitor the health and performance of your app, and Cloud Debugger and Error Reporting help diagnose and fix bugs quickly.

- **Application versioning** — Easily host different versions of your app, and easily create development, test, staging, and production environments.

- **Traffic splitting** — Route incoming requests to different app versions for A/B tests, incremental feature rollouts, and similar use cases.

- **Application security** — Helps safeguard your application by defining access rules with App Engine firewall and leverage managed SSL/TLS certificates by default on your custom domain at no additional cost.

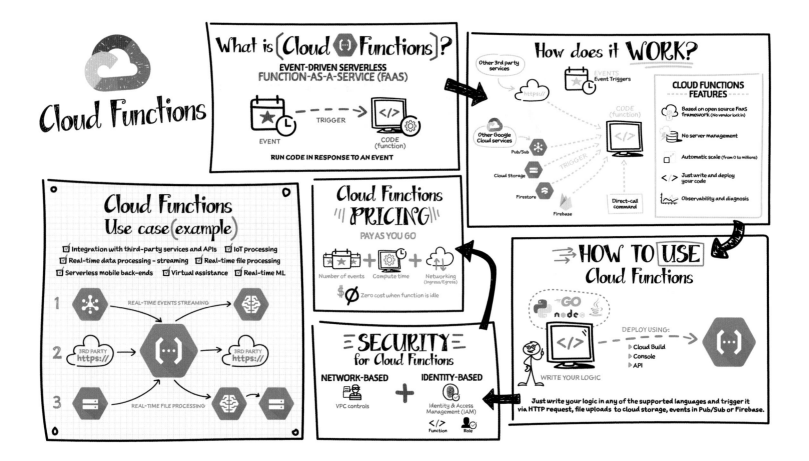

Cloud Functions

What is [Cloud 🔷 Functions]?
EVENT-DRIVEN SERVERLESS FUNCTION-AS-A-SERVICE (FAAS)

EVENT → TRIGGER → CODE (function)

RUN CODE IN RESPONSE TO AN EVENT

How does it WORK?
Other 3rd party services
https://
EVENTS — Event Triggers
Other Google Cloud services
Pub/Sub
Cloud Storage
Firestore
Firebase
CODE (function)
TRIGGER
Direct-call command

CLOUD FUNCTIONS FEATURES
- Based on open source FaaS framework (No vendor lock in)
- No server management
- Automatic scale (from 0 to millions)
- Just write and deploy your code
- Observability and diagnosis

Cloud Functions Use case (example)
- ☑ Integration with third-party services and APIs
- ☑ Real-time data processing - streaming
- ☑ Serverless mobile back-ends
- ☑ IoT processing
- ☑ Real-time file processing
- ☑ Virtual assistance
- ☑ Real-time ML

1 REAL-TIME EVENTS STREAMING
2 3RD PARTY https:// → → 3RD PARTY https://
3 REAL-TIME FILE PROCESSING

Cloud Functions PRICING
PAY AS YOU GO

Number of events + Compute time + Networking (Ingress/Egress)

$∅ Zero cost when function is idle

SECURITY for Cloud Functions
NETWORK-BASED + **IDENTITY-BASED**
VPC controls   Identity & Access Management (IAM)
</> Function   Role

HOW TO USE Cloud Functions
GO node (java)

</> WRITE YOUR LOGIC

DEPLOY USING:
▶ Cloud Build
▶ Console
▶ API

Just write your logic in any of the supported languages and trigger it via HTTP request, file uploads to cloud storage, events in Pub/Sub or Firebase.

What Is Cloud Functions?

Cloud Functions is a fully managed event-driven serverless function-as-a-service (FaaS). It is a serverless execution environment for building and connecting cloud services. With Cloud Functions you write simple, single-purpose functions that are attached to events emitted from your cloud infrastructure and services. Your function is a piece of code triggered when an event being watched is fired. Your code executes in a fully managed environment. There is no need to provision any infrastructure or worry about managing any servers in case of increase or decrease in traffic. Cloud Functions is also fully integrated with Cloud Operations for observability and diagnosis. Because Cloud Functions is based on an open source FaaS framework, it is easy to migrate.

How to Use Cloud Functions

To use Cloud Functions, just write the logic in any of the supported languages (Go, Python, Java, Node.js, PHP, Ruby, .NET); deploy it using the console, API, or Cloud Build; and then trigger it via HTTP(s) request from any service, file uploads to Cloud Storage, events in Pub/Sub, Firebase, or even a direct call through the command-line interface (CLI).

Cloud Functions augments existing cloud services and allows you to address an increasing number of use cases with arbitrary programming logic. It provides a connective layer of logic that lets you write code to connect and extend cloud services. Listen and respond to a file upload to Cloud Storage, a log change, or an incoming message on a Pub/Sub topic.

Pricing and Security

The pricing is based on number of events, compute time, memory, and ingress/egress requests and costs nothing if the function is idle. For security,

using Identity and Access Management (IAM) you can define which services or personnel can access the function, and using the VPC controls, you can define network-based access.

Some Cloud Functions Use Cases

- **Data processing/ETL** — Listen and respond to Cloud Storage events such as when a file is created, changed, or removed. Process images, perform video transcoding, validate and transform data, and invoke any service on the Internet from your Cloud Functions.

- **Webhooks** — Via a simple HTTP trigger, respond to events originating from third-party systems like GitHub, Slack, Stripe, or from anywhere that can send HTTP requests.

- **Lightweight APIs** — Compose applications from lightweight, loosely coupled bits of logic that are quick to build and that scale instantly. Your functions can be event-driven or invoked directly over HTTP/S.

- **Mobile backend** — Use Google's mobile platform for app developers or Firebase, and write your mobile backend in Cloud Functions. Listen and respond to events from Firebase Analytics, Realtime Database, Authentication, and Storage.

- **IoT** — Imagine tens or hundreds of thousands of devices streaming data into Pub/Sub, thereby launching Cloud Functions to process, transform, and store data. Cloud Functions lets you do so in a way that's completely serverless.

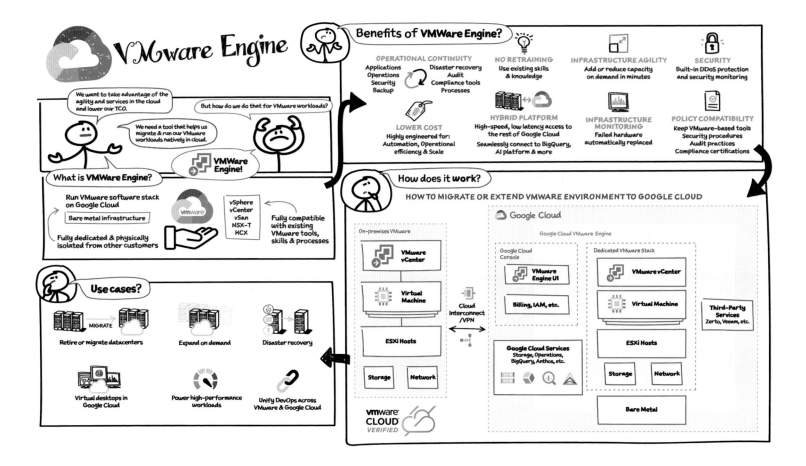

What Is Google Cloud VMware Engine?

If you have VMware workloads and you want to modernize your application to take advantage of cloud services to increase agility and reduce total cost of ownership (TCO), then Google Cloud VMware Engine is the service for you. It is a managed VMware service with bare-metal infrastructure that runs the VMware software stack on Google Cloud — fully dedicated and physically isolated from other customers.

Benefits of Google Cloud VMware Engine

One benefit is operational continuity. Your team can continue to utilize their existing processes, and they can use their existing skills and knowledge. The infrastructure also scales on demand in minutes when you need it. You get built-in DDoS protection and security monitoring, and you can continue to use the VMware-based compliance and security policies. You get reliability, with fully redundant and dedicated 100 Gbps networking, providing up to 99.99 percent availability to meet the needs of your VMware stack. There is also infrastructure monitoring so that failed hardware automatically gets replaced. With the hybrid platform, you get the benefits of high speed, low latency, and access to other resources within Google Cloud such as BigQuery, AI Platform, GCS, and more. Because the service is highly engineered for automation, operational efficiency, and scale, it is also cost effective.

How Does Google Cloud VMware Engine Work?

Google Cloud VMware Engine makes it easy to migrate or extend your VMware environment to Google Cloud. Here is how it works. You can easily migrate your on-premises VMware instances to Google Cloud, using included HCX licenses, via a cloud VPN or interconnect. The service consists of VMware vCenter, the virtual machines, ESXi host, storage, and network on bare metal. You can easily connect from the service to other Google Cloud services such as Cloud SQL, BigQuery, and Memorystore. You can access the service UI, billing, and Identity and Access Management all from the Google Cloud console as well as connect to other third-party disaster recovery and storage services such as Zerto and Veeam.

Google Cloud VMware Engine Use Cases

- **Retire or migrate data centers:** Scale data center capacity in the cloud and stop managing hardware refreshes. Reduce risk and cost by migrating to the cloud while still using familiar VMware tools and skills. In the cloud, use Google Cloud services to modernize your applications at your pace.

- **Expand on demand:** Scale capacity to meet unanticipated needs, such as new development environments or seasonal capacity bursts, and keep it only as long as you need it. Reduce your up-front investment, accelerate speed of provisioning, and reduce complexity by using the same architecture and policies across both on-premises and the cloud.

- **Disaster recovery and virtual desktops in Google Cloud:** High-bandwidth connections let you quickly upload and download data to recover from incidents.

- **Virtual desktops in Google Cloud:** Create virtual desktops infrastructure (VDI) in Google Cloud for remote access to data, apps, and desktops. Low-latency networks give you fast response times — similar to those of a desktop app.

- **Power high-performance applications and databases:** In Google Cloud you have a hyper-converged architecture designed to run your most demanding VMware workloads such as Oracle, Microsoft SQL Server, middleware systems, and high-performance NoSQL databases.

- **Unify DevOps across VMware and Google Cloud:** Optimize VMware administration by using Google Cloud services that can be applied across all your workloads, without having to expand your data center or rearchitect your applications. You can centralize identities, access control policies, logging, and monitoring for VMware applications on Google Cloud.

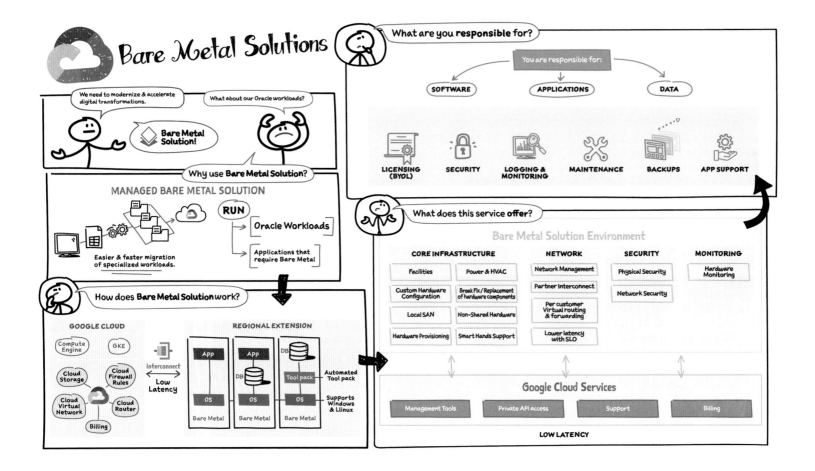

What Is Bare Metal Solution?

Enterprises are migrating to the cloud to reduce management overhead and increase business agility. There are many workloads that are easy to lift and shift to the cloud, but there are also specialized workloads (such as Oracle) that are difficult to migrate to a cloud environment due to complicated licensing, hardware, and support requirements. Bare Metal Solution provides a path to modernize the application infrastructure landscape while maintaining the existing investments and architecture. It enables an easier and a faster migration path.

Features

Bare Metal Solution offers a reliable, secure, and high-performance database infrastructure for your Oracle workloads

1. Seamlessly access all Oracle capabilities: Run Oracle databases the same way you do it on-premises. Install Oracle Real Application Clusters (RAC) on certified hardware for HA, use Oracle Data Guard for disaster recovery, and Oracle Recovery Manager (RMAN) for backups. Google Cloud's service catalog provides analogous topologies to all Oracle Maximum Availability Architecture templates.

2. Integrated support and billing: It offers a seamless experience with support for infrastructure, including defined SLAs for initial response, defined enterprise-grade SLA for infrastructure uptime and interconnect availability, 24/7 coverage for all Priority 1 and 2 issues, and unified billing across Google Cloud and Bare Metal Solution for Oracle.

3. Data protection: Helps meet compliance requirements with certifications such as ISO, PCI DSS, and HIPAA, plus regional certifications where applicable. Copy data management and backups provided by Actifio, fully integrated into Bare Metal Solution for Oracle.

4. Tools and services to simplify operations: Automate day-to-day operational database administrator tasks by either using Google's open source Ansible based toolkit or Google Cloud's Kubernetes operator for Oracle. You can integrate these tools with their existing automation framework of choice.

How Does It Work?

It provides purpose-built bare-metal machines in regional extensions that are connected to Google Cloud by a managed, high-performance connection with a low-latency network fabric. It supports Windows and Linux workloads. Google Cloud provides and manages the core infrastructure, the network, the physical and network security, and hardware monitoring capabilities in an environment from which you can access all of the Google Cloud services.

What Does the Bare Metal Solution Environment Include?

The core infrastructure includes secure, controlled-environment facilities, and power. Bare Metal Solution also includes the provisioning and maintenance of the custom, sole-tenancy hardware with local SAN, as well as smart hands support. The network, which is managed by Google Cloud, includes a low-latency Cloud Interconnect connection into your Bare Metal Solution environment. And you have access to other Google Cloud services such as private API access, management tools, support, and billing. When you use Google Cloud Bare Metal Solution, you can bring your own license of the specialized software such as Oracle, and you are responsible for your software, applications, and data. This includes maintenance, security, backups, and software monitoring.

Choosing the right infrastructure options to run your application is critical, both for the success of your application and for the team that is managing and developing it. This section breaks down some of the most important factors that you need to consider when deciding where you should run your stuff. Remember that no decision is necessarily final; you can always move from one option to another but it's important to consider all the relevant factors.

What Is the Level of Abstraction You Need?

You can run an application on VMs directly on Compute Engine, or build them for Serverless with Cloud Run or Cloud Functions, and in the middle is Kubernetes with Google Kubernetes Engine. As you move up the layers of abstraction from raw VMs (where you manage everything) → Kubernetes (container orchestration and management)→ Serverless (provide your code/container to run), your operations get easier as there's less for you to manage, but your deployment choices and flexibility are reduced at the same time. You're trading the flexibility to deploy things however you like, with the need to manage all that custom configuration.

- If you need more control over the underlying infrastructure (for example, the operating system/disk images, CPU, RAM, and disk) then it makes sense to use Compute Engine. This is a typical path for legacy application migrations and existing systems that require specific OS and underlying requirements.

- Containers provide a way to virtualize an OS so that multiple workloads can run on a single OS instance. They are fast and lightweight, and they provide portability. If your applications are containerized, then you have two main options. You can use Google Kubernetes Engine, or GKE, which gives you full control over the container down to the nodes with specific OS, CPU, GPU, disk, memory, and networking. GKE also offers Autopilot, when you need the flexibility and control but have limited ops and engineering support. If, on the other hand, you are just looking to run your application in containers without having to worry about scaling the

infrastructure, then use Cloud Run: you can just write your application code, optionally package it into a container, and deploy it.

- Regardless of your chosen abstraction, Cloud Functions provides a simple, lightweight solution for extending the behavior of the services you use. Think of it as the scripting engine of the cloud. You can use it to connect two services together, or transform data in-flight between services.

What Is Your Use Case?

- If you are migrating a **legacy application** with specific licensing, OS, kernel, or networking requirements such as Windows-based applications, genomics processing, or SAP HANA, use Compute Engine.

- If you are building a **cloud-native, microservices-based application** then GKE or Cloud Run are both great options. Choice would depend on your focus. If developer productivity is the focus, then use a serverless containerization approach with Cloud Run, and if you are building your own platform and tooling on a cloud-native basis, then GKE is a good fit.

- If your application needs a **specific OS or network protocols** beyond HTTP, HTTP/2, or gRPC, use GKE.

- If you are building an application for **hybrid and multi-cloud**, then portability is top of mind. GKE is a great fit for this use case because it is based on open source Kubernetes, which helps with keeping all your on-premise and cloud environments consistent. Additionally, Anthos is a platform specifically designed for hybrid and multi-cloud deployments. It provides single-pane-of-glass visibility across all clusters from infrastructure to application performance and topology.

- For **websites or APIs** use Cloud Run. Cloud Run supports containerized deployment and scaling an application in a programming language of your choice with HTTP/s or WebSocket support.

- For **data processing apps and webhooks** use Cloud Run or Cloud Functions. Consider applications that transform lightweight data as it arrives and store it as structured data. You can trigger these transformations from Google Cloud sources or HTTP requests.

- If your application is kicking off a task based on an **event**, Cloud Functions is a great choice. Think of use cases such as video transcoding or image processing once an asset is stored in a Cloud Storage bucket. In this case your code just does one thing based on an event/trigger such as Cloud Storage, Pub/Sub, Firebase, HTTP, and others.

Need Portability with Open Source?

If your requirement is based on portability and open source support, take a look at GKE, Cloud Run, and Cloud Functions. They are all based on open source frameworks that help you avoid vendor lock-in and give you the freedom to expand your infrastructure into hybrid and multi-cloud environments. GKE clusters are powered by the Kubernetes open source cluster management system, which provides the mechanisms through which you interact with your cluster. Cloud Run supports Knative, an open source project that supports serverless workloads on Kubernetes. Cloud Functions uses open source frameworks to run functions across multiple environments.

What Are Your Team Dynamics Like?

If you have a team of developers and you want their attention focused on the code, then Cloud Run and Cloud Functions are good choices because you won't need the team managing the infrastructure, scale, and operations.

If you are building your own platform for your developers to use, or your developers are already familiar with Kubernetes, then GKE is a good choice as it offers a managed service that handles much of the operation of Kubernetes while still providing the full range of capabilities available in Kubernetes.

Both Cloud Run and GKE run containers, so there is a natural portability between these environments, and using both platforms in combination is also a common pattern.

What Type of Billing Model Do You Prefer?

Compute Engine and GKE billing models are based on resources, which means you pay for the duration that the resource is provisioned. You can also take advantage of sustained and committed use discounts based on your usage pattern.

Cloud Run, Cloud Functions, and GKE Autopilot are "pay as you go," only charging for what you use, with a more granular pricing model.

CHAPTER TWO

Storage

Cloud storage is a simple, reliable, and scalable method for easily storing, retrieving, and sharing data in the cloud. Cloud providers offer managed data storage services that eliminate the need for buying and managing your own storage infrastructure. Cloud storage gives you the flexibility to scale your storage infrastructure as needed, globally and durably.

Fundamental characteristics of an effective cloud storage service include:

- **Security** — Data is stored securely (encrypted at rest and in transit).
- **Durability** — Data is stored redundantly, so it is not lost in the event of a disruption.
- **Availability** — Data is available at all times, whenever it's needed.

Common cloud storage use cases include:

- **Compliance and business continuity** — You can use cloud storage backup and recovery capabilities to help meet compliance and business continuity requirements.

- **Data lakes** — You can use data lakes based on cloud storage to store information in its raw/native form with metadata for selective access and data analysis.
- **Application development** — Storage is critical for development and testing. You can use cloud storage to store and serve static files (for websites) globally, create fast applications, and deploy shared file systems across teams.

This chapter covers the three types of cloud data storage: object storage, file storage, and block storage. It also covers the distinct advantages and use cases for each type, as well as the Google Cloud storage options that support them.

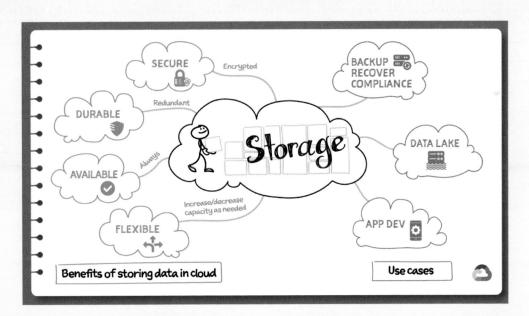

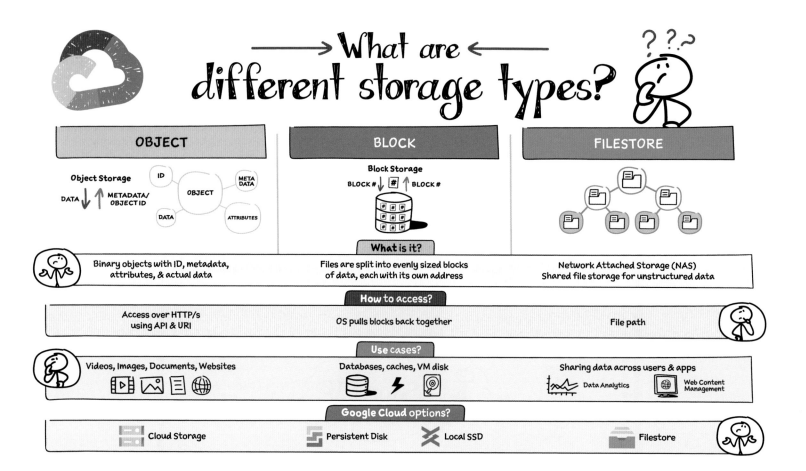

What Are the Different Storage Types?

There are three broad categories of storage that applications use: object store, block store, and file store.

Object Storage

Object store is used for binary and object data, blobs, and unstructured data such as media, documents, logs, backups, application binaries, and VM images. Objects are discrete units of data that are stored in a structurally flat data environment. The objects have an ID, metadata, attributes, and the actual data. The metadata could include things about security classification of the file, the applications that can access it, and similar information. This information enables an application to locate and access the object. You can add data to it or retrieve data from it as often as you need using a URI or API. Object storage is usually cloud-based; an example is Cloud Storage.

Block Storage

With block storage, files are split into evenly sized blocks of data, each with its own address but with no additional information such as the metadata used in object store or the file structure used in file store. To access any file, the server's operating system uses the unique address to pull the blocks back together into the file, which takes less time than navigating through directories and file hierarchies to access a file. Because block storage doesn't rely on a single path to the data, the data can be retrieved quickly. Each block lives on its own and can be partitioned so that it can be accessed in a different operating system, which gives the user complete freedom to configure their data. Because block storage can be directly accessed by the operating system as a mounted drive volume, it is used for applications requiring higher performance and low latency. Examples include databases, backups for running VMs, cache, analytics, and more! Persistent Disk and Local SSD are Google Cloud's block storage options.

File Storage

File storage is a shared filesystem where data is stored as a single piece of information inside a folder. In file storage, data is stored in files, the files are organized in folders, and the folders are organized under a hierarchy of directories and subdirectories. When you need to access a piece of data, your computer needs to know the path to find it. File storage is Network Attached Storage (NAS), which is a shared filesystem for unstructured data so that multiple clients can access a single shared folder. Managing file storage can become time consuming and cumbersome as the number of files increases, but cloud-based file storage such as Filestore helps mitigate that issue.

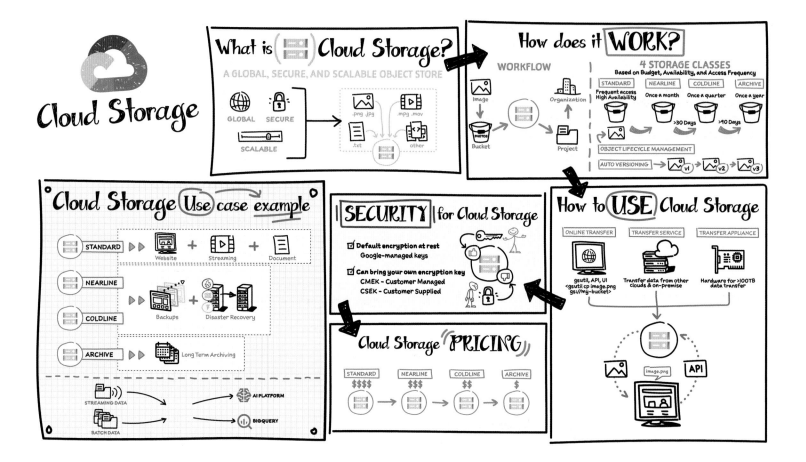

Cloud Storage

What is [🗄] Cloud Storage?
A GLOBAL, SECURE, AND SCALABLE OBJECT STORE

GLOBAL SECURE SCALABLE

.png .jpg .mpg .mov .txt other

How does it WORK?

WORKFLOW

Image → Bucket → Project → Organization

4 STORAGE CLASSES
Based on Budget, Availability, and Access Frequency

STANDARD	NEARLINE	COLDLINE	ARCHIVE
Frequent access High Availability	Once a month	Once a quarter	Once a year
	>30 Days	>90 Days	

OBJECT LIFECYCLE MANAGEMENT

AUTO VERSIONING → v1 → v2 → v3

Cloud Storage (Use) case example

- **STANDARD** ▷▷ Website + Streaming + Document
- **NEARLINE** ▷▷ Backups + Disaster Recovery
- **COLDLINE** ▷▷ Backups + Disaster Recovery
- **ARCHIVE** ▷▷ Long Term Archiving

STREAMING DATA → AI PLATFORM
BATCH DATA → BIG QUERY

SECURITY for Cloud Storage

☑ Default encryption at rest
   Google-managed keys

☑ Can bring your own encryption key
   CMEK – Customer Managed
   CSEK – Customer Supplied

Cloud Storage PRICING

STANDARD	NEARLINE	COLDLINE	ARCHIVE
$$$$	$$$	$$	$

How to USE Cloud Storage

ONLINE TRANSFER	TRANSFER SERVICE	TRANSFER APPLIANCE
gsutil, API, UI <gsutil cp image.png gs://my-bucket>	Transfer data from other clouds & on-premise	Hardware for >100TB data transfer

image.png API

Cloud Storage is a global, secure, and scalable object store for immutable data such as images, text, videos, and other file formats. You can add data to it or retrieve data from it as often as your application needs. The objects stored have an ID, metadata, attributes, and the actual data. The metadata can include all sorts of things, including the security classification of the file, the applications that can access it, and similar information. The ID, metadata, and attributes make object storage an appealing storage choice for a large variety of applications ranging from web serving to data analytics.

Storage Classes

You store objects in buckets that are associated with a project, which are, in turn, grouped under an organization. There are four storage classes that are based on budget, availability, and access frequency.

- Standard buckets, for high-performance, frequent access, and highest availability
  - Regional or dual-regional locations, for data accessed frequently or high-throughput needs
  - Multi-region, for serving content globally
- Nearline, for data accessed less than once a month
- Coldline, for data accessed roughly less than once a quarter
- Archive, for data that you want to put away for years (accessed less than once a year)

It costs a bit more to use standard storage because it is designed for short-lived and/or frequently accessed data. Nearline, coldline, and archive storage offer a lower monthly storage cost for longer-lived and less frequently accessed data.

Choosing a Location for Your Use Case

Cloud Storage lets you store your data in three types of locations:

- **Regional:** Data is stored redundantly in a single region; regional offers the lowest monthly storage price and is suitable for a wide range of use

cases, including high-performance analytics where it is important to co-locate your compute and storage in the same region.

- **Multi-region:** Availability is higher than regional because data is stored redundantly across a continent, but it's not visible which specific regions your data is in. It costs a little more than single regions, but is a great choice for serving web content across the internet.
- **Dual-regions:** These provide the best of regional and multi-region, with data stored in two specific regions. You get high availability and protection against regional failures while also getting the high-performance characteristics of regional storage. This option is best for business-critical workloads, data lakes for streaming, and batch uploading of data for big data and machine learning projects.

No matter the location that you select, all four storage classes are available to you so that you can optimize your costs over time, storing your most active "hot" data in standard and moving the data down to "colder" classes as it becomes older and less frequently accessed.

How to Use Cloud Storage

With Object Lifecycle Management, you can automatically transition your data to lower-cost storage classes when it reaches a certain age or when other lifecycle rules that you've set up apply. Cloud Storage also offers automatic object versioning, so you can restore older versions of objects—which can be especially helpful as protection against accidental deletion.

You can upload objects to the bucket and download objects from it using the console or gsutil tools, Storage Transfer Service, Transfer Appliance, or Transfer Online. Once you have stored the data, accessing it is easy with a single API call for all storage classes.

Security

By default 100% of data in Cloud Storage is automatically encrypted at rest and if needed, customers can bring their own encryption keys. You can grant permission to specific members and teams or make the objects fully public for use cases such as websites.

Options to move data to Google Cloud

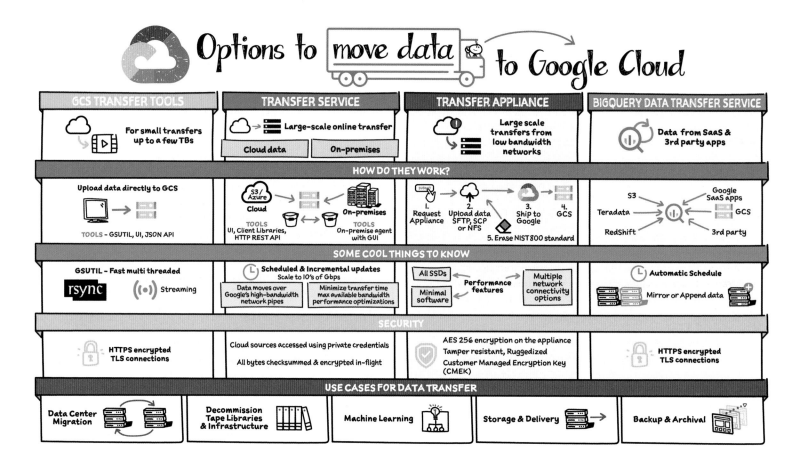

GCS TRANSFER TOOLS	TRANSFER SERVICE	TRANSFER APPLIANCE	BIGQUERY DATA TRANSFER SERVICE
For small transfers up to a few TBs	Large-scale online transfer — Cloud data / On-premises	Large scale transfers from low bandwidth networks	Data from SaaS & 3rd party apps

HOW DO THEY WORK?

Upload data directly to GCS. TOOLS - GSUTIL, UI, JSON API	S3/Azure Cloud ↔ On-premises. TOOLS UI, Client Libraries, HTTP REST API / TOOLS On-premise agent with GUI	1. Request Appliance 2. Upload data SFTP, SCP or NFS 3. Ship to Google 4. GCS 5. Erase NIST 800 standard	S3, Teradata, RedShift → ← Google SaaS apps, GCS, 3rd party

SOME COOL THINGS TO KNOW

GSUTIL – Fast multi threaded. rsync. Streaming	Scheduled & Incremental updates. Scale to 10's of Gbps. Data moves over Google's high-bandwidth network pipes / Minimize transfer time max available bandwidth performance optimizations	All SSDs / Minimal software — Performance features — Multiple network connectivity options	Automatic Schedule. Mirror or Append data

SECURITY

HTTPS encrypted TLS connections	Cloud sources accessed using private credentials. All bytes checksummed & encrypted in-flight	AES 256 encryption on the appliance. Tamper resistant, Ruggedized. Customer Managed Encryption Key (CMEK)	HTTPS encrypted TLS connections

USE CASES FOR DATA TRANSFER

Data Center Migration	Decommission Tape Libraries & Infrastructure	Machine Learning	Storage & Delivery	Backup & Archival

Data Transfer Reasons and Requirements

There can be multiple reasons to move data into Google Cloud, such as data center migration, machine learning, content storage, delivery, backup, and archival. Data is a critical piece for any application's functionality, so when moving data between locations it's important to think about reliability, predictability, scalability, security, and consistency of the data transfer. Google Cloud provides four major transfer solutions that fit all these requirements and varying use cases.

Google Cloud Data Transfer Options

You can get the data into Google Cloud using four major tools:

1. **Cloud Storage transfer tools** — These are a set of tools that help you upload data directly from your computer into Cloud Storage. You would typically use this option for small transfers up to a few terabytes. These include the Google Cloud Console UI, the JSON API, and the GSUTIL command-line interface. GSUTIL is an open source command-line utility for scripted transfers from your shell. It also enables you to manage GCS buckets. It can operate in rsync mode for incremental copies and in streaming mode for pushing script output for large multithreaded/multiprocessing data moves. Use it in place of the UNIX cp (copy) command, which is not multithreaded.

2. **Storage Transfer Service** — This service enables you to quickly import online data into Cloud Storage from other clouds, from on-premises sources, or from one bucket to another within Google Cloud. You can set up recurring transfer jobs to save time and resources, and it can scale to 10s of Gbps. To automate creation and management of transfer jobs, you can use the storage transfer API or client libraries in the language of your choice. As compared to GSUTIL, Storage Transfer Service is a managed solution that handles retries and provides detailed transfer logging. The data transfer is fast since the data moves over high-bandwidth network pipes. The on-premise transfer service minimizes the transfer time by utilizing the maximum available bandwidth and by applying performance optimizations.

3. **Transfer Appliance** — This is the option of choice if you want to migrate a large dataset and don't have high bandwidth to spare. Transfer Appliance enables seamless, secure, and speedy data transfer to Google Cloud. With low bandwidth, it can take a long time to transfer data. For example, a 1 PB data transfer can be completed in just over 40 days using the Transfer Appliance, as compared to an online data transfer over a typical network (100 Mbps), which would require three years. Transfer Appliance is a physical box that comes in two form factors: TA100 (90 TB) and TA480 (300 TB). The process is simple: First, you order the appliance through the Cloud Console and it is shipped to you. Then you copy your data to the appliance via a file copy over NFS; the data is encrypted and secured. Finally, you ship the appliance back to Google for data transfer into your GCS bucket, and the data is erased from the appliance. Transfer Appliance is highly performant because it uses all solid-state drives, minimal software, and multiple network connectivity options.

4. **BigQuery data transfer service** — Using this option, your analytics team can lay the foundation for a BigQuery data warehouse without writing a single line of code. The service automates data movement into BigQuery on a scheduled, managed basis. It supports several third-party transfers along with transfers from Google SaaS apps, external cloud storage providers, and data warehouses such as Teradata and Amazon Redshift. Once that data is in, you can use it right inside BigQuery for analysis, machine learning, or just warehousing.

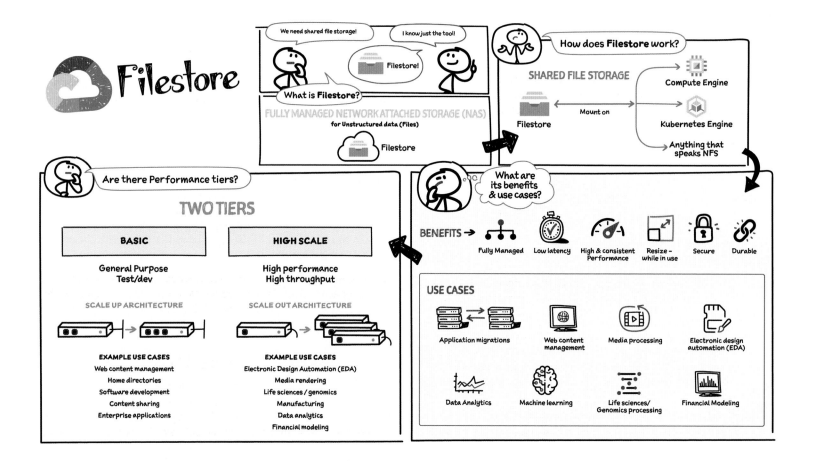

Filestore is high-performance, fully managed, NoOps shared file storage in the cloud. As the name indicates, it is used for files or unstructured data. You can easily mount file shares on Compute Engine VMs and Google Kubernetes Engine so that containers can reference the same shared data. Filestore can also be mounted on anything that speaks Network File System (NFS). Filestore accelerates and simplifies migration to the cloud without requiring you to rewrite your most business-critical applications.

Benefits of Filestore

Filestore is fully managed, high-performance file storage that offers really low latency. It provides concurrent access to tens of thousands of clients with scalable and predictable performance, along with the ability to scale capacity up and down based on demand. It keeps the data safe and secure by automatically encrypting it at rest and in transit.

Filestore Use Cases

Filestore offers low latency for file operations. It's designed for workloads that are latency sensitive, such as electronic design automation (EDA), media rendering, data analytics, or other metadata-intensive applications.

- **Data analytics** Compute complex financial models or analyze environmental data with Filestore. As capacity or performance needs change, easily grow or shrink your instances as needed. As a persistent and shareable storage layer, Filestore enables immediate access to data for high-performance, smart analytics without the need to lose valuable time on loading and off-loading data to clients' drives.

- **Genomics processing** Genome sequencing requires an incredible amount of raw data, on the order of billions of data points per person. This type of analysis requires speed, scalability, and security. Filestore meets the needs of companies and research institutions performing scientific research while also offering predictable prices for the performance.

- **Electronic design automation** EDA is all about data management. It requires the ability to batch workloads across thousands of cores and has large memory needs. Filestore offers the necessary capacity and scale to meet the needs of manufacturing customers doing intensive EDA and also makes sure files are universally accessible.

- **Web content management** Web developers and large hosting providers (such as WordPress hosting) rely on Filestore to manage and serve web content.

- **Media rendering** You can easily mount Filestore file shares on Compute Engine instances, enabling visual effects artists to collaborate on the same file share. As rendering workflows typically run across fleets ("render farms") of compute machines, all of which mount a shared filesystem, Filestore and Compute Engine can scale to meet your job's rendering needs.

- **Application migration** Many on-premises applications require a filesystem interface to data. As these applications continue to migrate to the cloud, Filestore can support a broad range of enterprise applications that need a shared filesystem.

Filestore Performance Tiers

You can choose Filestore based on your applications performance needs. The High Scale tier provides higher overall performance in multi-client scenarios. High performance is offered by using a scale-out architecture. If your workloads are performance-critical and spread over multiple clients, you may choose to deploy a High Scale tier instance for its performance benefits. For general-purpose applications such as test and development environments, use a basic version that offers good performance.

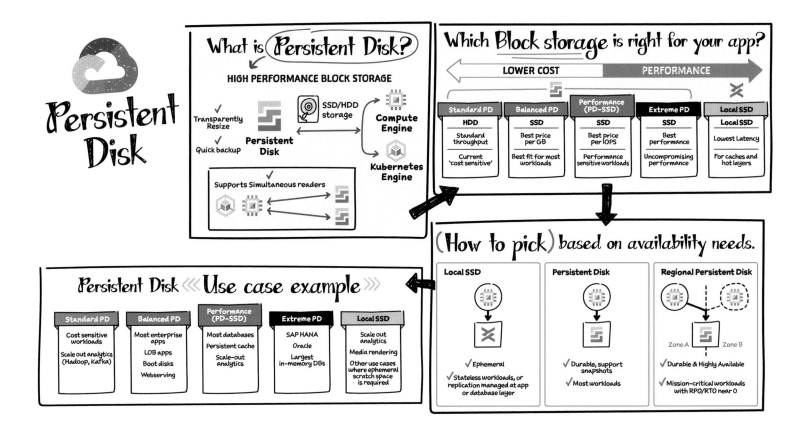

Persistent Disk

What is Persistent Disk?

HIGH PERFORMANCE BLOCK STORAGE

- ✓ Transparently Resize
- ✓ Quick backup

Persistent Disk — SSD/HDD storage → **Compute Engine** / **Kubernetes Engine**

✓ Supports Simultaneous readers

Which Block storage is right for your app?

← LOWER COST · PERFORMANCE →

Standard PD	Balanced PD	Performance (PD-SSD)	Extreme PD	Local SSD
HDD	SSD	SSD	SSD	Local SSD
Standard throughput	Best price per GB	Best price per IOPS	Best performance	Lowest Latency
Current 'cost sensitive'	Best fit for most workloads	Performance sensitive workloads	Uncompromising performance	For caches and hot layers

How to pick based on availability needs.

Local SSD
- ✓ Ephemeral
- ✓ Stateless workloads, or replication managed at app or database layer

Persistent Disk
- ✓ Durable, support snapshots
- ✓ Most workloads

Regional Persistent Disk
Zone A · Zone B
- ✓ Durable & Highly Available
- ✓ Mission-critical workloads with RPO/RTO near 0

Persistent Disk ≪ Use case example ≫

Standard PD	Balanced PD	Performance (PD-SSD)	Extreme PD	Local SSD
Cost sensitive workloads; Scale out analytics (Hadoop, Kafka)	Most enterprise apps; LOB apps; Boot disks; Webserving	Most databases; Persistent cache; Scale-out analytics	SAP HANA; Oracle; Largest in-memory DBs	Scale out analytics; Media rendering; Other use cases where ephemeral scratch space is required

Where Do Virtual Machines Store Data So They Can Access It When They Restart?

We need storage that is persistent in nature. That's where Persistent Disk comes in. Persistent Disk is a high-performance block storage service that uses solid-state drive (SSD) or hard disk drive (HDD) disks. These disks store data in blocks and are attached to virtual machines. In Google Cloud, that means they are attached to Compute Engine or Kubernetes Engine. You can attach multiple persistent disks to Compute Engine or GKE simultaneously, and you can configure quick, automatic, incremental backups or resize storage on the fly without disrupting your application.

Types of Block Storage

You can choose the best Persistent Disk option for you based on your cost and performance requirements.

- **Standard PD** is HDD and provides standard throughput. Because it is the most cost-effective option, it is best used for cost-sensitive applications and scale out analytics with Hadoop and Kafka.
- **Balanced PD** is SSD and is the best price per GB option. This makes it a good fit for common workloads such as line-of-business apps, boot disks, and web serving.

- **Performance PD** is SSD and provides the best price per IOPS (input/output operations per second). It is best suited for performance-sensitive applications such as databases, caches, and scale-out analytics.
- **Extreme PD** is SSD optimized for applications with uncompromising performance requirements. These applications include SAP HANA, Oracle, and the largest in-memory databases.
- **Local SSD** is recommended if your apps need really low latency. It is best for hot caches that offer best performance for analytics, media rendering, and other use cases that might require scratch space.

How to Pick Block Storage Based on Availability Needs

You can also choose a Persistent Disk based on the availability needs of your app. Use Local SSD if you just need ephemeral storage for a stateless app that manages the replication at the application or the database layer. For most workloads, you will be fine with Persistent Disk; it is durable and supports automated snapshots. But if your app demands even higher availability and is mission critical, then you have the option to use a regional persistent disk, which is replicated across zones for near-zero Recovery Point Objective (RPO) and Recovery Time Objective (RTO) values.

Which Storage Should I Use?

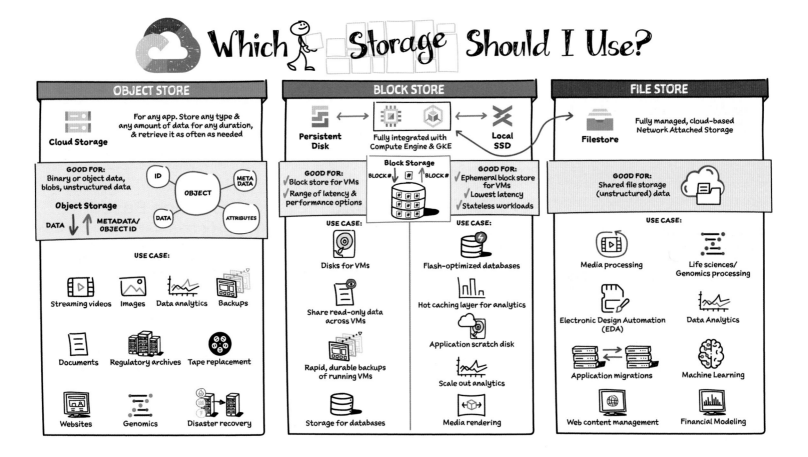

OBJECT STORE

Cloud Storage — For any app. Store any type & any amount of data for any duration, & retrieve it as often as needed

GOOD FOR: Binary or object data, blobs, unstructured data

Object Storage

DATA ↓ ↑ METADATA/ OBJECT ID

OBJECT — ID, METADATA, DATA, ATTRIBUTES

USE CASE:
- Streaming videos
- Images
- Data analytics
- Backups
- Documents
- Regulatory archives
- Tape replacement
- Websites
- Genomics
- Disaster recovery

BLOCK STORE

Persistent Disk ↔ Fully integrated with Compute Engine & GKE ↔ **Local SSD**

Block Storage
BLOCK # ↓ [#] ↑ BLOCK #

GOOD FOR:
- ✓ Block store for VMs
- ✓ Range of latency & performance options

GOOD FOR:
- ✓ Ephemeral block store for VMs
- ✓ Lowest latency
- ✓ Stateless workloads

USE CASE:
- Disks for VMs
- Share read-only data across VMs
- Rapid, durable backups of running VMs
- Storage for databases

USE CASE:
- Flash-optimized databases
- Hot caching layer for analytics
- Application scratch disk
- Scale out analytics
- Media rendering

FILE STORE

Filestore — Fully managed, cloud-based Network Attached Storage

GOOD FOR: Shared file storage (unstructured) data

USE CASE:
- Media processing
- Life sciences/ Genomics processing
- Electronic Design Automation (EDA)
- Data Analytics
- Application migrations
- Machine Learning
- Web content management
- Financial Modeling

Where Should Your Application Store Data?

Of course, the choice depends on the use case. Several different storage options are available within Google Cloud across three storage types: object storage, block storage, and file storage. We cover the use cases that are best suited for each storage option.

Object Storage — Cloud Storage

Cloud Storage is an object store for binary and object data, blobs, and unstructured data. You would typically use it for any app, any type of data that you need to store, for any duration. You can add data to it or retrieve data from it as often as you need. The objects stored have an ID, metadata, attributes, and the actual data. The metadata can include security classification of the file, the applications that can access it, and similar information.

Object storage use cases include applications that need data to be highly available and highly durable, such as streaming videos, serving images and documents, and websites. It is also used for storing large amounts of data for use cases such as genomics and data analytics. You can also use object storage for storing backups and archives for compliance with regulatory requirements. Or, use it to replace old physical tape records and move them over to cloud storage. Object storage is also widely used for disaster recovery because it takes practically no time to switch to a backup bucket to recover from a disaster.

There are four storage classes that are based on budget, availability, and access frequency.

- **Standard buckets**, for high-performance, frequent access, and highest availability
  - Regional or dual-regional locations, for data accessed frequently or high-throughput needs
  - Multi-region, for serving content globally
- **Nearline,** for data accessed less than once a month
- **Coldline,** for data accessed roughly less than once a quarter
- **Archive,** for data that you want to put away for years

It costs a bit more to use standard storage because it allows for automatic redundancy and frequent access options. Nearline, coldline, and archive storage offer 99% availability and costs significantly less.

Block Storage — Persistent Disk and Local SSD

Persistent Disk and Local SSD are block storage options. They are integrated with Compute Engine virtual machines and Kubernetes Engine. With block storage, files are split into evenly sized blocks of data, each with its own address but with no additional information (metadata) to provide more context for what that block of data is. Block storage can be directly accessed by the operating system as a mounted drive volume.

Persistent Disk is a block store for VMs that offers a range of latency and performance options. The use cases of Persistent Disk include disks for VMs and shared read-only data across multiple VMs. It is also used for rapid, durable backups of running VMs. Because of the high-performance options available, Persistent Disk is also a good storage option for databases.

Local SSD is also block storage but it is ephemeral in nature, and therefore typically used for stateless workloads that require the lowest available latencies. The use cases include flash optimized databases, host caching layers for analytics, or scratch disks for any application, as well as scale-out analytics and media rendering.

File Storage - Filestore

Now, Filestore! As fully managed Network Attached Storage (NAS), Filestore provides a cloud-based shared filesystem for unstructured data. It offers really low latency and provides concurrent access to tens of thousands of clients with scalable and predictable performance up to hundreds of thousands of IOPS, tens of GB/s of throughput, and hundreds of TBs. You can scale capacity up and down on-demand. Typical use cases of Filestore include high-performance computing (HPC), media processing, electronic design automation (EDA), application migrations, web content management, life science data analytics, and more!

CHAPTER THREE

Databases

A cloud database is a database service that is built and deployed on cloud infrastructure. Easily via the internet, cloud databases serve the same functions as any other modern relational or nonrelational databases, but with the added flexibility that comes with cloud computing. With a cloud database, you don't have to buy any dedicated hardware, and you don't have to worry about the infrastructure to run and scale the database. Depending on your needs and your team's abilities, you can choose a fully managed or a self-managed service.

Advantages of databases in the cloud:

- **Managed:** Cloud databases offer options to automate database provisioning, storage capacity management, and other time-consuming management tasks.
- **Scalable:** As the amount of data stored in your cloud database grows or shrinks, the storage capacity can be adjusted at runtime to accommodate the changes.
- **Easy to access:** Cloud databases can be easily accessed over the internet via APIs or a web console.

- **Disaster recovery:** Managed databases offer automated backups and recovery to restore instances to an earlier state.
- **Secure:** Cloud databases are secure, offering data encryption at rest and in transit, along with private connectivity to the applications that interact with them.

This chapter covers the two broad categories of cloud databases (relational and nonrelational), their advantages and common use cases, and options available for running them on Google Cloud.

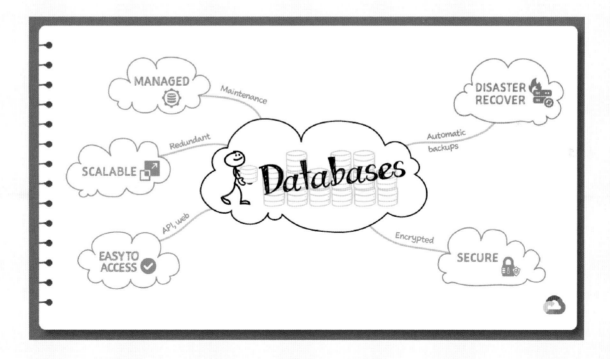

Introduction to Databases

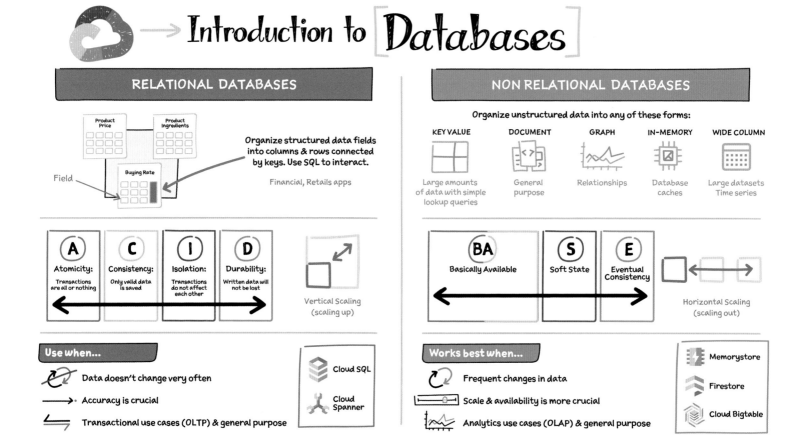

RELATIONAL DATABASES

Organize structured data fields into columns & rows connected by keys. Use SQL to interact.

Financial, Retails apps

Field

Product Price

Product Ingredients

Buying Rate

A Atomicity: Transactions are all or nothing

C Consistency: Only valid data is saved

I Isolation: Transactions do not affect each other

D Durability: Written data will not be lost

Vertical Scaling (scaling up)

Use when...

Data doesn't change very often

Accuracy is crucial

Transactional use cases (OLTP) & general purpose

Cloud SQL

Cloud Spanner

NON RELATIONAL DATABASES

Organize unstructured data into any of these forms:

KEY VALUE — Large amounts of data with simple lookup queries

DOCUMENT — General purpose

GRAPH — Relationships

IN-MEMORY — Database caches

WIDE COLUMN — Large datasets Time series

BA Basically Available

S Soft State

E Eventual Consistency

Horizontal Scaling (scaling out)

Works best when...

Frequent changes in data

Scale & availability is more crucial

Analytics use cases (OLAP) & general purpose

Memorystore

Firestore

Cloud Bigtable

Databases are critical parts of an application; they store data so that the application can easily access it when needed. For example: On a retail website you are browsing products to purchase. These items are stored in a database and rendered on the page when you request them. There are two broad categories of databases: relational (SQL) and nonrelational (NoSQL) databases.

Relational Databases

In relational databases information is stored in tables, rows, and columns, an arrangement that typically works best for structured data. As a result, they are used for applications in which the structure of the data does not change often. SQL (Structured Query Language) is used when interacting with most relational databases. They offer ACID consistency mode for the data, which means:

- **Atomic:** All operations in a transaction succeed or the operation is rolled back.
- **Consistent:** On the completion of a transaction, the database is structurally sound.
- **Isolated:** Transactions do not contend with one another. Contentious access to data is moderated by the database so that transactions appear to run sequentially.
- **Durable:** The results of applying a transaction are permanent, even in the presence of failures.

Because of these properties, relational databases are used in applications that require high accuracy and for transactional queries such as financial and retail transactions. For example: In banking when a customer makes a funds transfer request, you want to make sure that the transaction is possible and that it happens on the most up-to-date account balance; in this case, an error or resubmit request is likely fine but stale response is not.

Nonrelational databases

Nonrelational databases (or NoSQL databases) store complex, unstructured data in a nontabular form such as documents. Nonrelational databases are often used when large quantities of complex and diverse data need to be organized, or where the structure of the data is regularly evolving to meet new business requirements. Unlike relational databases, they perform faster because a query doesn't have to access several tables to deliver an answer, making them ideal for storing data that may change frequently or for applications that handle many different kinds of data. For example: An apparel store might have a database in which shirts have their own document containing all their information, including size, brand, and color, with room for adding more parameters such as sleeve size and collars later.

Qualities that make NoSQL databases fast:

- **Optimized:** They are typically optimized for a specific workload pattern (i.e., key-value, graph, wide-column).
- **Horizontal scaling:** They use range or hashed distributions to provide horizontal scaling.
- **Eventual consistency:** Many NoSQL stores usually exhibit consistency at some later point (e.g., lazily at read time). However, Firestore offers strong global consistency.
- **Transactions:** A majority of NoSQL stores don't support cross-shard transactions or flexible isolation modes. However, Firestore provides ACID transactions across shards with serializable isolation.

Because of these properties, nonrelational databases are used in applications that require reliability, availability, and large-scale, frequent data changes. They can easily scale horizontally by adding more servers, unlike some relational databases, which scale vertically by increasing the machine size as the data grows (although some relational databases such as Cloud Spanner support scale-out and strict consistency). Nonrelational databases can store a variety of unstructured data such as documents, key-value, graphs, wide columns, and more.

Which One Is Best?

Choosing a relational or a nonrelational database largely depends on the use case. Generally, if your application requires ACID transactions and your data is not going to change much, select a relational database. If your data may change later and if scale and availability is a bigger requirement than consistency, then a nonrelational database is a preferable choice.

In this chapter we will explore various types of databases available in Google Cloud and their use cases.

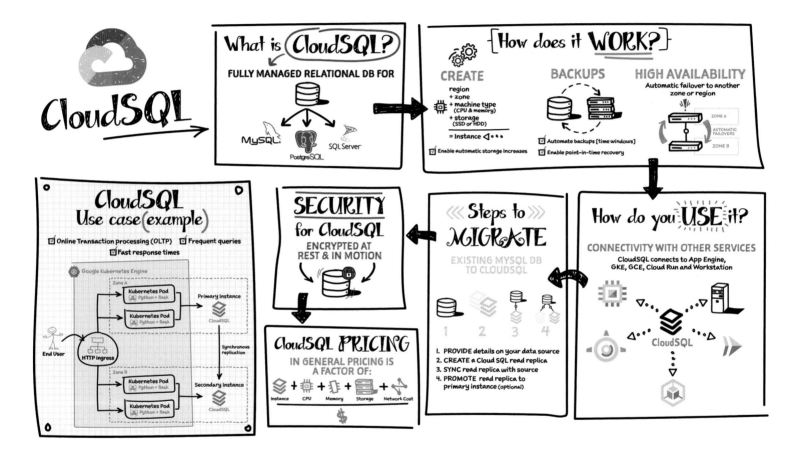

CloudSQL

What is CloudSQL?

FULLY MANAGED RELATIONAL DB FOR

MySQL · PostgreSQL · SQL Server

How does it WORK?

CREATE
region
+ zone
+ machine type (CPU & memory)
+ storage (SSD or HDD)
= Instance ◁ • • •
☑ Enable automatic storage increases

BACKUPS
☑ Automate backups [time windows]
☑ Enable point-in-time recovery

HIGH AVAILABILITY
Automatic failover to another zone or region
ZONE A
AUTOMATIC FAILOVERS
ZONE B

CloudSQL Use case (example)
☑ Online Transaction processing (OLTP) ☑ Frequent queries
☑ Fast response times

Google Kubernetes Engine
Zone A
Kubernetes Pod — Python + flask
Kubernetes Pod — Python + flask
Primary Instance — CloudSQL
End User — HTTP ingress
Synchronous replication
Zone B
Kubernetes Pod — Python + flask
Kubernetes Pod — Python + flask
Secondary Instance — CloudSQL

SECURITY for CloudSQL
ENCRYPTED AT REST & IN MOTION

CloudSQL PRICING
IN GENERAL PRICING IS A FACTOR OF:
Instance + CPU + Memory + Storage + Network Cost
$

Steps to MIGRATE
EXISTING MYSQL DB TO CLOUDSQL
1 2 3 4
1. PROVIDE details on your data source
2. CREATE a Cloud SQL read replica
3. SYNC read replica with source
4. PROMOTE read replica to primary instance (optional)

How do you USE it?
CONNECTIVITY WITH OTHER SERVICES
CloudSQL connects to App Engine, GKE, GCE, Cloud Run and Workstation
CloudSQL

When you are building an application, chances are you will need a relational database for transaction processing. That's where Cloud SQL comes in. It is a fully managed relational database for MySQL, Post-greSQL, and SQL Server. It reduces maintenance cost and automates database provisioning, storage capacity management, backups, and out-of-the-box high availability and disaster recovery/failover. Cloud SQL offers quick setup with standard connection drivers and built-in migration tools.

How to Set Up Cloud SQL

Cloud SQL is easy to set up:

- Select the region and zone where you would like the instances to be and they are created.

- Configure the machine type with the right number of CPU and the amount of memory your application needs.

- Choose the storage type, solid-state or hard disk drives, depending on latency, queries per second (QPS), and cost requirements.

Reliability and Availability

Cloud SQL also offers automated backups and point-in-time recovery options. You can set time slots and locations for backups. For production applications, it is recommended that you enable the built-in high availability (HA) option, which supports 99.95% SLA. With this, Google Cloud continuously monitors the Cloud SQL instance with a heartbeat signal, and when a primary fails, an automatic failover is triggered to another zone in your selected region in case of an outage. You can also create replicas across regions to protect from regional failure. And you can enable automatic storage increase so that more storage is added when nearing capacity.

Cloud SQL Insights, a free tool, helps detect, diagnose, and identify problems in a query for Cloud SQL databases. It provides self-service, intuitive monitoring, and diagnostic information that goes beyond detection to help you identify the root cause of performance problems.

Migrating an Existing MySQL Database to Cloud SQL

If you have an existing application that you are moving to the cloud, chances are you need to migrate your existing SQL database to Cloud SQL. Database Migration Service (DMS) simplifies the migration of MySQL and PostgreSQL databases from on-premises, Google Compute Engine, and other clouds to Cloud SQL. It is serverless, easy to set up, and available at no additional cost. It replicates data continuously for minimal downtime migrations.

Here's how it works:

- Provide your data source details—type of database engine, such as MySQL, PostgreSQL, Amazon RDS, or others. Pick one time or continuous replication for minimal downtime.

- Create a Cloud SQL instance as your destination.

- DMS makes connectivity to the source instance easy by providing multiple options. You can allow-list an IP address, create a reverse SSH tunnel via a cloud-hosted virtual machine, or set up VPC peering.

- Finally, test and promote the migrated instance to the primary Cloud SQL instance.

Security and Compliance

The data in Cloud SQL is automatically encrypted at rest and in transit. External connections can be enforced to be SSL-only. For secure connectivity you can also use Cloud SQL Proxy, a tool that helps you connect to your Cloud SQL instance from your local machine. You can control network access with firewall protection.

Cloud SQL in Action

Cloud SQL can be used in multiple use cases in conjunction with different compute options. You can use it in any application as a transactional database, long-term analytics backend with BigQuery, predictive analytics with Vertex AI, and event-driven messaging with Pub/Sub. Cloud SQL, when combined with Datastream (Change Data Capture), makes a great real-time analysis solution for any incoming data. Some examples include web/mobile apps, gaming, predictive analytics and inventory tracking.

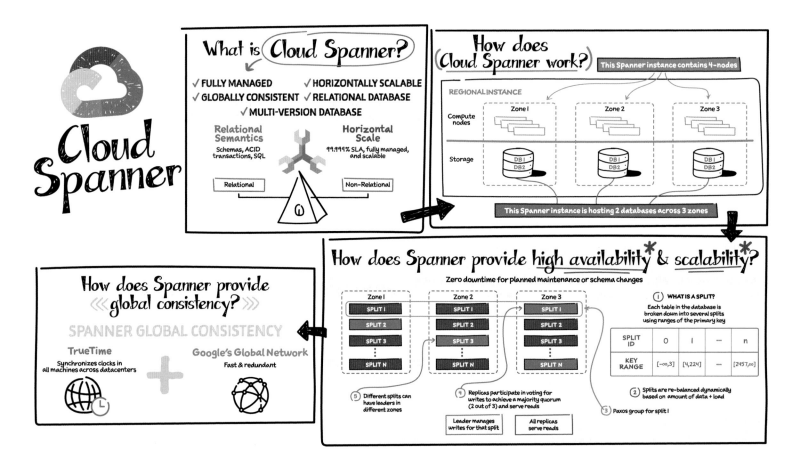

Cloud Spanner

What is Cloud Spanner?

✓ FULLY MANAGED   ✓ HORIZONTALLY SCALABLE
✓ GLOBALLY CONSISTENT ✓ RELATIONAL DATABASE
✓ MULTI-VERSION DATABASE

Relational Semantics
Schemas, ACID transactions, SQL

Horizontal Scale
99.999% SLA, fully managed, and scalable

Relational — Non-Relational

How does Cloud Spanner work?

This Spanner instance contains 4-nodes

REGIONAL INSTANCE

Compute nodes — Zone 1 | Zone 2 | Zone 3

Storage — DB1 DB2 | DB1 DB2 | DB1 DB2

This Spanner instance is hosting 2 databases across 3 zones

How does Spanner provide high availability* & scalability*?

Zero downtime for planned maintenance or schema changes

Zone 1	Zone 2	Zone 3
SPLIT 1	SPLIT 1	SPLIT 1
SPLIT 2	SPLIT 2	SPLIT 2
SPLIT 3	SPLIT 3	SPLIT 3
SPLIT N	SPLIT N	SPLIT N

5. Different splits can have leaders in different zones

4. Replicas participate in voting for writes to achieve a majority quorum (2 out of 3) and serve reads

Leader manages writes for that split

All replicas serve reads

1. WHAT IS A SPLIT?
Each table in the database is broken down into several splits using ranges of the primary key

SPLIT ID	0	1	...	n
KEY RANGE	[−∞,3]	[4,224]	...	[2457,∞]

2. Splits are re-balanced dynamically based on amount of data + load

3. Paxos group for split 1

How does Spanner provide global consistency?

SPANNER GLOBAL CONSISTENCY

TrueTime
Synchronizes clocks in all machines across datacenters

Google's Global Network
Fast & redundant

Databases are part of virtually every application you run in your organization, and great apps need great databases. This section is focused on one such great database: **Cloud Spanner**.

Cloud Spanner is the only enterprise-grade, globally distributed, and strongly consistent database service built for the cloud, specifically to combine the benefits of relational database structure with nonrelational horizontal scale. It is a unique database that combines transactions, SQL queries, and relational structure with the scalability that you typically associate with nonrelational or NoSQL databases.

How Does Spanner Work?

You can deploy your Cloud Spanner instance in a configuration of your choice with a specific number of nodes, databases, and zones. In the image you see a four-node regional Cloud Spanner instance hosting two databases. A *node* is a measure of compute in Spanner. Node servers serve the read and write/commit transaction requests, but they don't store the data. Each node is replicated across three zones in the region. The database storage is also replicated across the three zones. Nodes in a zone are responsible for reading and writing to the storage in their zone. The data is stored in Google's underlying Colossus distributed replicated filesystem. This provides huge advantages when it comes to redistributing load, because the data is not linked to individual nodes. If a node or a zone fails, the database remains available, being served by the remaining nodes. No manual intervention is needed to maintain availability.

How Does Spanner Provide High Availability and Scalability?

Each table in the database is stored, sorted by primary key. Tables are divided by ranges of the primary key, and these divisions are known as *splits*. Each split is managed completely independently by different Spanner nodes.

The number of splits for a table varies according to the amount of data; empty tables have only a single split. The splits are rebalanced dynamically depending on the amount of data and the load (dynamic resharding). But remember that the table and nodes are replicated across three zones. How does that work?

Everything is replicated across the three zones; the same goes for split management. Split replicas are associated with a group (Paxos) that spans zones. Using Paxos consensus protocols, one of the zones is determined to be a *leader*. The leader is responsible for managing write transactions for that split, whereas the other replicas can be used for reads. If a leader fails, the consensus is redetermined, and a new leader may be chosen. For different splits, different zones can become leaders, thus distributing the leadership roles among all the Cloud Spanner compute nodes. Nodes will likely be both leaders for some splits and replicas for others. Using this distributed mechanism of splits, leaders, and replicas, Cloud Spanner achieves both high availability and scalability.

How Do Reads and Writes Work?

There are two types of reads in Cloud Spanner:

Strong reads are used when the absolute latest value needs to be read. Here's how it works:

1. The Cloud Spanner API identifies the split, looks up the Paxos group to use for the split, and routes the request to one of the replicas (usually in the same zone as the client). In this example, the request is sent to the read-only replica in zone 1.

2. The replica requests from the leader if it is OK to read, and it asks for the TrueTime timestamp of the latest transaction on this row.

3. The leader responds, and the replica compares the response with its own state.

How do reads & writes work in Spanner?

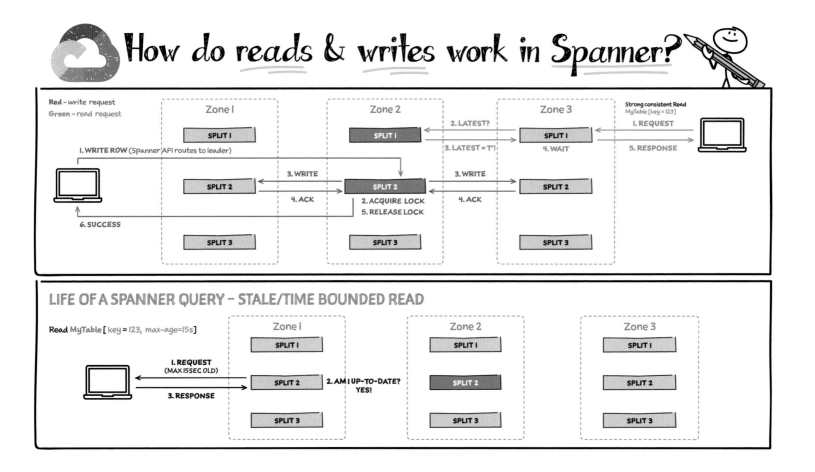

Red – write request
Green – read request

Strong consistent Read
MyTable [key = 123]

Zone 1 — SPLIT 1 — SPLIT 2 — SPLIT 3

Zone 2 — SPLIT 1 — SPLIT 2 — SPLIT 3

Zone 3 — SPLIT 1 — SPLIT 2 — SPLIT 3

2. LATEST?
3. LATEST = T'!
1. REQUEST
5. RESPONSE
4. WAIT

1. WRITE ROW (Spanner API routes to leader)

3. WRITE
4. ACK
2. ACQUIRE LOCK
5. RELEASE LOCK
6. SUCCESS

LIFE OF A SPANNER QUERY – STALE/TIME BOUNDED READ

Read MyTable [key = 123, max-age=15s]

Zone 1 — SPLIT 1 — SPLIT 2 — SPLIT 3

Zone 2 — SPLIT 1 — SPLIT 2 — SPLIT 3

Zone 3 — SPLIT 1 — SPLIT 2 — SPLIT 3

1. REQUEST (MAX 15SEC OLD)
2. AM I UP-TO-DATE? YES!
3. RESPONSE

4. If the row is up-to-date, it can return the result. Otherwise, it needs to wait for the leader to send updates.

5. The response is sent back to the client.

In some cases—for example, when the row has just been updated while the read request is in transit—the state of the replica is sufficiently up-to-date that it does not even need to ask the leader for the latest transaction.

Stale reads are used when low read latency is more important than getting the latest values, so some data staleness is tolerated. In a stale read, the client does not request the absolute latest version, just the data that is most recent (e.g., up to n seconds old). If the staleness factor is at least 15 seconds, the replica in most cases can return the data without even querying the leader since its internal state will show that the data is sufficiently up-to-date. You can see that in each of these read requests, no row locking was required—the ability for any node to respond to reads is what makes Cloud Spanner so fast and scalable.

How Does Spanner Provide Global Consistency?

TrueTime is essential to make Spanner work as well as it does…so, what is it, and how does it help?

TrueTime is a way to synchronize clocks in all machines across multiple datacenters. The system uses a combination of GPS and atomic clocks, each correcting for the failure modes of the other. Combining the two sources (using multiple redundancy, of course) gives an accurate source of time for all Google applications. But clock drift on each machine can still occur, and even with a sync every 30 seconds, the difference between the server's clock and the reference clock can be as much as 2 ms. The drift will look like a sawtooth graph, with the uncertainty increasing until corrected by a clock sync. Since 2 ms is quite a long duration (in computing terms, at least), TrueTime includes this uncertainty as part of the time signal.

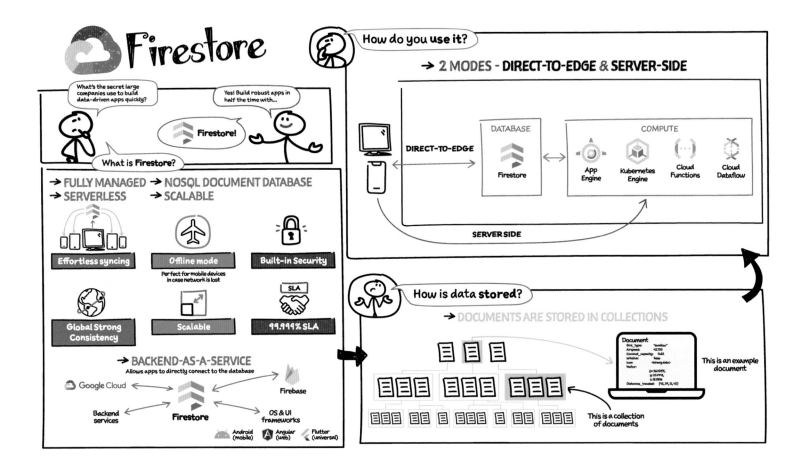

Firestore

What's the secret large companies use to build data-driven apps quickly?

Yes! Build robust apps in half the time with...

Firestore!

What is **Firestore?**

→ FULLY MANAGED → NOSQL DOCUMENT DATABASE
→ SERVERLESS → SCALABLE

Effortless syncing

Offline mode
Perfect for mobile devices in case network is lost

Built-in Security

Global Strong Consistency

Scalable

SLA
99.999% SLA

→ BACKEND-AS-A-SERVICE
Allows apps to directly connect to the database

Google Cloud

Firebase

Backend services

Firestore

OS & UI frameworks

Android (mobile)   Angular (web)   Flutter (universal)

How do you **use it?**

→ 2 MODES - **DIRECT-TO-EDGE** & **SERVER-SIDE**

DATABASE

COMPUTE

DIRECT-TO-EDGE

Firestore

App Engine

Kubernetes Engine

Cloud Functions

Cloud Dataflow

SERVER SIDE

How is data **stored?**

→ DOCUMENTS ARE STORED IN COLLECTIONS

Document
Bird_Type: "swallow"
Airspeed: 42.733
Coconut_capacity: 0.62
isHollow: true
Icon: <binarydata>
Vector:
              (n: 56.4255,
              z: 25.9412,
              z: 51.8916
Distance_traveled: [42, 34, 11, 43]

This is an example document

This is a collection of documents

Your product teams may wonder why it takes so long to build a new feature or application. One reason that building applications is such a heavy lift is technical complexity, which includes the complexity of backend services that are used to manage and store data. Time spent dealing with this technical complexity is a distraction from delivering on core business value. Firestore eliminates this distraction by having Google Cloud manage backend complexity through a complete backend-as-a-service! Firestore acts as a glue that intelligently brings together the complete Google Cloud backend ecosystem, in-app services from Firebase, and core UI frameworks and OS from Google.

What Is Firestore?

Firestore is a serverless, fully managed NoSQL document database that scales from zero to global scale without configuration or downtime. Here's what makes Firestore unique:

- Ideal for rapid, flexible, and scalable web and mobile development with direct connectivity to the database.
- Supports effortless real-time data synchronization with changes in your database as they happen.
- Robust support for offline mode, so your users can keep interacting with your app even when the internet isn't available or is unreliable.
- Fully customizable security and data validation rules to ensure data is always protected.
- Built-in strong consistency, elastic scaling, high performance, and best-in-class 99.999% availability.
- Integration with Firebase and Google Cloud services like Cloud Functions and BigQuery.

- In addition to a rich set of Google Cloud service integrations, Firestore offers deep one-click integrations with a growing set of third-party partners via Firebase Extensions to help you build applications even more rapidly.

Document-Model Database

Firestore is a document-model database. All of your data is stored in *documents* and then *collections*. You can think of a document as a JSON object. It's a dictionary with a set of key-value mappings, where the values can be several different supported data types, including strings, numbers, or binary values.

Documents are stored in collections. Documents can't directly contain other documents, but they can point to subcollections that contain other documents, which can point to subcollections, and so on. This structure brings with it a number of advantages. For starters, all queries that you make are shallow, meaning that you can grab a document without worrying about grabbing all the data underneath it. And this means that you can structure your data hierarchically in a way that makes sense to you logically, without having to worry about grabbing tons of unnecessary data.

How Do You Use Firestore?

Firestore can be used in two modes:

- **Firestore in Native mode:** This mode is differentiated by its ability to directly connect your web and mobile apps to Firestore. Native Mode supports up to **10K** writes per second and over a **million** connections.
- **Firestore in Datastore mode:** This mode supports only server-side usage of Firestore, but it supports unlimited scaling, including writes.

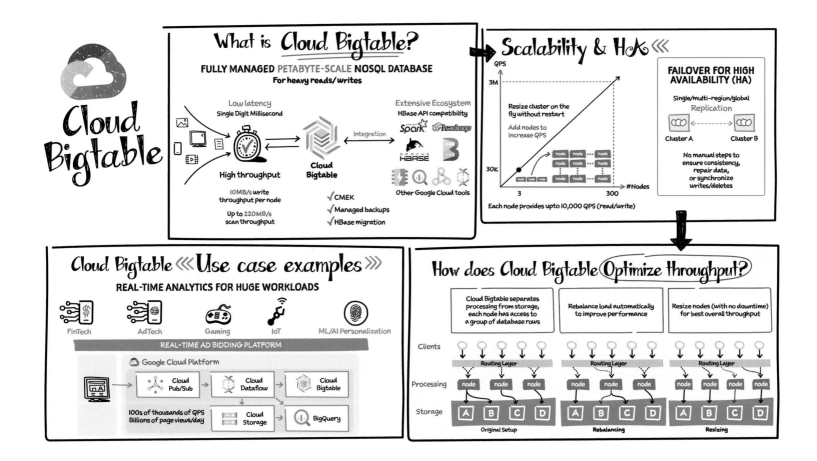

What is Cloud Bigtable?

FULLY MANAGED PETABYTE-SCALE NOSQL DATABASE
For heavy reads/writes

Low latency
Single Digit Millisecond

Cloud Bigtable

Integration

Extensive Ecosystem
HBase API compatibility

Spark · hadoop

HBASE · B

Other Google Cloud tools

High throughput

IOMB/s write throughput per node

Up to 220MB/s scan throughput

✓ CMEK
✓ Managed backups
✓ HBase migration

Scalability & HA

QPS
3M
30K
Resize cluster on the fly without restart
Add nodes to increase QPS

node node ··· node

3   300   #Nodes

Each node provides upto 10,000 QPS (read/write)

FAILOVER FOR HIGH AVAILABILITY (HA)

Single/multi-region/global
Replication

Cluster A   Cluster B

No manual steps to ensure consistency, repair data, or synchronize writes/deletes

Cloud Bigtable « Use case examples »

REAL-TIME ANALYTICS FOR HUGE WORKLOADS

FinTech   AdTech   Gaming   IoT   ML/AI Personalization

REAL-TIME AD BIDDING PLATFORM

Google Cloud Platform

Cloud Pub/Sub → Cloud Dataflow → Cloud Bigtable

100s of thousands of QPS
Billions of page views/day

Cloud Storage → BigQuery

How does Cloud Bigtable Optimize throughput?

Cloud Bigtable separates processing from storage, each node has access to a group of database rows

Rebalance load automatically to improve performance

Resize nodes (with no downtime) for best overall throughput

Clients

Routing Layer

Processing

node node node

Storage

A B C D

Original Setup

Routing Layer

node node node

A B C D

Rebalancing

Routing Layer

node node node node

A B C D

Resizing

Building an application that needs low latency and high throughput? You need a database that can scale for a large number of reads and writes. Cloud Bigtable is designed to handle just that.

Cloud Bigtable is a fully managed wide-column NoSQL database that scales to petabyte-scale. It's optimized for low latency, large numbers of reads and writes, and maintaining performance at scale. It offers really low latency of the order of single-digit milliseconds. It is an ideal data source for time series and MapReduce-style operations. Bigtable supports the open source HBase API standard to easily integrate with the Apache ecosystem, including HBase, Beam, Hadoop, and Spark. It also integrates with the Google Cloud ecosystem, including Memorystore, BigQuery, Dataproc, Dataflow, and more.

Some Cloud Bigtable Features

- Data is by default encrypted with Google managed encryption keys, but for specific compliance and regulatory requirements if customers need to manage their own keys, customer managed encryption keys (CMEKs) are also supported.

- Bigtable backups let you save a copy of a table's schema and data, then restore from the backup to a new table at a later time. Backups can help you recover from application-level data corruption or from operator errors such as accidentally deleting a table.

Scale and High Availability (HA)

How BIG is Bigtable? Bigtable has nearly 10 exabytes of data under management.

It delivers highly predictable performance that is linearly scalable. Throughput can be adjusted by adding/removing nodes—each node provides up to 10,000 operations per second (read and write). You can use Bigtable as the storage engine for large-scale, low-latency applications as well as throughput-intensive data processing and analytics. It offers high availability with an SLA of 99.9% for zonal instances. It's strongly consistent in a single cluster; replication between clusters adds eventual consistency. If you leverage Bigtable's multicluster routing across two clusters, the SLA increases to 99.99%, and if that routing policy is utilized across clusters in three different regions, you get a 99.999% uptime SLA.

Replication for Cloud Bigtable enables you to increase the availability and durability of your data by copying it across multiple regions or multiple zones within the same region. To use replication in a Bigtable instance, just create an instance with more than one cluster or add clusters to an existing instance. Bigtable supports up to four replicated clusters located in Google Cloud zones where Bigtable is available. Placing clusters in different zones or regions enables you to access your data even if one zone or region becomes unavailable. Bigtable treats each cluster in your instance as a primary cluster, so you can perform reads and writes in each cluster. You can also set up your instance so that requests from different types of applications are routed to different clusters. The data and changes to data are synchronized automatically across clusters.

How Does It Optimize Throughput?

Through separation of processing and storage, Cloud Bigtable is able to automatically configure throughput by adjusting the association of nodes and data. In the rebalancing example, if Node A is experiencing a heavy load, the routing layer can move some of the traffic to a less heavily loaded node, improving overall performance. Resizing comes into play when a node is added to again ensure a balanced load across nodes, ensuring best overall throughput.

Choice of app profile and traffic routing can also affect performance. An app profile with multicluster routing automatically routes requests to the closest cluster in an instance from the perspective of the application, and the writes are then replicated to the other clusters in the instance. This automatic choice of the shortest distance results in the lowest possible latency. An app profile that uses single-cluster routing can be optimal for certain use cases, like separating workloads or having read-after-write semantics on a single cluster, but it will not reduce latency in the way multicluster routing does.

Replication can improve read throughput, especially when you use multicluster routing. And it can reduce read latency by placing your data geographically closer to your users. Write throughput does not increase with replication because write to one cluster must be replicated to all other clusters in the instance, resulting in each cluster spending the CPU resources to pull changes from the other clusters.

Memorystore

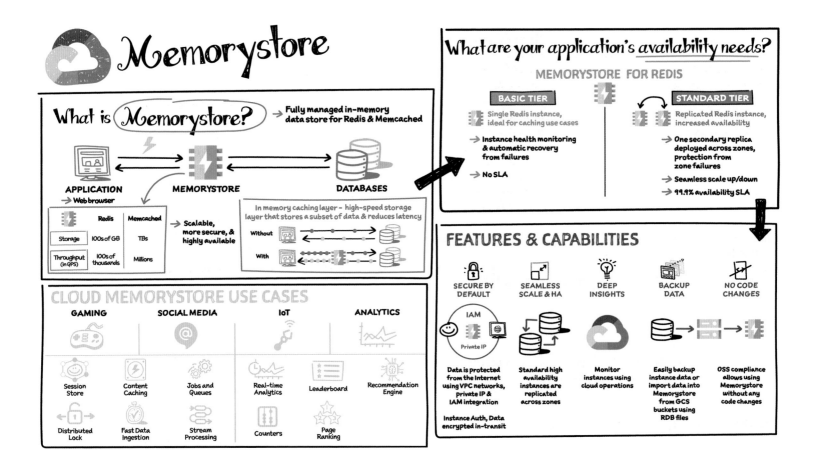

What is Memorystore?

→ Fully managed in-memory data store for Redis & Memcached

APPLICATION
→ Web browser

MEMORYSTORE

DATABASES

	Redis	Memcached
Storage	100s of GB	TBs
Throughput (in QPS)	100s of thousands	Millions

→ Scalable, more secure, & highly available

In memory caching layer - high-speed storage layer that stores a subset of data & reduces latency

Without

With

CLOUD MEMORYSTORE USE CASES

GAMING
- Session Store
- Distributed Lock

SOCIAL MEDIA
- Content Caching
- Fast Data Ingestion
- Jobs and Queues
- Stream Processing

IoT
- Real-time Analytics
- Counters
- Leaderboard
- Page Ranking

ANALYTICS
- Recommendation Engine

What are your application's availability needs?

MEMORYSTORE FOR REDIS

BASIC TIER
- Single Redis instance, ideal for caching use cases
→ Instance health monitoring & automatic recovery from failures
→ No SLA

STANDARD TIER
- Replicated Redis instance, increased availability
→ One secondary replica deployed across zones, protection from zone failures
→ Seamless scale up/down
→ 99.9% availability SLA

FEATURES & CAPABILITIES

SECURE BY DEFAULT

SEAMLESS SCALE & HA

DEEP INSIGHTS

BACKUP DATA

NO CODE CHANGES

IAM
Private IP

Data is protected from the Internet using VPC networks, private IP & IAM integration

Instance Auth, Data encrypted in-transit

Standard high availability instances are replicated across zones

Monitor instances using cloud operations

Easily backup instance data or import data into Memorystore from GCS buckets using RDB files

OSS compliance allows using Memorystore without any code changes

Many of today's applications, ranging from gaming, to cybersecurity, to social media, require processing data at sub-millisecond latency to deliver real-time experiences. To meet demands of low latency at increased scale and reduced cost, you need an in-memory data store. Redis and Memcached are among the most popular. Memorystore is a fully managed in-memory data store service for Redis and Memcached at Google Cloud. Like any other Google Cloud service, it is fast, scalable, highly available, and secure. It automates the complex tasks of provisioning, replication, failover, and patching so that you can spend more time on other activities. It comes with a 99.9% SLA and integrates seamlessly with your apps within Google Cloud.

Memorystore is used for different types of in-memory caches and transient stores. Memorystore for Redis is also used as a highly available key-value store. This serves multiple use cases, including web content caches, session stores, distributed locks, stream processing, recommendations, capacity caches, gaming leaderboards, fraud/threat detection, personalization, and AdTech.

What are Your Application's Availability Needs?

Memorystore for Redis offers Basic and Standard tiers. The Basic tier is best suited for applications that use Redis as a cache and that can withstand a cold restart and full data flush. Standard tier instances provide high availability using replication and automatic failover.

Memorystore for Memcached instances are provisioned on a node basis with vCPU and memory per cores per node, which means you can select them based on your specific application requirements.

Features and Capabilities

Secure: Memorystore is protected from the internet using VPC networks and private IP and comes with IAM integration to protect your data. Memorystore for Redis also offers instance-level AUTH and in-transit encryption. It is also compliant with major certifications (e.g., HIPAA, FedRAMP, and SOC2).

Observability: You can monitor your instance and set up custom alerts with Cloud Monitoring. You can also integrate with OpenCensus to get more insights into client-side metrics.

Scalable: Start with the lowest tier and smallest size and then grow your instance as needed. Memorystore provides automated scaling using APIs and optimized node placement across zones for redundancy. Memorystore for Memcached can support clusters as large as 5 TB, enabling millions of QPS at very low latency.

Highly available: Memorystore for Redis instances are replicated across two zones and provide a 99.9% availability SLA. Instances are monitored constantly and with automatic failover—applications experience minimal disruption.

Migrate with no code changes: Memorystore is open source software compliant, which makes it easy to switch your applications with no code changes.

Backups: Memorystore for Redis offers an import/export feature to migrate Redis instances to Google Cloud using RDS snapshots.

Use Cases

Memorystore is great for use cases that require fast, real-time processing of data. Simple caching, gaming leaderboards, and real-time analytics are just a few examples.

Caching: Caches are an integral part of modern application architectures. Memorystore is used in caching use cases such as session management, frequently accessed queries, scripts, and pages.

Gaming: With data structures like Sorted Set, Memorystore makes it easy to maintain a sorted list of scores for a leaderboard while providing uniqueness of elements. Redis hash makes it fast and easy to store and access player profiles.

Stream Processing: Whether processing a Twitter feed or stream of data from IoT devices, Memorystore is a perfect fit for streaming solutions combined with Dataflow and Pub/Sub.

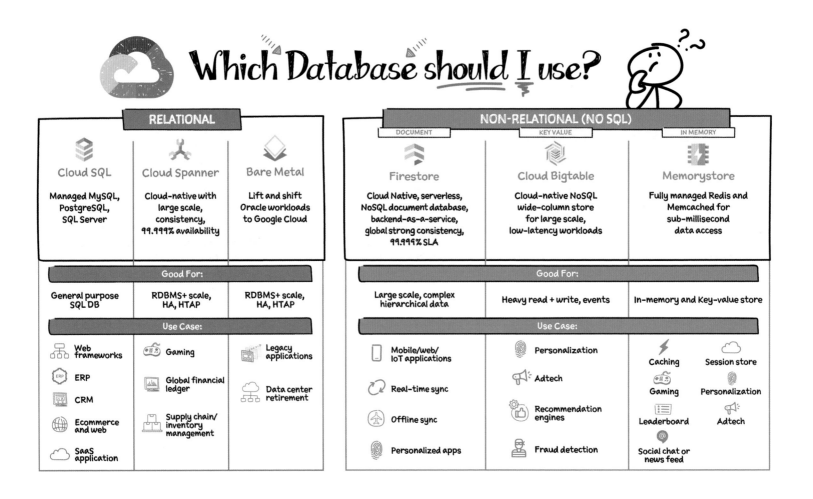

Which Database should I use?

RELATIONAL

Cloud SQL	Cloud Spanner	Bare Metal
Managed MySQL, PostgreSQL, SQL Server	Cloud-native with large scale, consistency, 99.999% availability	Lift and shift Oracle workloads to Google Cloud

Good For:

General purpose SQL DB	RDBMS+ scale, HA, HTAP	RDBMS+ scale, HA, HTAP

Use Case:

Web frameworks	Gaming	Legacy applications
ERP	Global financial ledger	Data center retirement
CRM	Supply chain/ inventory management	
Ecommerce and web		
SaaS application		

NON-RELATIONAL (NO SQL)

DOCUMENT	KEY VALUE	IN MEMORY
Firestore	**Cloud Bigtable**	**Memorystore**
Cloud Native, serverless, NoSQL document database, backend-as-a-service, global strong consistency, 99.999% SLA	Cloud-native NoSQL wide-column store for large scale, low-latency workloads	Fully managed Redis and Memcached for sub-millisecond data access

Good For:

Large scale, complex hierarchical data	Heavy read + write, events	In-memory and Key-value store

Use Case:

Mobile/web/ IoT applications	Personalization	Caching / Session store
Real-time sync	Adtech	Gaming / Personalization
Offline sync	Recommendation engines	Leaderboard / Adtech
Personalized apps	Fraud detection	Social chat or news feed

Picking the right database for your application is not easy. The choice depends on the use case: transactional processing, analytical processing, in-memory database, and so forth. In the beginning of this chapter, you learned when to use relational (SQL) and nonrelational (NoSQL) databases, and throughout this chapter we covered each of the databases in Google Cloud. Here let's stack them side by side to get a clear understanding of the use cases they support.

We have three different relational database options:

- **Cloud SQL:** Provides managed MySQL, PostgreSQL, and SQL Server databases on Google Cloud. It reduces maintenance cost and automates database provisioning, storage capacity management, backups, and out-of-the-box high availability and disaster recovery/failover. For these reasons, it is best for general-purpose web frameworks, CRM, ERP, SaaS, and e-commerce applications.

- **Cloud Spanner:** Cloud Spanner is an enterprise-grade, globally distributed, and strongly consistent database that offers up to 99.999% availability, built specifically to combine the benefits of relational database structure with nonrelational horizontal scale. It is a unique database that combines ACID transactions, SQL queries, and relational structure with the scalability that you typically associate with nonrelational or NoSQL databases. As a result, Spanner is best used for applications such as gaming, payment solutions, global financial ledgers, retail banking, and inventory management that require the ability to scale limitlessly with strong consistency and high availability.

- **Bare Metal Solution:** Provides hardware to run specialized workloads with low latency on Google Cloud. This is specifically useful if there is an Oracle database that you want to lift and shift into Google Cloud. This enables data center retirements and paves a path to modernize legacy applications. For specifics on Bare Metal solution, refer to Chapter 1 where we covered this in detail.

We have three nonrelational databases in Google Cloud:

- **Firestore:** Firestore is a serverless document database that scales on demand, is strongly consistent, supports ACID transactions, offers up to 99.999% availability, and acts as a backend-as-a-service. It is a DBaaS that is optimized for building applications. It is perfect for all general-purpose use cases such as e-commerce, gaming, IoT, and real-time dashboards. With Firestore, users can interact with and collaborate on live and offline data, making it great for real-time application and mobile apps.

- **Cloud Bigtable:** Cloud Bigtable is a sparsely populated table that can scale to billions of rows and thousands of columns, enabling you to store terabytes or even petabytes of data. It is ideal for storing large amounts of single-keyed data with very low latency. It supports high read and write throughput at single-digit-millisecond latency, and it is an ideal data source for MapReduce operations. It also supports the open source HBase API standard, so it easily integrates with the Apache ecosystem, including HBase, Beam, Hadoop, and Spark, along with Google Cloud ecosystem.

- **Memorystore:** Memorystore is a fully managed in-memory data store service for Redis and Memcached at Google Cloud. It is best for in-memory and transient data stores and automates the complex tasks of provisioning, replication, failover, and patching so that you can spend more time coding. Because it offers extremely low latency and high performance, Memorystore is great for web and mobile, gaming, leaderboard, social, chat, and newsfeed applications.

CHAPTER FOUR

Data Analytics

The amount of data being collected — and then being made available for data analytics — is growing rapidly. So too is the need to employ effective pipelines that can take all that collected data and transform it into meaningful insights. Building these pipelines in the cloud comes with significant advantages. In addition to virtually unlimited scalability, the cloud offers managed services that eliminate the hassles and risks of managing your own infrastructure and hardware.

A typical data analytics pipeline starts with a data lake — a centralized repository for storing all your structured and unstructured data at scale in its raw form. The pipeline processes the data, cleaning, enriching, and transforming it to make it useful for downstream applications. A data warehouse stores the processed data in a relational format accessible via SQL. Analytics, business intelligence, and data science teams access the data in the data warehouse to create dashboards, machine learning (ML) models for predictions, and more.

This chapter covers the different steps involved in a typical data analytics pipeline, and options available for running them on Google Cloud in a scalable way.

Every application generates data, but what does that data mean? This is a question all data scientists are hired to answer. There is no doubt that this information is the most precious commodity for a business. But making sense of data, creating insights, and turning them into decisions is even more important. As the data keeps growing in volume, the data analytics pipelines have to be scalable to adapt to the rate of change. And for this reason, choosing to set up the pipeline in the cloud makes perfect sense, since the cloud offers on-demand scalability and flexibility.

In this chapter we will demystify how to build a scalable and adaptable data processing pipeline in Google Cloud. Let's start here by discussing the general concepts of a data pipeline that are applicable in any cloud or on-premise data pipeline.

5 Steps to Create a Data Analytics Pipeline

1. *Capture:* First you ingest the data from various data sources. These sources could be either batch or real-time data.

   a. Batch data is the data that is stored at a regular period of time and further processed in bulk.

   b. Real-time data is generated from websites such as clickstream data or IoT devices sending streams of data for processing.

2. *Process:* Once the data is ingested, it is processed and enriched so that the downstream system can utilize them in the format it

understands best. Business logic is applied on the data in the processing stage, and then the data is dropped into a *sink*, which is a storage device for the enriched and processed data. For example: Your business logic requires the input data to be maked and tokenized for security reasons and then dumps the tokenized data into a storage device.

3. ***Store:*** After the data is processing, it needs to be stored so that it can enable analytics projects. There are two types of storage options you can use at this stage of the pipeline:

    a. **Data warehouse** is a repository for structured, filtered data that has already been processed for a specific purpose. For example: specific reporting, analysis, data marts, machine learning.

    b. **Data lake** is a vast pool of raw data, the purpose for which is either interim or not yet defined. A data lake is a centralized repository designed to securely store large amounts of structured, semi-structured, and unstructured data. It can store data in its native format and process any variety of it, ignoring size limits.

4. ***Analyze:*** Data stored in a data warehouse can then be used by the downstream systems for analysis. This is the stage where data analysts and data scientists can run queries on the data to explore it for their purposes.

5. ***Use:*** Once the data is in a data warehouse, it can be used by multiple different internal customers such as data analysts and data scientists. Analysts can analyze the data, and the data scientists can pull the same data into a Jupyter Notebook or train a machine learning model with it. They could create data marts, dashboards, and reports for business purposes or integrate it with external data and reporting systems.

A few factors apply across all these stages of the data analytics pipeline:

- **Data integration** — Data is always in multiple different places; at any stage you might need a data integration service that brings data from other systems in one place such as a data lake.

- **Metadata management** — Data scientists and data analysts need to be able to quickly discover, understand, and manage all your data in one place. This is where having a metadata management system enables you to democratize data and insights for both technical and business users.

- **Workflow orchestration** — Data pipelines are not run just once; most pipelines have to be scheduled and run over a period of time and tasks need to be defined. Across these tasks a workflow orchestration tool is needed to easily author, schedule, and monitor pipelines.

Extract, Transform, and Load (ETL)

You might have come across the term ETL (extract, transform, and load) in the context of data pipelines. ETL is essentially a data processing pipeline that works on a batch of data. Data pipelines don't necessarily have to end in loading data to a storage or analytics system; they can be used to trigger a business process via a webhook.

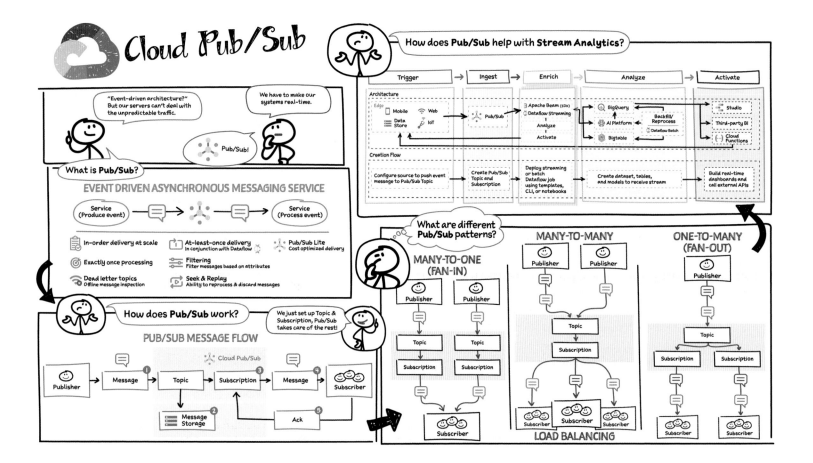

So, you've said goodbye to the monolithic application and refactored it into services. You are shipping faster and the code is cleaner. But the complexity of communication between the services is causing performance issues. And every time a new team needs to integrate, it's a whole lot of meetings. The time has come to consider asynchronous communication, where services publish and listen for events that flow through a messaging system. The services are decoupled and you can keep scaling. That is where Pub/Sub comes in — a set of fully managed messaging services. You can use Pub/Sub as messaging-oriented middleware or event ingestion and delivery for streaming analytics pipelines. Pub/Sub comes in two flavors:

Pub/Sub:

- It provides messaging and event ingestion for real-time analytics.
- It is serverless, it autoscales, and it auto-provisions as needed.
- It provides the ability to publish and subscribe to events regardless of geography.
- You can create up to 10,000 subscriber apps per topic; it provides independent capacity and billing for publishers and subscribers.
- It supports the push delivery model and is especially useful for communication between microservices

Pub/Sub Lite:

- Optimizes for cost over reliability
- Is up to 90% cheaper than Pub/Sub
- Requires you to manage your capacity and offers less available storage than Pub/Sub

How Does Pub/Sub Work?

A publisher application creates and sends messages to a topic. Subscriber applications create a subscription to a topic to receive messages from it. Communication can be one-to-many (fan-out), many-to-one (fan-in), and many-to-many.

1. A publisher application creates a topic in the Pub/Sub service and sends messages to the topic. A message contains a payload and optional attributes that describe the payload content.

2. The service ensures that published messages are retained on behalf of subscriptions. A published message is retained for a subscription until it is acknowledged by any subscriber consuming messages from that subscription.

3. Pub/Sub forwards messages from a topic to all of its subscriptions individually.

4. A subscriber receives messages either by Pub/Sub pushing them to the subscriber's chosen endpoint, or by the subscriber pulling them from the service.

5. The subscriber sends an acknowledgment to the Pub/Sub service for each received message.

6. The service removes acknowledged messages from the subscription's message queue.

Pub/Sub Features

- **Global routing:** You can publish messages to a topic anywhere in the world. It is persisted locally for low latency. On the other end, subscribers, deployed in any region, receive messages from all publish locations without doing anything special.

- **Partition-less in-order delivery:** If messages have the same ordering key and are in the same region, you can enable message ordering and receive the messages in the order that the Pub/Sub service receives them.

- **Dead letter topics:** If the Pub/Sub service attempts to deliver a message but the subscriber can't acknowledge it, Pub/Sub can forward the undeliverable message to a dead-letter topic to attempt delivery at a later time.

- **Seek and replay:** There could be times when you need to alter the acknowledgment stage of messages in bulk; the seek and replay feature allows you to do that.

- **Filtering:** You can filter messages by message attributes, and when you receive messages from a subscription with a filter, you only receive the messages that match the filter. Pub/Sub automatically acknowledges the messages that don't match the filter.

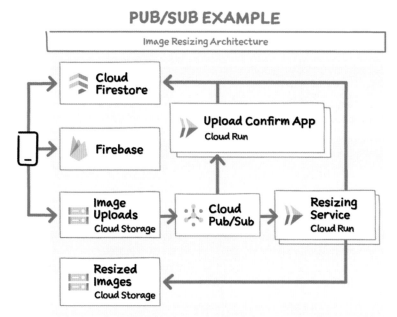

EVENT-DRIVEN SYSTEMS

PUB/SUB EXAMPLE

Pub/Sub Use Cases

Asynchronous service integration: Pub/Sub works as a messaging middleware for traditional service integration or a simple communication medium for modern microservices. Push subscriptions deliver events to serverless webhooks on Cloud Functions, App Engine, Cloud Run, or custom environments on Google Kubernetes Engine or Compute Engine. Low-latency pull delivery is available when exposing webhooks is not an option or for efficient handling of higher throughput streams.

Stream analytics: Data ingestion is the foundation for analytics and machine learning, whether you are building stream, batch, or unified pipelines. Cloud Pub/Sub provides a simple and reliable staging location for your event data on its journey to processing, storage, and analysis. Use Cloud Dataflow with Cloud Pub/Sub to enrich, deduplicate, order, aggregate, and land events. Mix real-time and batch processing via Cloud Pub/Sub's durable storage.

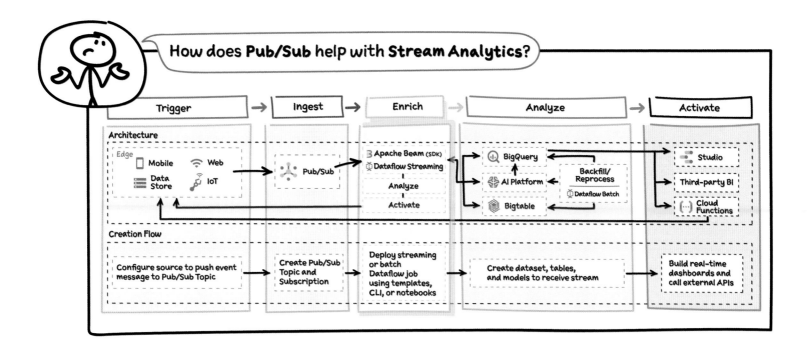

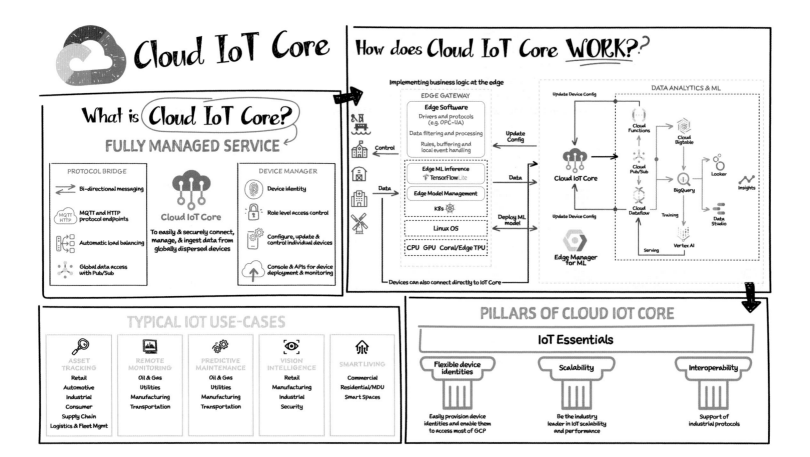

Cloud IoT Core

What is Cloud IoT Core?

FULLY MANAGED SERVICE

PROTOCOL BRIDGE

- Bi-directional messaging
- MQTT and HTTP protocol endpoints
- Automatic load balancing
- Global data access with Pub/Sub

Cloud IoT Core

To easily & securely connect, manage, & ingest data from globally dispersed devices

DEVICE MANAGER

- Device identity
- Role level access control
- Configure, update & control individual devices
- Console & APIs for device deployment & monitoring

How does Cloud IoT Core WORK?

Implementing business logic at the edge

EDGE GATEWAY

Edge Software
Drivers and protocols (e.g. OPC-UA)
Data filtering and processing
Rules, buffering and local event handling

Edge ML inference
TensorFlow Lite

Edge Model Management
K8s

Linux OS

CPU GPU Coral/Edge TPU

Control

Data

Update Config

Deploy ML model

Cloud IoT Core

Edge Manager for ML

Devices can also connect directly to IoT Core

DATA ANALYTICS & ML

Update Device Config

Cloud Functions

Cloud Bigtable

Cloud Pub/Sub

Cloud Dataflow

BigQuery

Looker

Insights

Training

Vertex AI

Data Studio

Serving

Update Device Config

TYPICAL IOT USE-CASES

ASSET TRACKING
Retail
Automotive
Industrial
Consumer
Supply Chain
Logistics & Fleet Mgmt

REMOTE MONITORING
Oil & Gas
Utilities
Manufacturing
Transportation

PREDICTIVE MAINTENANCE
Oil & Gas
Utilities
Manufacturing
Transportation

VISION INTELLIGENCE
Retail
Manufacturing
Industrial
Security

SMART LIVING
Commercial
Residential/MDU
Smart Spaces

PILLARS OF CLOUD IOT CORE

IoT Essentials

Flexible device identities

Easily provision device identities and enable them to access most of GCP

Scalability

Be the industry leader in IoT scalability and performance

Interoperability

Support of industrial protocols

The ability to gain real-time insights from IoT data can redefine competitiveness for businesses. Intelligence allows connected devices and assets to interact efficiently with applications and with human beings in an intuitive and nondisruptive way. After your IoT project is up and running, many devices will be producing lots of data. You need an efficient, scalable, affordable way to both manage those devices and handle all that information.

IoT Core is a fully managed service for managing IoT devices. It supports registration, authentication, and authorization inside the Google Cloud resource hierarchy as well as device metadata stored in the cloud, and offers the ability to send device configuration from other GCP or third-party services to devices.

Main Components

The main components of Cloud IoT Core are the device manager and the protocol bridges:

- The device manager registers devices with the service, so you can then monitor and configure them. It provides:
  - Device identity management
  - Support for configuring, updating, and controlling individual devices
  - Role-level access control
  - Console and APIs for device deployment and monitoring
- Two protocol bridges (MQTT and HTTP) can be used by devices to connect to Google Cloud Platform for:
  - Bi-directional messaging
  - Automatic load balancing
  - Global data access with Pub/Sub

How Does Cloud IoT Core Work?

Device telemetry data is forwarded to a Cloud Pub/Sub topic, which can then be used to trigger Cloud Functions as well as other third-party apps to consume the data. You can also perform streaming analysis with Dataflow or custom analysis with your own subscribers.

Cloud IoT Core supports direct device connections as well as gateway-based architectures. In both cases the real-time state of the device and the operational data is ingested into Cloud IoT Core and the key and certificates at the edge are also managed by Cloud IoT Core. From Pub/Sub the raw input is fed into Dataflow for transformation, and the cleaned output is populated in Cloud Bigtable for real-time monitoring or BigQuery for warehousing and machine learning. From BigQuery the data can be used for visualization in Looker or Data Studio, and it can be used in Vertex AI for creating machine learning models. The models created can be deployed at the edge using Edge Manager (in experimental phase). Device configuration updates or device commands can be triggered by Cloud Functions or Dataflow to Cloud IoT Core, which then updates the device.

Design Principles of Cloud IoT Core

As a managed service to securely connect, manage, and ingest data from global device fleets, Cloud IoT Core is designed to be:

- Flexible, providing easy provisioning of device identities and enabling devices to access most of Google Cloud
- The industry leader in IoT scalability and performance
- Interoperable, with supports for the most common industry-standard IoT protocols

Use Cases

IoT use cases range across numerous industries. Here are some typical examples:

- Asset tracking, visual inspection, and quality control in retail, automotive, industrial, supply chain, and logistics
- Remote monitoring and predictive maintenance in oil and gas, utilities, manufacturing, and transportation
- Connected homes and consumer technologies
- Vision intelligence in retail, security, manufacturing, and industrial sectors
- Smart living in commercial, residential, and smart spaces
- Smart factories with predictive maintenance and real-time plant floor analytics

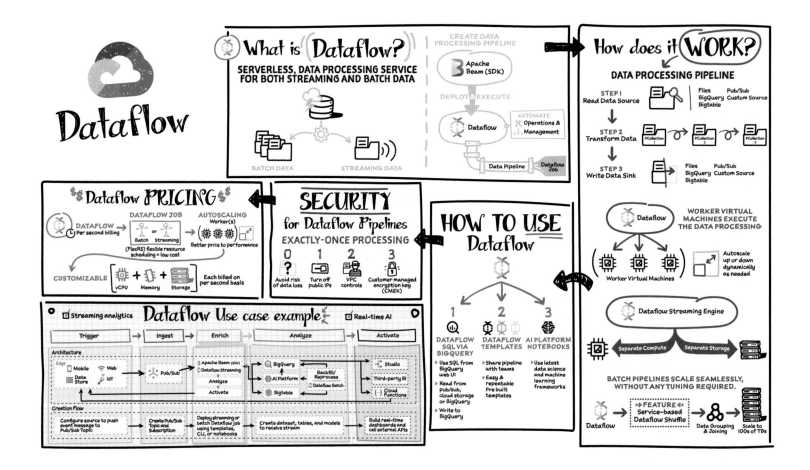

Data is generated in real-time from websites, mobile apps, IoT devices, and other workloads. Capturing, processing, and analyzing this data is a priority for all businesses. But data from these systems is not often in the format that is conducive for analysis or for effective use by downstream systems. That's where Dataflow comes in. Dataflow is used for processing and enriching batch or stream data for use cases such as analysis, machine learning, or data warehousing.

Dataflow is a serverless, fast, and cost-effective service that supports both stream and batch processing. It provides portability with processing jobs written using the open source Apache Beam libraries and removes operational overhead from your data engineering teams by automating the infrastructure provisioning and cluster management.

How Does Data Processing Work?

In general a data processing pipeline involves three steps: you read the data from a source, transform it, and write the data back into a sink.

- The data is read from the source into a PCollection. The P stands for "parallel" because a PCollection is designed to be distributed across multiple machines.

- Then it performs one or more operations on the PCollection, which are called transforms. Each time it runs a transform, a new PCollection is created. That's because PCollections are immutable.

- After all of the transforms are executed, the pipeline writes the final PCollection to an external sink.

Once you have created your pipeline using Apache Beam SDK in the language of your choice, Java or Python, you can use Dataflow to deploy and execute that pipeline, which is called a Dataflow job. Dataflow then assigns the worker virtual machines to execute the data processing; you can customize the shape and size of these machines. And, if your traffic pattern is spiky, Dataflow autoscaling automatically increases or decreases the number of worker instances required to run your job. Dataflow streaming engine separates compute from storage and moves parts of pipeline execution out of the worker VMs and into the Dataflow service backend. This improves autoscaling and data latency.

How to Use Dataflow

You can create Dataflow jobs using the cloud console UI, gcloud CLI, or the API. There are multiple options to create a job.

- Dataflow templates offer a collection of prebuilt templates with an option to create your own custom ones. You can then easily share them with others in your organization.

- Dataflow SQL lets you use your SQL skills to develop streaming pipelines right from the BigQuery web UI. You can join streaming data from Pub/Sub with files in Cloud Storage or tables in BigQuery, write results into BigQuery, and build real-time dashboards for visualization.

- Using Vertex AI notebooks from the Dataflow interface, you can build and deploy data pipelines using the latest data science and machine learning frameworks.

Dataflow inline monitoring lets you directly access job metrics to help with troubleshooting pipelines at both the step and the worker levels.

Dataflow Governance

When using Dataflow, all the data is encrypted at rest and in transit. To further secure data processing environment you can:

- Turn off public IPs to restrict access to internal systems.

- Leverage VPC Service Controls that help mitigate the risk of data exfiltration.

- Use your own custom encryption keys, or customer-managed encryption keys (CMEKs).

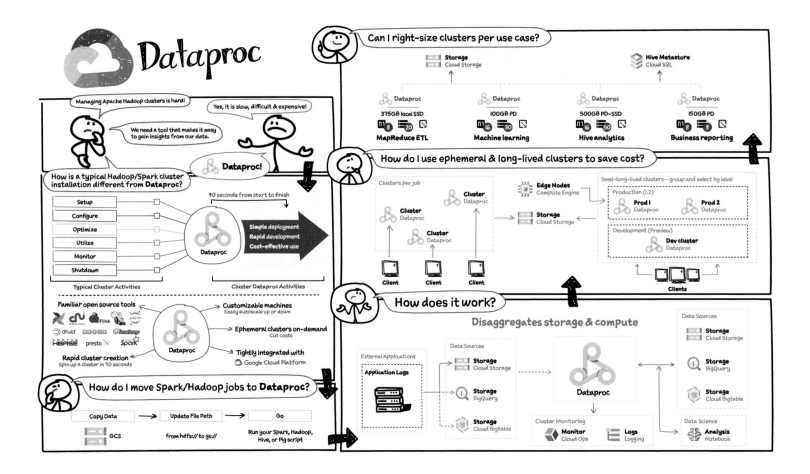

If you are analyzing your data in the on-premise Hadoop and Spark ecosystem, then you know that is costly and time consuming and requires a lot of manual management. That's where Dataproc comes in. It is a fully managed Apache Spark and Apache Hadoop service.

Dataproc Features

- Dataproc clusters take 90 seconds or less, on average, to start, scale, and shut down, making it simple, fast, and cost effective to gain insights as compared to traditional cluster management activities.

Dataproc is much more cost effective than an on-premise data lake because it takes away the cluster creation and management responsibilities so teams can focus more on using the data instead of worrying about infrastructure.

- Dataproc clusters can include on-demand ephemeral preemptible instances that have lower compute prices, saving you money.
- It supports the familiar open source tools and data analytics ecosystem — Hadoop, Spark, Hive, Presto, and Flink.
- It is tightly integrated with the Google Cloud services, including BigQuery, Bigtable, and Cloud Storage.
- When you create a Dataproc cluster, you can enable Hadoop Secure Mode via Kerberos to provide multi-tenancy via user authentication, isolation, and encryption inside a Dataproc cluster.
- You don't need to learn new tools or APIs to use Dataproc, making it easy to move existing projects into Dataproc without redevelopment. And you can interact with your data using Notebooks, Looker, or any BI tools.
  - Dataproc enables data science users through integrations with Vertex AI, BigQuery, and Dataplex
- To move an existing Hadoop/Spark jobs, all you do is copy your data into Cloud Storage, update your file paths from Hadoop File system (HDFS) to Cloud Storage, and you are ready!

How Does Dataproc Work?

Dataproc disaggregates storage and compute, which helps manage your costs and be more flexible in scaling your workloads. Assume a use case where an external application is sending logs for analysis. You store them in a data store such as Cloud Storage, BigQuery, or Bigtable. From there the data is consumed by Dataproc for processing, which then stores it back into Cloud Storage, BigQuery (BQ), or Bigtable (BT). You could also use the data for analysis in a notebook and send logs to Cloud Monitoring. Since storage is separate, for a long-lived cluster you could have one cluster per job, but to save costs you could use ephemeral clusters that are grouped and selected by labels. You could also use the right amount of memory, CPU, and disk space to fit the needs of your application.

Migrating HDFS Data from On-Premises to Google Cloud

Plan to migrate data incrementally so you can leave time to migrate jobs, experiment, and test after moving each body of data.

There are two different migration models you should consider for transferring HDFS data to the cloud: push and pull. The push model is the simplest where the source cluster on-premises runs the distcp jobs on its data nodes and pushes files directly to Cloud Storage. The pull model is more complex, but has some advantages. An ephemeral Dataproc cluster runs the distcp jobs on its data nodes, pulls files from the source cluster on-premises, and copies them to Cloud Storage.

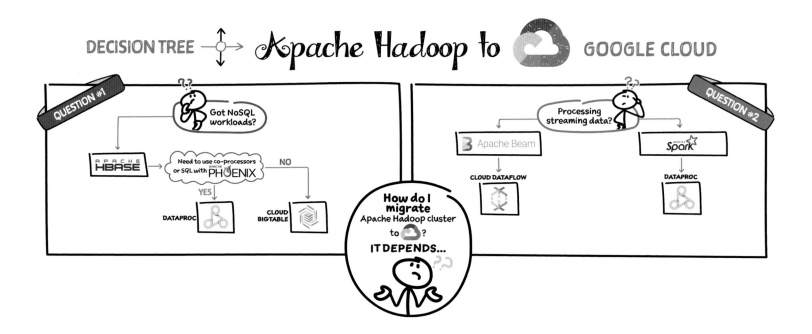

Here are four common scenarios that can help you decide how to migrate Apache Hadoop Cluster to Google Cloud:

- If you are migrating NoSQL workloads and if you use Hbase, then check if you need to use co-processors or SQL with Phoenix. In that case, Dataproc is the best option. If not, then Bigtable is a good choice, because it is a managed wide-column NoSQL database.

- If you are processing streaming data and you use Apache Beam, it makes sense to use Dataflow because it is based on the Apache Beam SDK. If you are using Spark or Kafka, then Dataproc is best, since it manages all Spark and Hadoop workloads.

- If you are doing interactive data analysis or ad hoc querying in Spark with an interactive notebook, then Dataproc is great in combination with managed Jupyter notebooks in Vertex AI or Zeppelin. If you are doing data analysis with SQL in Hive or Presto *and* want to keep it that way, then also Dataproc is perfect. But if you are interested in a managed solution for this interactive data analysis, then use BigQuery, a fully managed data analysis and warehousing solution.

- If you are doing ETL or batch processing using mapreduce, pig, spark, or hive, then use Dataproc. Similarly, if you use the workflow orchestration tool such as Apache Airflow or Oozie and want to keep the jobs as they are, Dataproc is perfect. But if you want to pick a managed solution, then use Cloud Composer, a managed Apache Airflow service.

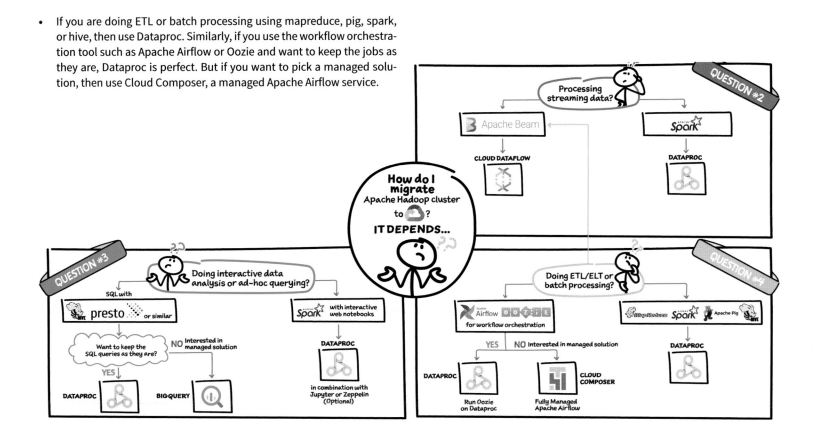

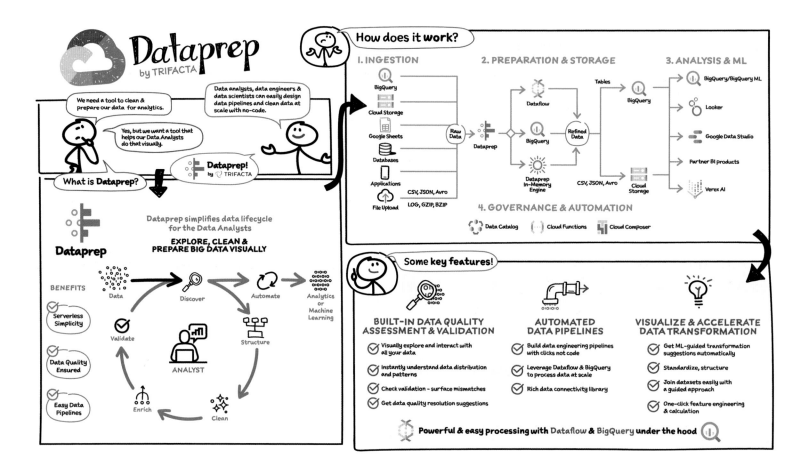

Whether you are in a leadership position leveraging data for decision-making or in a support role to deliver clean and trustworthy data, you know how much effort (and often frustration) it takes to prepare data and make it ready for consumption. Where is the data? How do I access it? What's in the data? Can I trust the data? How can I turn it into a format that I can use? How do I combine it with other sets of data? How do I automate all this process? Let's see how you can turn this cumbersome and painful process into a seamless and fun experience with Dataprep!

Dataprep by Trifacta is a serverless and native Google Cloud data preparation solution as part of the broader Google Cloud Smart Analytics portfolio. Dataprep allows data analysts, business analysts, data engineers, and data scientists to visually explore, clean, and prepare big data.

What Is Data Preparation?

Data preparation, also known as data wrangling, is a self-service activity to access, assess, and convert disparate, raw, messy data into a clean and consistent view for your analytics and data science needs. Preparing data is critical but time-intensive; data teams spend up to 80% of their time converting raw data into a high-quality, analysis-ready output.

The work of preparing raw data into a pristine asset consists of five iterative steps:

Discover

How do I access the data? What is in the data? Can I trust it? Dataprep helps you access diverse data sources and discover features of the data to quickly determine its value.

Structure

Can the data be used with its current format? Structuring refers to actions that change the form or schema of your data. Splitting columns, pivoting rows, and deleting fields are all forms of structuring. Dataprep predicts and suggests the next best transformation based on the data you're working with and the type of interaction you applied to the data.

Clean

Are all the dates valid? Is the category correct? Is a SKU missing? During the cleaning stage, Dataprep surfaces data quality issues, such as missing or mismatched values, and suggests the appropriate transformations.

Enrich

Do you want to keep your data alone or augment it with other datasets from public or internal repositories? The data you need may be spread across multiple files, applications, and databases. With Dataprep you can quickly execute lookups to data dictionaries or perform joins and unions with disparate datasets.

Validate

Do you trust the transformations you applied to your data? Is this an accurate result? Dataprep profiles and provides data quality indicators across the complete transformed dataset. Here, you can do a final check for any data inaccuracy that wasn't initially identified.

When your data has been successfully structured, cleaned, enriched, and validated, it's time to publish your wrangled output for use in downstream analytics processes.

How Does Dataprep Work?

Dataprep connects to BigQuery, Cloud Storage, Google Sheets, and hundreds of other cloud applications and traditional databases so that you can transform and clean any data you want.

Dataprep is built on top of Dataflow and BigQuery. That means any data transformation and cleaning rules you design can easily scale to transform any data, big or small, by translating Dataprep data transformation recipes into Dataflow jobs or BigQuery SQL statements.

Once your data is ready in BigQuery or Cloud Storage, you can analyze it with Data Studio or Looker, train ML models with Vertex AI services, or get insight with other analytics partner solutions such as Qlik or Tableau.

Dataprep, as a native service to Google Cloud, can be governed and automated via APIs to be controlled by Cloud Composer and Cloud Functions, for example.

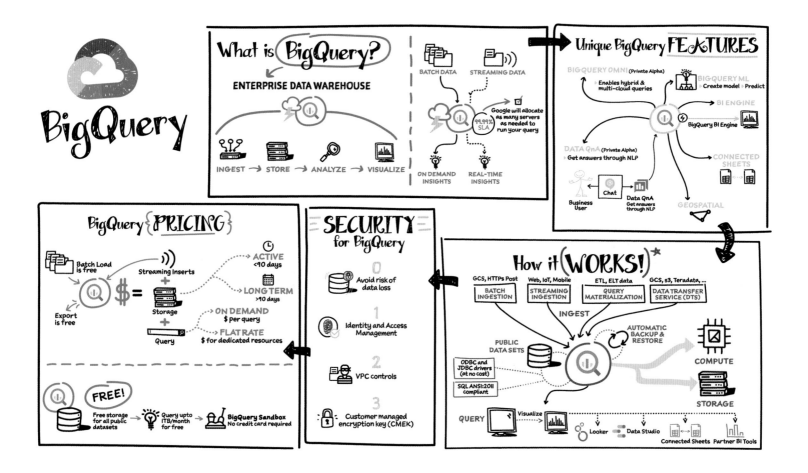

Organizations rely on data warehouses to aggregate data from disparate sources, process it, and make it available for data analysis and to support strategic decision-making. BigQuery is Google Cloud's enterprise data warehouse designed to help organizations run large-scale analytics with ease and quickly unlock actionable insights. You can ingest data into BigQuery either through batch uploading or streaming data directly to unlock real-time insights. As a fully managed data warehouse, Google takes care of the infrastructure so you can focus on analyzing your data up to petabyte scale. BigQuery supports Structured Query Language (SQL) for analyzing your data, which you may be familiar with if you've worked with ANSI-compliant relational databases.

BigQuery Unique Features

BI Engine — BigQuery BI Engine is a fast, in-memory analysis service that enables sub-second query response time with high concurrency. BI Engine integrates with Google Data Studio and Looker for visualizing query results and enables integration with other popular business intelligence (BI) tools.

BigQuery ML — BigQuery ML is unlocking machine learning for millions of data analysts. It allows data analysts or data scientists to build and operationalize machine learning models directly within BigQuery by using simple SQL.

BigQuery Omni — BigQuery Omni is a flexible, multi-cloud analytics solution powered by Anthos that lets you cost-effectively access and securely analyze data across Google Cloud, Amazon Web Services (AWS), and Azure, without leaving the BigQuery user interface (UI). Using standard SQL and the same BigQuery APIs, you can break down data silos and gain critical business insights from a single pane of glass.

Data QnA — Data QnA enables self-service analytics for business users on BigQuery data as well as federated data from Cloud Storage, Bigtable, Cloud SQL, or Google Drive. It uses Dialogflow and allows users to formulate free-form text analytical questions with auto-suggested entities while users type a question.

Connected Sheets — This native integration between Sheets and BigQuery makes it possible for all business stakeholders, who are already quite familiar with spreadsheet tools, to get their own up-to-date insights whenever they need it.

Geospatial data — BigQuery offers accurate spatial analysis with geography data type over GeoJSON and WKT formats. It supports core GIS functions — measurements, transforms, constructors, etc. — using familiar SQL.

How Does It Work?

Here's how it works: You ingest your own data into BigQuery or use data from the public datasets. Storage and compute are decoupled and can scale independently on-demand. This offers immense flexibility and cost control for your business since you don't need to keep your expensive compute resources up and running all the time. This is very different than the traditional node-based cloud data warehouse solutions or on-premise systems. Backup and restore of data are performed automatically so you don't have to.

You can ingest data into BigQuery in batches or stream real-time data from web, IoT, or mobile devices via Pub/Sub. You can also use Data Transfer Service to ingest data from other clouds, on-premise systems, or third-party services. BigQuery also supports ODBC and JDBC drivers to connect with existing tools and infrastructure.

Interacting with BigQuery to load data, run queries, or even create ML models can be done in three different ways. You can use the UI in the Cloud Console, the BigQuery command-line tool, or the API using client libraries available in several languages.

When it comes time to visualize your data, BigQuery integrates with Looker as well as several other business intelligence tools across our partner ecosystem.

BigQuery Storage Internals

BigQuery offers fully managed storage, meaning you don't have to provision servers. Sizing is done automatically and you only pay for what you use. Because BigQuery was designed for large scale data analytics data is stored in columnar format.

Traditional relational databases, like Postgres and MySQL, store data row-by-row in record-oriented storage. This makes them great for transactional updates and OLTP (Online Transaction Processing) use cases because they only need to open up a single row to read or write data. However, if you want to perform an aggregation like a sum of an entire column, you would need to read the entire table into memory.

BigQuery uses columnar storage where each column is stored in a separate file block. This makes BigQuery an ideal solution for OLAP (Online Analytical Processing) use cases. When you want to perform aggregations you only need to read the column that you are aggregating over.

Dremel: BigQuery's query engine

Dremel is made up of a cluster of workers. Each one of these workers executes a part of a task independently and in parallel. BigQuery uses a distributed memory shuffle tier to store intermediate data produced from workers at various stages of execution. The shuffle leverages some fairly interesting Google technologies, such as our very fast petabit network technology, and RAM wherever possible. Each shuffled row can be consumed by workers as soon as it's created by the producers.

This makes it possible to execute distributed operations in a pipeline. Additionally, if a worker has partially written some of its output and then terminated (for example, the underlying hardware suffered a power event), that unit of work can simply be re-queued and sent to another worker. A failure of a single worker in a stage doesn't mean all the workers need to re-run.

When a query is complete, the results are written out to persistent storage and returned to the user. This also enables us to serve up cached results the next time that query executes.

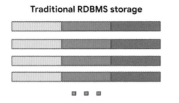

Traditional RDBMS storage · BigQuery storage

Record-oriented storage · Columnar storage

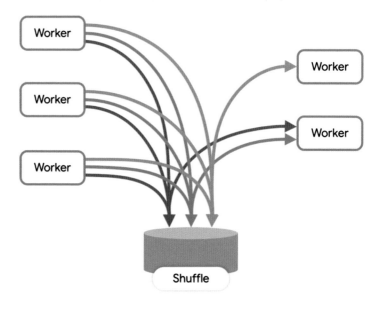

Security

BigQuery offers built-in data protection at scale. It provides security and governance tools to efficiently govern data and democratize insights within your organization.

- Within BigQuery, users can assign dataset-level and project-level permissions to help govern data access. Secure data sharing ensures you can collaborate and operate your business with trust.
- Data is automatically encrypted while in transit and at rest, which ensures that your data is protected from intrusions, theft, and attacks.
- Cloud DLP helps you discover and classify sensitive data assets.
- Cloud IAM provides access control and visibility into security policies.
- Data Catalog helps you discover and manage data.

Cost

The BigQuery sandbox lets you explore BigQuery capabilities at no cost and confirm that it fits your needs. BigQuery makes data analysts more productive with flexible and predictable price performance. With BigQuery, you pay for storing and querying data, and streaming inserts. Loading and exporting data are free of charge. Storage costs are based on the amount of data stored and have two rates based on how often the data is changing. Query costs can be either:

- On-demand; you are charged per query by the amount of data processed.
- Flat-rate, if you want to purchase dedicated resources.

Whether initiative-based, ramping over a planned duration, or performing a complete migration of the EDW, choose the model that fits best:

- Start with pay-as-you-go, and move to flat-rate.
- Start with flat-rate, understand usage, and move to pay-as-you-go models for additional workloads .
- Use data warehouse bundles for a fixed monthly cost.

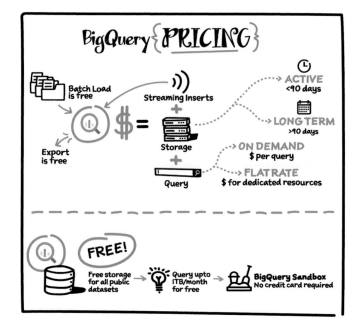

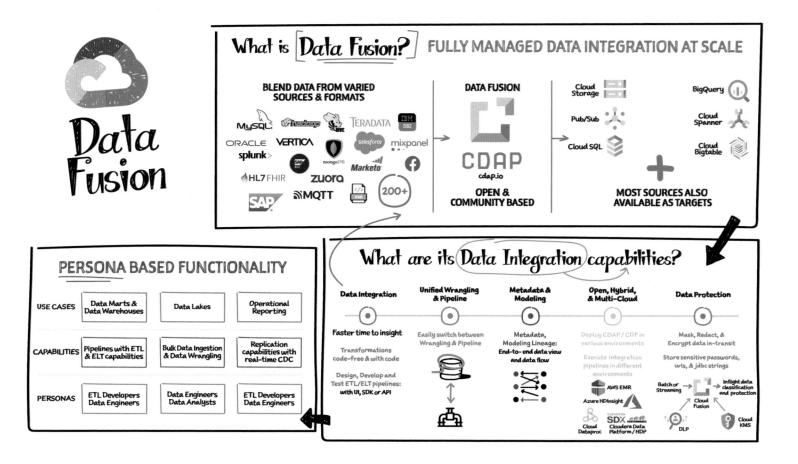

A huge challenge with data analytics is that the data is all over the place and is in different formats. As a result, you often need to complete numerous integration activities before you can start to gain insights from your data. Data Fusion offers a one-stop shop for all enterprise data integration activities, including ingestion, extract transform load (ETL), extract load transform (ELT), and streaming, and with an execution engine optimized for SLAs and cost. It is designed to make lives easier for ETL developers, data analysts, and data engineers.

Data Fusion is Google's cloud-native, fully managed, scalable enterprise data integration platform. It enables bringing transactional, social, or machine data in various formats from databases, applications, messaging systems, mainframes, files, SaaS, and IoT devices; offers an easy to use virtual interface and provides deployment capabilities to execute data pipelines on ephemeral or dedicated Dataproc clusters in Spark. Cloud Data Fusion is powered by open source CDAP, which makes the pipelines portable across Google Cloud or hybrid or multicloud environments.

Data Integration Capabilities

Data Fusion integration capabilities include data integration, unified wrangling and pipeline, metadata and modeling, data protection, and also open, hybrid, and multicloud functionality.

Data Integration

Data Fusion provides data integration for optimized analytics and accelerated data transformations. It supports a broad set of more than 200 connectors and formats, which enable you to extract and wrangle data. You can develop data pipelines in a visual environment to improve productivity. It provides extensive REST API to design, automate, orchestrate, and manage the data pipeline life cycle. It supports all data delivery modes, including batch, streaming, or real-time. It provides operational insights to monitor data integration processes, manage SLAs and help optimize integration jobs. It provides capabilities to parse and enrich unstructured data using Vertex AI, such as converting audio files to text, extracting features from images, documents and more.

Unified Wrangling and Pipeline

Data Fusion builds confidence in business decision-making with advanced data consistency features. It minimizes the risk of mistakes by providing structured ways of specifying transformations, data quality checks, and predefined directives. Data formats change over time, so Data Fusion helps you handle data drift with the ability to identify change and customize error handling.

Metadata and Modeling

Data Fusion makes it easy to gain insights with metadata. You can collect technical, business, and operational metadata for datasets and pipelines and easily discover metadata with a search. It provides end-to-end data views to help you understand the data model and to profile data, flows, and relationships of datasets. It enables exchange of metadata between catalogs and integration with end-user workbenches using REST APIs.

The Data Fusion data lineage feature enables you to understand the flow of your data and how it is prepared for business decisions.

Open, Hybrid, and Multicloud

Data Fusion is cloud-native and powered by CDAP, a 100% open source framework for building on-premises and cloud data analytics applications. This means you can deploy and execute integration pipelines in different environments without any changes to suit business needs.

Data Protection

Data Fusion ensures data security in the following ways:

- It provides secure access to on-premises data with private IP.
- It encrypts data at rest by default or with customer managed encryption keys (CMEKs) to control across all user data in supported storage systems.
- It provides data exfiltration protection via VPC Service Controls, a security perimeter around platform resources.
- You can store sensitive passwords, URLs, and JDBC strings in Cloud KMS, and integrate with external KMS systems.
- It integrates with Cloud DLP to mask, redact, and encrypt data in transit.

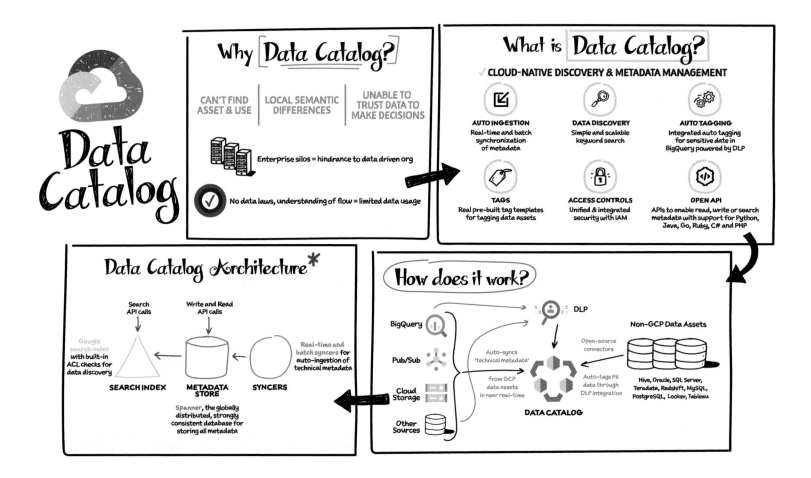

Data Catalog

Why Data Catalog?

CAN'T FIND ASSET & USE | LOCAL SEMANTIC DIFFERENCES | UNABLE TO TRUST DATA TO MAKE DECISIONS

Enterprise silos = hindrance to data driven org

✓ No data laws, understanding of flow = limited data usage

What is Data Catalog?

✓ CLOUD-NATIVE DISCOVERY & METADATA MANAGEMENT

AUTO INGESTION
Real-time and batch synchronization of metadata

DATA DISCOVERY
Simple and scalable keyword search

AUTO TAGGING
Integrated auto tagging for sensitive date in BigQuery powered by DLP

TAGS
Real pre-built tag templates for tagging data assets

ACCESS CONTROLS
Unified & integrated security with IAM

OPEN API
APIs to enable read, write or search metadata with support for Python, Java, Go, Ruby, C# and PHP

Data Catalog Architecture*

Search API calls

Write and Read API calls

Google search index with built-in ACL checks for data discovery

Real-time and batch syncers for auto-ingestion of technical metadata

SEARCH INDEX | **METADATA STORE** | **SYNCERS**

Spanner, the globally distributed, strongly consistent database for storing all metadata

How does it work?

BigQuery

DLP

Non-GCP Data Assets

Pub/Sub

Auto-syncs 'technical metadata'

Open-source connectors

from GCP data assets in near real-time

Cloud Storage

Auto-tags PII data through DLP integration

Hive, Oracle, SQL Server, Teradata, Redshift, MySQL, PostgreSQL, Looker, Tableau

Other Sources

DATA CATALOG

People struggle to find analytic content. The harder it is to find content, the higher the likelihood of business initiative failures. This is why every company, including yours, is on a mission to democratize data and insights by making data discoverable. Due to enterprise silos, teams can't find the assets they need, so they create localized semantics that make it hard to integrate with the rest of the organization and diminishes trust in data quality. These are likely just some of the major challenges hindering your data analytics journey. But how can you make your data easily discoverable? Use Data Catalog!

Data Catalog is a fully managed and scalable metadata management service that empowers you to quickly discover, understand, and manage all your data in one place. It makes data discoverable and democratizes data and insights for both technical and business users, fostering a culture of data-driven decision-making. Data Catalog provides the following:

- A unified view of all your data assets in Google Cloud and in external systems.

- A simple and easy-to-use search interface to quickly and easily discover data assets using the same search technology as Gmail.

- A flexible and powerful system for capturing both technical metadata (automatically) and business metadata (tags) in a structured format.

- Schematized tags, which provide rich and organized business metadata. Tag structure helps you define an implicit relationship between the tag and all the key-value pairs contained within so that you get all the relevant information in a structured form in one glance, which would otherwise have involved looking up multiple tags and deciphering the relationship between them.

- A UI for seamlessly creating and applying business metadata tags.

- Full API access for writing, reading, and searching metadata, as well as for bulk uploads and integration with other systems.

How Does Data Catalog Work?

Data Catalog provides unified search across all projects, systems, and regions. It does this by:

- Automatically syncing technical metadata from Cloud Storage, Pub/Sub, BigQuery, and other Google Cloud sources

- Providing open source connectors to bring in metadata from external data sources

- Auto-tagging personally identifiable information (PII) data through DLP integration

Data Catalog Architecture

- **Syncers:** Real-time and batch syncers auto-ingest your technical metadata.

- **Metadata store:** Spanner, the globally distributed, strongly consistent database, stores all your metadata.

- **Search Index:** Google Search Index has built-in ACL checks for data discovery using the same technology that powers Gmail and Google Drive.

Data Governance

Data Catalog helps enforce data security policies and maintain compliance through Cloud IAM (Identity and Access Management) and Cloud DLP integrations, which help ensure that only the right people gain access to the right data and sensitive data is protected. Before searching, discovering, or displaying Google Cloud resources, Data Catalog checks that the user has been granted an IAM role with the metadata read permissions required by BigQuery, Pub/Sub, Dataproc Metastore, or other source systems to access the resource.

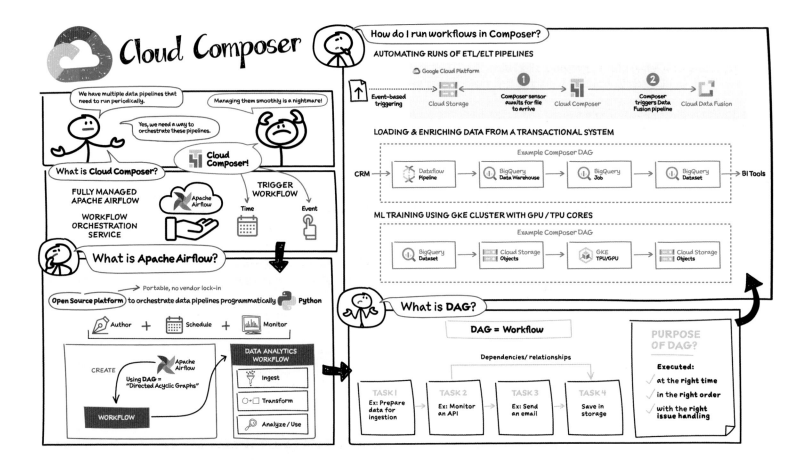

When you are building data pipelines, you need to manage and monitor the workflows in the pipeline and often automate them to run periodically. Cloud Composer is a fully managed workflow orchestration service built on Apache Airflow that helps you author, schedule, and monitor pipelines spanning hybrid and multicloud environments.

By using Cloud Composer instead of managing a local instance of Apache Airflow, you can benefit from the best of Airflow with no installation, management, patching, and backup overhead because Google Cloud takes care of that technical complexity. Cloud Composer is also enterprise-ready and offers a ton of security features so you don't have to worry about it. Last but not least, the latest version of Cloud Composer supports autoscaling, which provides cost efficiency and additional reliability for workflows that have bursty execution patterns.

How Does Cloud Composer Work?

In data analytics, a workflow represents a series of tasks for ingesting, transforming, analyzing, or utilizing data. In Airflow, workflows are created using directed acyclic graphs (DAGs).

A DAG is a collection of tasks that you want to schedule and run, in a way that reflects their relationships and dependencies. DAGs are created in Python scripts, which define the DAG structure (tasks and their dependencies) using code. The purpose of a DAG is to ensure that each task is executed at the right time, in the right order, and with the right issue handling.

Each task in a DAG can represent almost anything — for example, one task might perform data ingestion, another sends an email, and yet another runs a pipeline.

How to Run Workflows in Cloud Composer

After you create a Cloud Composer environment, you can run any workflows your business case requires. The Composer service is based on a distributed architecture running in GKE and other Google Cloud services. You can schedule a workload at a specific time, or you can start a workflow when a specific condition is met, such as when an object is saved to a storage bucket. Cloud Composer comes with built-in integration to almost all Google Cloud products, including BigQuery and Dataproc; it also supports integration (enabled by provider packages from vendors) with applications running on-premises or on another cloud. Here is a list of built-in integration and provider packages.

Cloud Composer Security Features

- **Private IP:** Using Private IP means that the compute node in Cloud Composer is not publicly accessible and therefore is protected from the public Internet. Developers can access the Internet but the compute node cannot be accessed from the public internet.

- **Private IP + Web Server ACLs:** The user interface for Airflow is protected by authentication. Only authenticated customers can access the specific Airflow user interface. For additional network-level security, you can use web server access controls along with Private IP, which helps limit access from the outside world by whitelisting a set of IP addresses.

- **VPC Native Mode:** In conjunction with other features, VPC native mode helps limit access to Composer components in the same VPC network, keeping the components protected.

- **VPC Service Controls:** Provides increased security by enabling you to configure a network service perimeter that prevents access from the outside world and also prevents access to the outside world.

- **Customer-Managed Encryption Keys (CMEKs):** Enabling CMEK lets you provide your own encryption keys to encrypt/decrypt environment data.

- **Restricting Identities By Domain:** This feature enables you to restrict the set of identities that can access Cloud Composer environments to specific domain names, such as @yourcompany.com.

- **Integration with Secrets Manager:** You can use built-in integration with Secrets Manager to protect keys and passwords used by your DAGs for authentication to external systems.

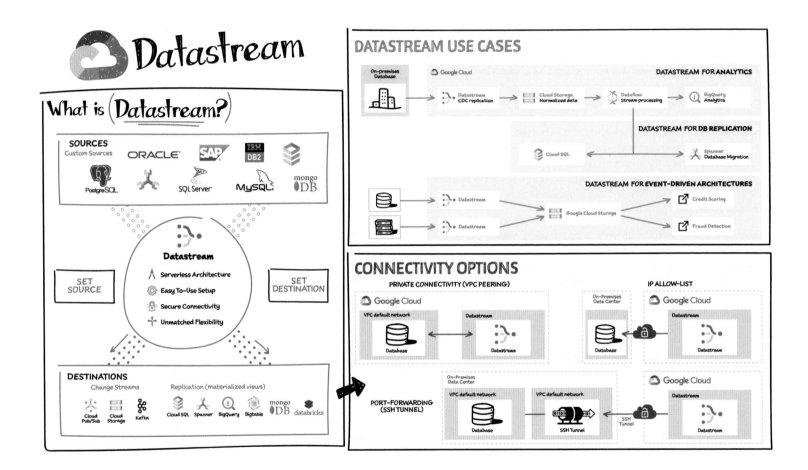

What is (Datastream?)

SOURCES
Custom Sources — ORACLE · SAP · IBM DB2 · PostgreSQL · SQL Server · MySQL · mongoDB

Datastream
- Serverless Architecture
- Easy To-Use Setup
- Secure Connectivity
- Unmatched Flexibility

SET SOURCE · SET DESTINATION

DESTINATIONS
Change Streams — Cloud Pub/Sub · Cloud Storage · Kafka
Replication (materialized views) — Cloud SQL · Spanner · BigQuery · Bigtable · mongoDB · databricks

DATASTREAM USE CASES

DATASTREAM FOR ANALYTICS
On-premises Database → Google Cloud → Datastream CDC replication → Cloud Storage Normalized data → Dataflow Stream processing → BigQuery Analytics

DATASTREAM FOR DB REPLICATION
Cloud SQL → Spanner Database Migration

DATASTREAM FOR EVENT-DRIVEN ARCHITECTURES
Datastream → Google Cloud Storage → Credit Scoring
Datastream → Fraud Detection

CONNECTIVITY OPTIONS

PRIVATE CONNECTIVITY (VPC PEERING)
Google Cloud — VPC default network — Database ↔ Datastream

IP ALLOW-LIST
On-Premises Data Center — Database → Google Cloud — Datastream

PORT-FORWARDING (SSH TUNNEL)
On-Premises Data Center — VPC default network — Database → VPC default network — SSH Tunnel → SSH Tunnel → Google Cloud — Datastream

With data volumes constantly growing, many companies find it difficult to use data effectively and gain insights from it. Often these organizations are burdened with cumbersome and difficult-to-maintain data architectures.

One way that companies are addressing this challenge is with *change streaming*: the movement of data changes as they happen from a source (typically a database) to a destination. Powered by change data capture (CDC), change streaming has become a critical data architecture building block. Google Cloud recently announced Datastream, a serverless change data capture and replication service. Datastream's key capabilities include:

- **Replicate and synchronize data across your organization with minimal latency** — You can synchronize data across heterogeneous databases and applications reliably, with low latency, and with minimal impact to the performance of your source. Unlock the power of data streams for analytics, database replication, cloud migration, and event-driven architectures across hybrid environments.

- **Scale up or down with a serverless architecture seamlessly** — Get up and running fast with a serverless and easy-to-use service that scales seamlessly as your data volumes shift. Focus on deriving up-to-date insights from your data and responding to high-priority issues, instead of managing infrastructure, performance tuning, or resource provisioning.

- **Integrate with the Google Cloud data integration suite** — Connect data across your organization with Google Cloud data integration products. Datastream leverages Dataflow templates to load data into BigQuery, Cloud Spanner, and Cloud SQL; it also powers Cloud Data Fusion's CDC Replicator connectors for easier-than-ever data pipelining.

How Does It Work?

1. Create a source connection profile.
2. Create a destination connection profile.
3. Create a stream using the source and destination connection profiles, and define the objects to pull from the source.
4. Validate and start the stream.

Once started, a stream continuously streams data from the source to the destination. You can pause and then resume the stream.

Connectivity Options

To use Datastream to create a stream from the source database to the destination, you must establish connectivity to the source database. Datastream supports the IP allow list, forward SSH tunnel, and VPC peering network connectivity methods.

Private connectivity configurations enable Datastream to communicate with a data source over a private network (internally within Google Cloud, or with external sources connected over Cloud VPN or Cloud Interconnect). This communication happens through a Virtual Private Cloud (VPC) peering connection.

Datastream Use Cases

Datastream captures change streams from Oracle, MySQL, and other sources for destinations such as Cloud Storage, Pub/Sub, BigQuery, Spanner, and more. Here are some Datastream use cases:

- For analytics, use Datastream with a prebuilt Dataflow template to create up-to-date replicated tables in BigQuery in a fully managed way.

- For database replication, use Datastream with prebuilt Dataflow templates to continuously replicate and synchronize database data into Cloud SQL for PostgreSQL or Cloud Spanner to power low-downtime database migration or hybrid-cloud configuration.

- For building event-driven architectures, use Datastream to ingest changes from multiple sources into object stores like Cloud Storage or, in the future, messaging services such as Pub/Sub or Apache Kafka.

- Streamline a real-time data pipeline that continually streams data from legacy relational data stores (like Oracle and MySQL) using Datastream into MongoDB.

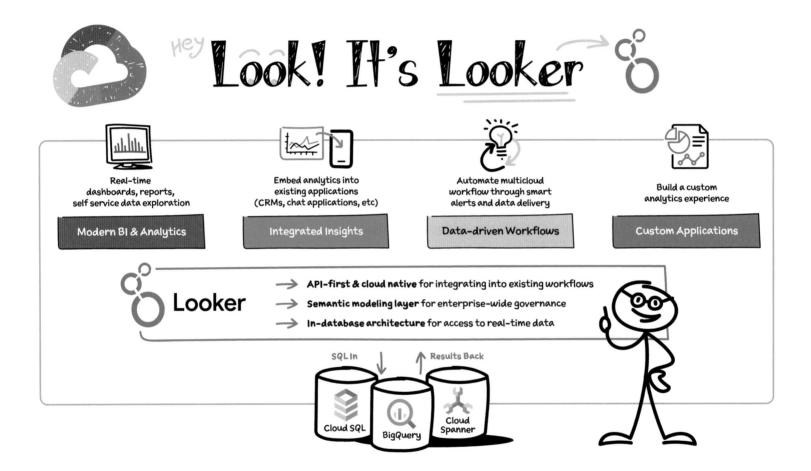

Most companies have data siloed across various applications. Siloed data gets stale quickly because you have to bring it all together from multiple applications and by the time you start analyzing it, the data has often already changed or updated. Additionally, when data is in silos, it can also be hard to ensure data governance — making sure data is easily accessible, credible, and secure. Silos also make it difficult to get a holistic view of the data and to garner fresh insights. To overcome these challenges, companies often centralize their data in a modern data store — such as a database, data warehouse, or data lake — to help enable fast queries as well as optimize performance and cost across various datasets.

Looker's Platform

To make the most of your investment in a modern data warehouse such as BigQuery, you need a modern business intelligence (BI) and analytics solution. That's where Looker comes in. Looker, was built to leverage the power of modern data storage and provide governed access to real-time metrics — helping users gain an accurate and up-to-date understanding of their business.

All of this is powered by Looker's platform and its unique architecture, which differentiates itself from other BI tools with a combination of in-database architecture, a semantic modeling layer, and by being cloud-native.

In-Database Architecture

Looker is a 100% cloud-native application that takes advantage the modern enterprise data warehouse (EDW) platforms. Looker sits on top of the database of your choice and leverages its unique functionality, such as creating nested tables in BigQuery or even creating materialized views. This helps provide fast query times over massive datasets, because the computational power comes straight from your warehouse. It also helps provides access to unique features such as geospatial analytics (GIS) and user-defined functions (UDFs). Additionally, the information that you see in Looker is as fresh as what you see in your data warehouse. This means that business users are always making informed decisions, as opposed to working off stale extracts of information. Additionally, Looker's

multicloud platform supports more than 50 distinct versions of SQL, so you can maintain the choice and flexibility to host data in the way that works best for you.

Semantic Modeling Layer

With Looker, data teams can build a unified semantic layer using its modeling language, LookML. This enables you to have one definition of metrics and KPIs shared across your organization and easily accessible to everyone who uses data. LookML's integration with Git allows analysts to easily collaborate on metric definitions and provides full version control. Results remain consistent and trust in the data grows internally with your key stakeholders. In addition, you control who accesses what data and how, right down to the row or column level. With LookML, end users can create their own queries on datasets you give them access to without having to know SQL. This empowers your business stakeholders to get real-time access to pressing questions and frees up your data team to focus on driving value and innovation for the business.

Cloud Native

As a cloud-native technology, Looker has rich, extensible APIs that let you send data to where your stakeholders are, such as email or mobile, allowing them to take immediate action on what they see in real-time. With Looker's API and embed capabilities, organizations can build robust data applications that can open up additional revenue streams with limited engineering effort. Using Looker actions, business users can automate operational workflows, thus saving time and ensuring the data is used to make meaningful decisions.

Because of these key differentiators, organizations can leverage Looker's platform to deliver data experiences tailored to the needs of the user. These data experiences range from modern business intelligence and analytics with reports and dashboards to

- integrating insights into user workflows
- creating data-driven workflows with automation
- creating completely new applications that are powered by data

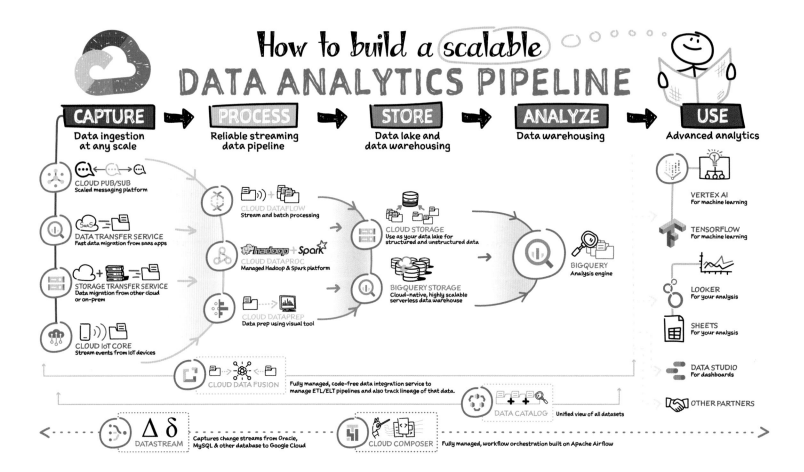

As you saw in the introduction of this chapter, there are roughly five steps to building a data analytics pipeline: capture data, process it, store the resulting enriched data in a data warehouse, analyze it, and finally use it to make meaningful business decisions. Let's see the Google Cloud tools you can use at each step:

Capture

Depending on where your data is coming from, you can have multiple options to ingest them.

Real-time data ingestion:

- You can stream real-time data from applications with Pub/Sub messaging service. You configure a data source to push event messages into Pub/Sub from where a subscriber picks up the message and takes appropriate action on it.

- If you have IoT devices, they can stream real-time data using Cloud IoT Core, which supports the MQTT protocol for the IoT devices. You can also send IoT data to Pub/Sub as events for further processing.

Batch data ingestion:

- There are multiple data migration tools you can use to migrate data from on-premises or from one cloud to another. You can use storage transfer services to transfer data from another cloud or on-premises, and use transfer appliances to transfer large amounts of data from a low-bandwidth or no-Internet location.

- To ingest data from your third-party SaaS services, you can use the BigQuery data transfer service and APIs to store data into BigQuery. You can load data from SaaS applications such as YouTube, Google Ads, Amazon S3, Teradata, RedShift, and more. For more details on these options, check out Chapter 2.

Process

Once the data is ingested, you can process or enrich it in order to make it useful for the downstream systems. There are three main tools that help you do that in Google Cloud:

- Dataproc is a managed Hadoop service. If you use the Hadoop ecosystem, then you know that it can be complicated to set up, involving hours and even days. Dataproc can spin up a cluster in 90 seconds so that you can start analyzing the data quickly.

- Dataprep is an intelligent graphical user interface tool that helps data analysts process data quickly without having to write any code.

- Dataflow is a serverless data processing service for streaming and batch data. It is based on the Apache Beam open source SDK and makes your pipelines portable. The service separates storage from computing, which allows it to scale seamlessly.

Store

Once the data is processed, you have to store it in a data lake or data warehouse for either long-term archival or for reporting and analysis. There are two main tools that help you do that in Google Cloud:

- Cloud Storage is an object store for images, videos, files, and other structured and unstructured data that comes with multiple classes depending on access frequency and use cases — such as standard for high-frequency data access, nearline for lower-cost storage for at least 30 days, coldline for very low cost and at least 90 days storage, and archive for lowest-cost storage for regulatory archives.

- BigQuery is a serverless data warehouse that scales seamlessly to petabytes of data without having to manage or maintain any server. You can store and query data in BigQuery using SQL. Then you can easily share the data and queries with others on your team. It also houses hundreds of free public datasets that you can use in your analysis. And it provides built-in connectors to other services so that data can be easily ingested into it and extracted out of it for visualization or further processing/analysis.

Analyze

Once the data is processed and stored in a data lake or data warehouse, it is ready to be analyzed. If you are using BigQuery to store the data, then you can directly analyze that data in BigQuery using SQL. If you use Cloud Storage to store, then you can easily move the data into BigQuery for analysis. BigQuery also offers machine learning features with BigQueryML, which you can use to create models and predict right from the BigQuery UI using SQL.

Use

Once the data is in the data warehouse, you can visualize the data and use it to gain insights by making predictions using machine learning.

- **Machine learning (ML)** — For further processing and predictions, you can use the TensorFlow framework and Vertex AI, depending on your needs. TensorFlow is an end-to-end open source ML platform with tools, libraries, and community resources. Vertex AI makes it easy for developers, data scientists, and data engineers to streamline their ML workflows. It includes tools for each stage of the ML life cycle, starting with preparation, moving to build, then validation, and finally deployment.

- **Data visualization** — There are lots of different tools for data visualization, and most of them have a connector to BigQuery so that you can easily create charts in the tool of your choice. Google Cloud provides a few tools that you might find helpful to consider:

  ◦ Data Studio is free and connects not just to BigQuery but also to many other services for easy data visualization.

  ◦ If you have used Google Drive, sharing charts and dashboards are exactly like that — extremely easy.

  ◦ Looker is an enterprise platform for business intelligence, data applications, and embedded analytics.

Services Spanning the Pipeline

- **Data Fusion** — Data integration platform powered by open source CDAP, making pipelines portable across hybrid and multicloud

- **Data Catalog** — Managed metadata management service that helps you quickly discover, understand, and manage all your data in one place

- **Composer** — Managed workflow orchestration service based on Apache Airflow that lets you author, schedule, and monitor data pipelines

- **Datastream** — Captures change data streams from Oracle, MySQL, and other sources for destinations such as Cloud Storage, Pub/Sub, BigQuery, Spanner, and more to support use cases such as analytics, database replication, and event-driven architectures.

CHAPTER FIVE

Application Development and Modernization Opening

While virtually all applications share the same basic elements (compute, storage, database access, and networking), there are different ways to develop and deploy those applications in the cloud depending on your specific requirements. You can migrate an existing on-premises application to the cloud, deploy your application to a hybrid or multicloud environment, or build a cloud-native, serverless application. Most modern applications benefit from a microservices-based, event-driven architecture. In this type of architecture, each microservice can be developed and deployed independent of other services, which offers flexibility to developers and increases development velocity. Building or modernizing an application requires:

- Service orchestration and choreography
- DevOps for continuous integration and continuous delivery from code to deployed applications
- Operations to monitor, log, and troubleshoot applications
- Security to secure the data and the infrastructure

This chapter covers the Google Cloud tools used to develop and modernize an application, whether you're migrating, deploying to hybrid and multi-cloud environments, or creating cloud-native, microservices-based applications.

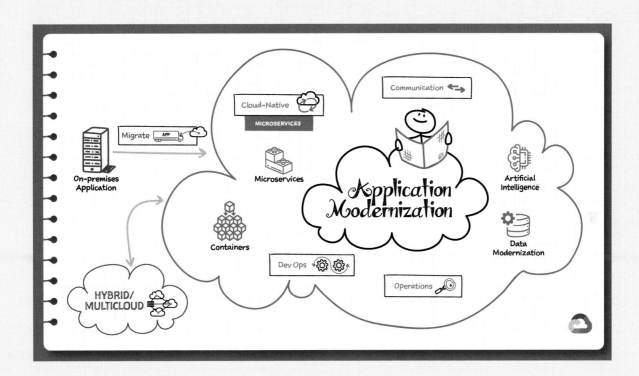

Introduction to Application Development & Modernization

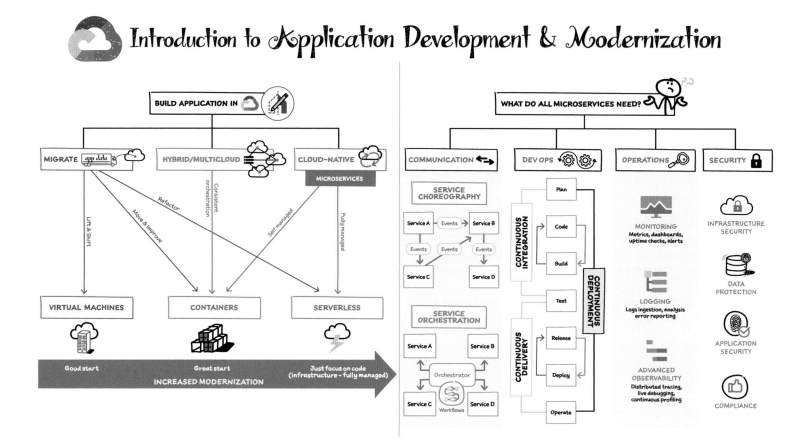

Picture this: You are building or enhancing an application to fulfill a business need. You know that you want to deploy this application in the cloud. At the start, you'll need to answer a few questions that will shape the entire effort and the tools you will need:

- Will you migrate an existing on-premises application to the cloud and then add additional functionality?
- Will you deploy to a hybrid or a multicloud environment?
- Will you build a cloud-native application?

Building and Modernizing Cloud Applications

Migrating an application to the cloud: Migrating an existing application can increase the speed of deployment, while enabling you to capitalize on the benefits of the cloud, modernize your application in the process, and focus more on day 2 operations like maintenance and optimization.

Hybrid and multicloud applications: Sometimes simple migration is not the best way forward. You may have applications that need to be deployed across multiple clouds and on-premises. To support such applications, you must be able to build, deploy, and optimize them consistently, with ease and security across hybrid and multicloud environments.

Cloud-native applications: Cloud-native applications are built to run in the cloud, focusing more on services and code than on the underlying infrastructure that is used to run them. Often based on a microservices architecture, they typically rely on containers for packaging and deployment of code. This speeds delivery and supports better DevOps practices where development and operations teams work closely together.

You can deploy cloud-native applications in fully managed serverless environments where you develop, deploy, and scale applications rapidly and securely without having to manage the infrastructure as you scale. This helps reduce time-to-market and simplifies the developer experience.

Microservices or Monolith?

Whether you are building an application from scratch or migrating and enhancing it, you want to think about modernizing your application for scale, agility, manageability, and delivery speed. Most modern-day requirements call for a microservices architecture because:

- Services are standalone or modular and can be reused across multiple applications.
- There is no single point of failure.
- You can independently release services.
- Development teams can be diverse, using different programming languages.
- DevOps practices have matured to support the speed of microservices deployments.

Monolithic application is built as a single unit; to make any changes to the system, a developer must build and deploy an updated version of the server-side application. When you are migrating a monolithic application to the cloud, you can approach it three ways:

- **Lift and shift:** You can migrate the entire monolith to a virtual machine or needed hardware in the cloud. This is often the fastest, simplest way to migrate, but it is not likely a long-term solution.
- **Move and improve:** You could migrate one service at a time, decoupling the service and its dependencies while containerizing your applications and adopting a microservices architecture. This approach takes longer, but you will modernize your application in the process, helping you reap the benefits of cloud.
- **Refactor:** If you choose to refactor your application, you can adopt serverless deployments with even more benefits.

What Do Most Microservices Need?

Hybrid and multicloud applications are often deployed in containers so that they can be orchestrated consistently across multiple environments. But these microservices need to communicate with each other, need a proper DevOps process for continuous deployment, and have to be monitored and secured.

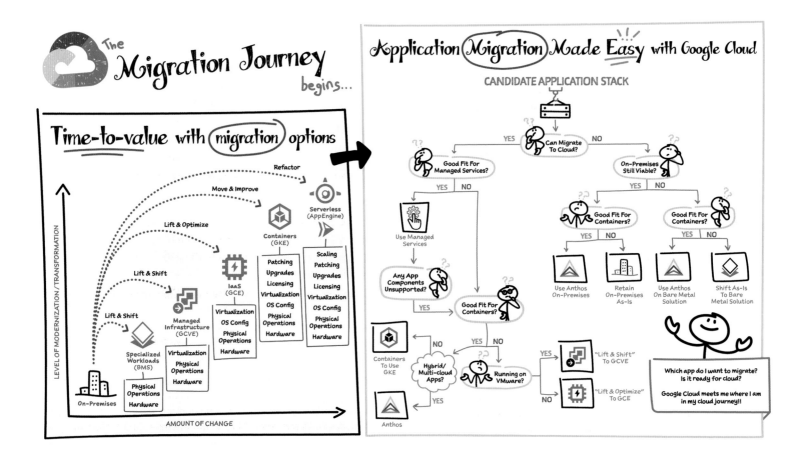

Where to Begin?

Understanding your starting point is essential to planning and executing a successful application migration strategy. Take a comprehensive approach, including not only technical requirements, but also consideration of your business goals (both present and future), any critical timelines, and your own internal capabilities. Depending on your situation you might fall in any of the below categories as it relates to time-to-value. There is no one-size-fits-all approach to migration, but the key here is to know that whichever path you choose, there is always a way to build on top of that and continue to enjoy more advantages of the cloud in an incremental fashion.

Should You Migrate to Google Cloud?

To determine whether your application can and should migrate to cloud, begin by asking yourself the following questions:

1. Are the components of my application stack virtualized or virtualizable?

2. Can my application stack run in a cloud environment while still supporting any and all licensing, security, privacy, and compliance requirements?

3. Can all application dependencies (e.g., third-party languages, frameworks, libraries) be supported in the cloud?

If you answer "no" to any of these questions, you should evaluate whether it is feasible to replace those application components with a cloud offering. If not, leave those components on-premises during the initial phase of your digital transformation while you focus on the migration of your other application components.

If retention on-premises is no longer viable (e.g., if you must completely shut down your data center) or if you want to increase proximity to cloud resources, then recommended alternatives include taking advantage of Google Cloud's Bare Metal Solution, or shifting to a co-location facility (colo) adjacent to the appropriate cloud region.

Which Migration Path Is Right for You?

As you embark on your transformation journey, we recommend considering five key types of migration to Google Cloud:

1. Migrating to Google Cloud managed services

2. Migrating to containers on Google Kubernetes Engine (GKE) or Anthos

3. Migrating to VMs ("Lift and Shift") on GCE (Google Compute Engine)

4. Migrating to Google Cloud VMware Engine

5. Migrating to the Google Cloud Bare Metal Solution

Here are example scenarios:

If you are dealing with aggressive timelines, "lift and shift" might be a good choice to gain immediate infrastructure modernization via relocation to cloud. And you can follow up with additional modernization at a later time.

If you seek to take immediate advantages from moving to cloud but are still under a constrained time and skills, then "lift and optimize" is a great choice. Using compute virtual machines or VMware Engine in the cloud, you use the same virtualized familiar environment but can now take advantage of cloud elasticity and scale.

If you are seeking to immediately leverage the full benefits of cloud (e.g., elasticity, scale, managed services), it might be most efficient to modernize more aggressively (such as by adopting container technology) in conjunction with migration. "Move and improve" and "refactoring" are great fits in this situation, but know that it will take a bit longer to execute either strategy due to some changes required in the current apps to make them container friendly and/or serverless.

This decision tree will help you decide which path is right for your application.

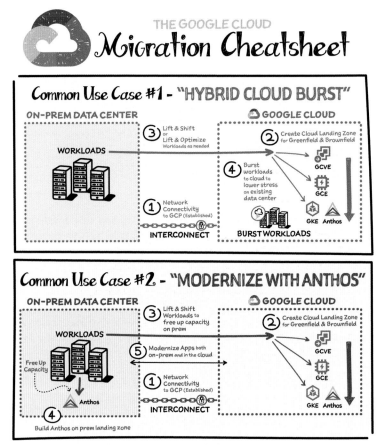

Common Cloud Migration Use Cases

Use Case 1: Hybrid Cloud Burst

- Set up the connectivity between on-premises and the cloud using Cloud Interconnect.
- Create a cloud landing zone; this includes creating the project and the resources such as Google Compute Engine (GCE), Google Kubernetes Engine (GKE), Google Cloud VMware Engine (GCVE), or Anthos.
- Then "lift and shift" or "lift and optimize" from on-premises to the cloud in the appropriate resource.
- At this point, you are ready to send the traffic bursts or excess traffic to Google Cloud to lower the stress on the existing data center.

Use Case 2: Modernize with Anthos

- Establish network connectivity to Google Cloud using Cloud Interconnect.
- Create the cloud landing zone.
- Then, "lift and shift" workloads to free up capacity on-premises.
- Build Anthos on-premises landing zone.
- Then, modernize apps both on-premises and in the cloud.

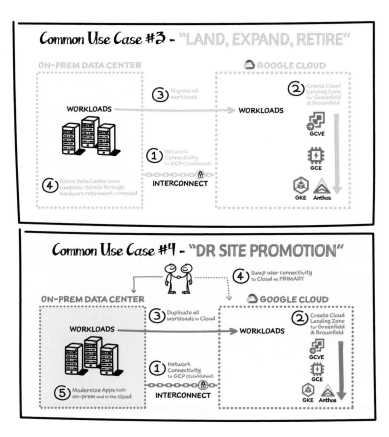

Use Case 3: Land, Expand, Retire

- Establish network connectivity to Google Cloud using Cloud Interconnect.
- Create the cloud landing zone.
- Then, migrate all workloads.
- Finally, retire the data center once complete. Iterate through hardware retirement as needed.

Use Case 4: DR Site Promotion

- Establish network connectivity to Google Cloud using Cloud Interconnect.
- Create the cloud landing zone.
- You are then ready to duplicate all workloads in the cloud.
- Then, swap user connectivity to the cloud as Primary.
- Finally, retire the colo all at once.

Whether you are starting or in the middle of your digital transformation journey, Google Cloud meets you wherever you are and makes it easy for you to move toward a more flexible and agile infrastructure. Hopefully, these steps act as a starting point in your journey and make your digital transformation journey easier.

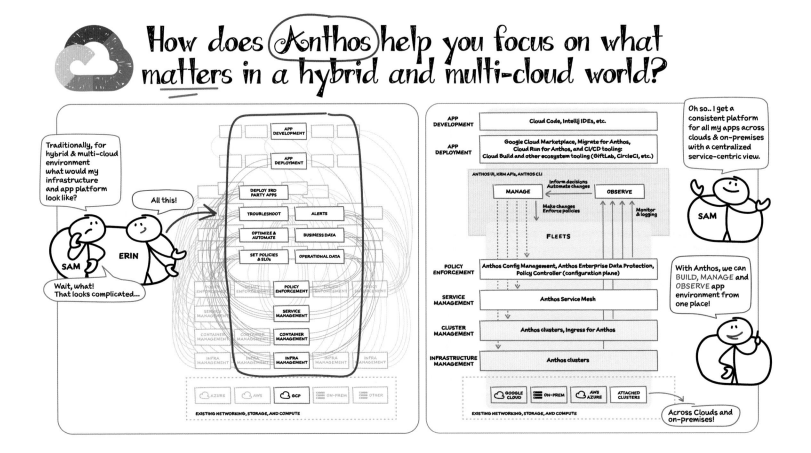

Most enterprises have applications in disparate locations — in their own data centers, in multiple public clouds, and at the edge. These apps run on different proprietary technology stacks, which reduces developer velocity, wastes computing resources, and hinders scalability. How can you consistently secure and operate existing apps while developing and deploying new apps across hybrid and multicloud environments? How can you get centralized visibility and management of the resources? Well, that is why Anthos exists. Here we explore why traditional hybrid and multicloud deployments are difficult, and then see how Anthos makes it easy to manage applications across multiple environments.

Why Is Traditional Hybrid and Multicloud Difficult?

In hybrid and multicloud environments, you need to manage infrastructure. Let's say you use containers on the clouds, and you develop apps using services on Google Cloud and Amazon Web Services (AWS). Regardless of environment, you will need policy enforcement across your IT footprint. To manage your apps across the environment, you require monitoring and logging systems. You must integrate that data into meaningful categories, like business data, operational data, and alerts.

Digging further, you might use operational data and alerts to inform optimizations, implement automations, and set policies or service-level objectives (SLOs). You might use business data to do all those things and to deploy third-party apps. Then, to actually enact the changes you decide to implement, you must act on different parts of the system. That means digging into each tool for policy enforcement, securing services, orchestrating containers, and managing infrastructure. Don't forget, all of this work is *in addition* to what it takes to develop and deploy your own apps.

Now, consider repeating this set of tasks across a hybrid and multicloud landscape. It becomes very complex, very quickly. Your platform admins, site reliability engineering (SRE), and DevOps teams who are responsible for security and efficiency have to do manual, cluster-by-cluster management, data collection, and information synthesis. With this complexity, it's hard to stay current, to understand business implications, and to ensure compliance (not to mention the difficulty of onboarding a new hire). Anthos helps solve these challenges!

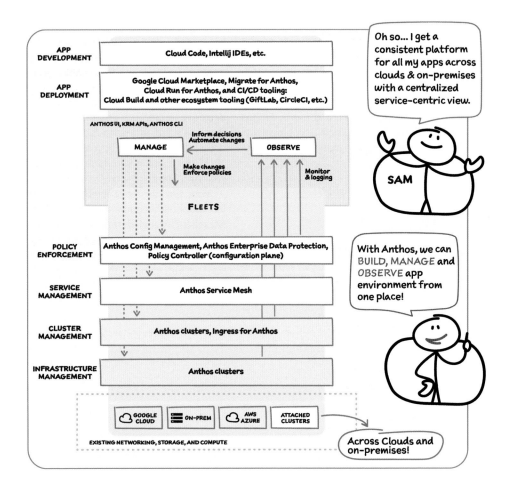

How Does Anthos Make Hybrid and Multicloud Easy?

With Anthos, you get a consistent way to manage your infrastructure using open source, with similar infrastructure management, container management, service management, and policy enforcement across your landscape.

As a result, you have observability across all your platforms in one place, including access to business information, alerts, and operations information. With this information you might decide to optimize, automate, and set policies or SLOs.

Digging Deeper into Anthos

Fleets　You may have different regions that need different policies, and also have different development, staging, or production environments that need different permissions. Some parts of your work may need more security. That's where fleets come in! Environs are a way to create logical sets of underlying Kubernetes clusters, regardless of which platform those clusters live on. By considering grouping and managing sets of clusters as logical environs, you can think about and work with your applications at the right level of detail for what you need to do, be it acquiring business insights over the entire system, updating settings for a dev environment, or troubleshooting data for a specific cluster. Using environs, each part of the functional stack can take declarative direction about configuration, compliance, and more.

Modernize Application Development　Anthos also helps modernize application development because it uses environs to enforce policies and processes, and abstracts away the cluster and container management from application teams. Anthos enables you to easily abstract away infrastructure from application teams, making it easy for them to incorporate a wide variety of continuous integration and continuous delivery (CI/CD) solutions on top of environs. It lets you view and manage your applications at the right level of detail, be it business insights for services across the entire system, or troubleshooting data for a specific cluster. Anthos also works with container-based tools like buildpacks (transform your application source code into images that can run on any cloud) to simplify the packaging process. It offers Migrate for Anthos to take those applications out of the VMs and move them to a more modern hosting environment.

What's in It for Platform Administrators?　Anthos provides platform administrators with a single place to monitor and manage their landscape, with policy control and marketplace access. This reduces person-hours needed for management, enforcement, discovery, and communication. Anthos also provides administrators with an out-of-the-box structured view of their entire system, including services, clusters, and more, so they can improve security, use resources more efficiently, and demonstrate measurable success. Administrators also save time and effort by managing declaratively, and they can communicate the success, cost savings, and efficiency of the platforms without having to manually combine data.

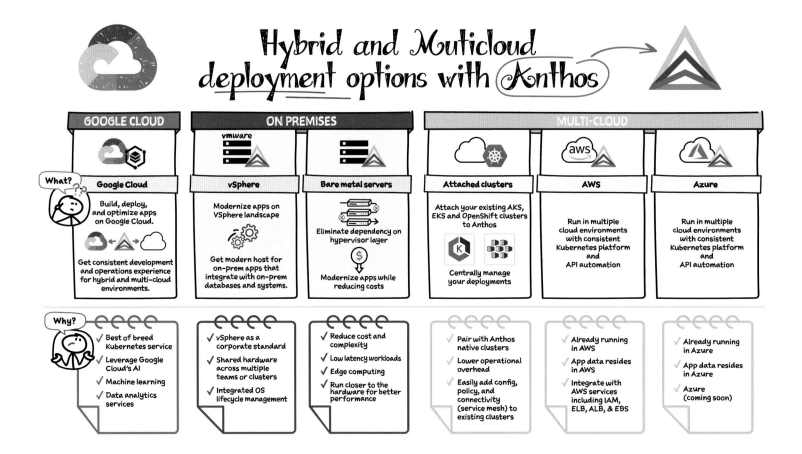

Anthos is a managed application platform that extends Google Cloud services and engineering practices to your environments so that you can modernize apps faster and establish operational consistency across them. With Anthos, you can build enterprise-grade containerized applications faster with managed Kubernetes on Google Cloud, on-premises, and other cloud providers. In this section, we outline each of Anthos's deployment options:

1. Google Cloud
2. VMware vSphere
3. Bare-metal servers
4. Anthos attached clusters
5. AWS
6. Microsoft Azure

Deployment Option 1: Google Cloud

One way to improve your apps' performance is to run your compute closer to your data. So, if you are already running your services on Google Cloud, then it's best to use Anthos to build, deploy, and optimize your containerized workloads directly on Google Cloud. You can take advantage of Google Cloud AI, machine learning, and data analytics services to gain critical business insights, improve decision-making, and accelerate innovation.

Deployment Option 2: VMware vSphere

If you are using VMware vSphere in your own environment, then you can choose to run Anthos clusters on VMware, which enables you to create, manage, and upgrade Kubernetes clusters on your existing infrastructure. This is a good option if vSphere is a corporate standard for your organization

and if you have shared hardware across multiple teams or clusters and with integrated OS life cycle management. With Anthos clusters on VMware, you can keep all your existing workloads on-premises without significant infrastructure updates. At the same time, you can modernize legacy applications by transforming them from VM-based to container-based using Migrate for Anthos. Going forward, you might decide to keep the newly updated, containerized apps on-premises or move them to the cloud. Either way, Anthos helps you manage and modernize your apps with ease and at your own pace.

Deployment Option 3: Bare-Metal Servers

Though virtual machines are unquestionably useful for a wide variety of workloads, a growing number of organizations are running Kubernetes on bare-metal servers to take advantage of reduced complexity, cost, and hypervisor overhead. Anthos on bare metal lets you run Anthos on physical servers, deployed on an operating system provided by you, without a hypervisor layer. Anthos on bare metal comes with built-in networking, life cycle management, diagnostics, health checks, logging, and monitoring. Mission-critical applications often demand the highest levels of performance and lowest latency from the compute, storage, and networking stack. By removing the latency introduced by the hypervisor layer, Anthos on bare metal lets you run computationally intensive applications such as GPU-based video processing, machine learning, and more, in a cost-effective manner. Anthos on bare metal allows you to leverage existing investments in hardware, OS, and networking infrastructure. There are minimal system requirements to run Anthos on bare metal at the edge on resource-constrained hardware. This means that you can capitalize on all the benefits of Anthos — centralized management, increased flexibility, and developer agility — even for your most demanding applications.

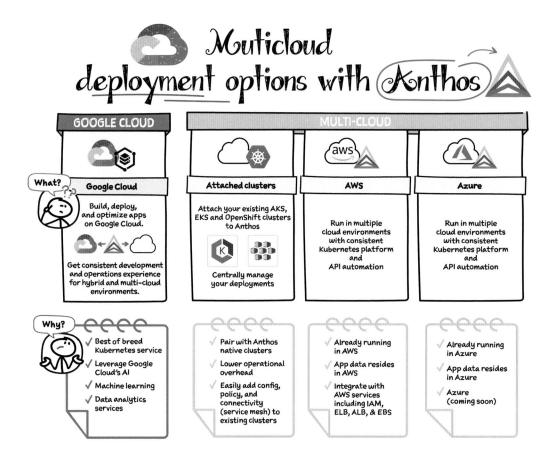

Deployment Option 4: Anthos Attached Clusters

When thinking about deploying Anthos, you may be wondering about what you'll do with your existing Kubernetes clusters. With Anthos attached clusters, you can retain your existing Kubernetes clusters while taking advantage of key Anthos features. Whether you're running Amazon EKS, Microsoft AKS, or Red Hat OpenShift, you can attach your existing clusters to Anthos. That means you can centrally manage your deployments in Google Cloud Console, enforce policies and configuration using Anthos Config Management, and centrally monitor and collect logs. Of course, Anthos doesn't manage everything; you still must manually maintain your clusters and keep them up to date. This deployment option does, however, enable you to begin your Anthos journey at a pace that works well for you, and it eases the transition to Anthos in other cloud environments.

Deployment Option 5: AWS

If your organization has more than a few teams, chances are pretty good that they're using different technologies, and perhaps even different cloud platforms. Anthos is designed to abstract these details and provide you with a consistent application platform. Anthos on AWS enables you to create

Google Kubernetes–based clusters with all the Anthos features you'd expect on Google Cloud. This includes easy deployment using Kubernetes-native tooling, Anthos Config Management for policy and configuration enforcement, and Anthos Service Mesh for managing the increasing sprawl of microservices. When you use the Google Cloud Console, you have a single pane of glass that you can use to manage your applications all in one place no matter where they are deployed.

Deployment Option 6: Microsoft Azure

Google Cloud are always extending Anthos to support more kinds of workloads, in more kinds of environments, and in more locations. Google announced last year that Anthos is coming to Azure. Support for Microsoft Azure is currently in preview, so stay tuned for more details!

So there you have it — six different hybrid and multicloud deployment options for Anthos! Depending on where your infrastructure and data is today, one or perhaps a combination of these options will help you power your application modernization journey, with a modern application platform that *just works* on-premises or in a public cloud, ties in seamlessly with legacy data center infrastructure, enables platform teams to cost-optimize, and supports a modern security posture anywhere.

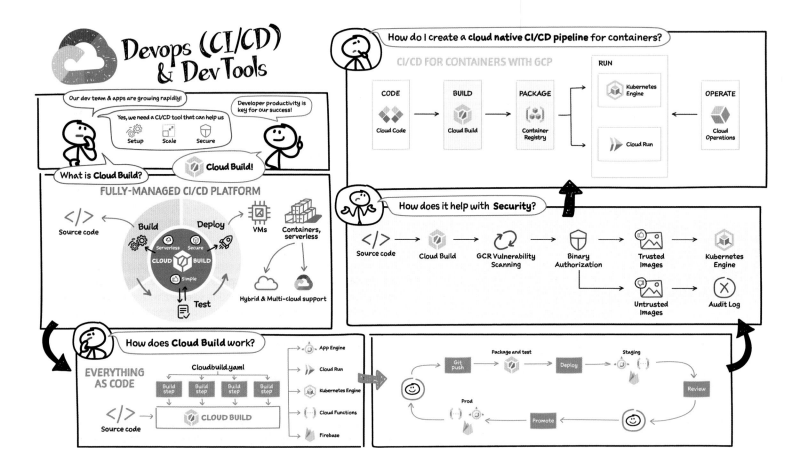

Continuous integration (CI) is the process of identifying and correcting problems early in the development process. With CI, you integrate your work frequently, instead of waiting for one large integration later on. Each integration is verified with an automated build, which enables you to detect integration issues as quickly as possible and reduce problems downstream.

Continuous delivery (CD) extends CI. CD is about packaging and preparing the software with the goal of delivering incremental changes to users. Deployment strategies such as red/black and canary deployments can help reduce release risk and increase confidence in releases. CD lowers risk and makes the release process safer, faster, and when done well, boring. Once deployments are made painless with CD, developers can focus on writing code, not tweaking deployment scripts.

How Has the Application Development Landscape Changed?

Much has changed in the app development space recently, and you'll want to take these changes into account as part of your CI/CD strategy.

- Hybrid and multicloud deployments — Large enterprises want to deploy applications in hybrid cloud environments, with tools and services that don't lock them into a specific vendor.

- The shift from monolith to microservices — Teams are breaking down large monoliths into microservices for greater agility. This makes it possible for different teams to use different languages, tech stacks, and development life cycles, which means deployment patterns, tooling needs, and scaling patterns are changing.

- Cloud-native applications — It's not just VMs anymore; companies are shifting paradigms and embracing serverless, containers, and Kubernetes. While simplifying some aspects of app development, this move adds complexity in other areas.

Ideally, developers should be focused on their code, not on ushering their changes through a CI/CD process. CI/CD steps should be triggered and run behind the scenes as soon as code is checked in. So, your CI/CD pipeline should support Packaging of source code, Automated unit and integration tests, Consistent build environments, Approvals before deploying to production, Blue/green and canary rollouts. That's where Cloud Build comes in.

Cloud Build

Cloud Build is a fully managed CI/CD platform that lets you build, test, and deploy across hybrid and multicloud environments that include VMs, serverless, Kubernetes, and Firebase. Cloud Build can import source code from Cloud Storage, Cloud Source Repositories, GitHub, or Bitbucket; execute a build to your specifications; and produce artifacts such as Docker container images or Java archives.

Cloud Build executes your build as a series of build steps, with each step run in a Docker container. A build step can do anything that can be done from a container regardless of the environment. To perform your tasks, you can either use the supported build steps provided by Cloud Build or write your own build steps. As a part of the build step, Cloud Build deploys the app to a platform of your choice. You also have the ability to perform deep security scans within the CI/CD pipeline using Binary Authorization and ensure only trusted container images are deployed to production.

Cloud Build private pools help you meet enterprise security and compliance requirements. These are private, dedicated pools of workers that offer greater customization over the build environment, including the ability to access resources in a private network. For instance, you can trigger fully managed DevOps workflows from source code repositories hosted in private networks, including GitHub Enterprise.

Cloud Code

If you are working entirely in a cloud-native environment, then you'll want to use Cloud Code to kick off your CI/CD pipeline. Use Cloud Code in your IDE; it comes with tools to help you write, run, and debug cloud-native applications quickly and easily. Then push your code to Cloud Build for the build process, package it in the Artifact Registry, and run it on GKE or Cloud Run. You can get all the visibility and metrics you want for the deployment in Google Cloud's operations suite.

Cloud Deploy

Google Cloud Deploy (In preview at the time of this writing) is a managed, continuous delivery service that makes continuous delivery to GKE easier, faster, and more reliable. It has built-in security controls and can be integrated with your existing DevOps ecosystem.

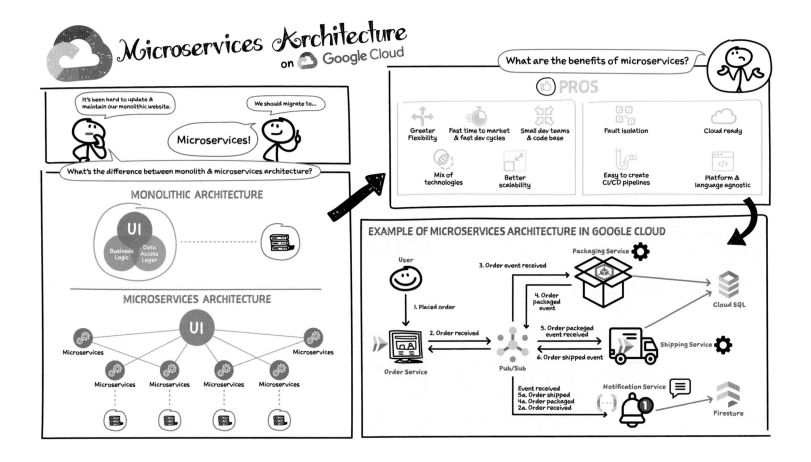

The evolution of technologies such as containerization, container orchestration, and cloud-native serverless services has given us the ability to develop distributed solutions based on microservices architectures that are both more scalable and more reliable.

What Is Microservices Architecture?

Microservices architecture (often shortened to *microservices*) refers to an architectural style for developing applications. Microservices enable you to break down a large application into smaller independent services, with each service having its own realm of responsibility. To serve a single user request, a microservices-based application can call on many individual microservices to compose its response.

Containers are well suited to microservices, since they let you focus on developing the services without worrying about dependencies. Modern cloud-native applications are usually built as microservices using containers.

When you use Google Cloud, you can easily deploy microservices using either the managed container service, Google Kubernetes Engine (GKE), or the fully managed serverless offering, Cloud Run. Depending on your use case, Cloud SQL and other Google Cloud products and services can be integrated to support your microservices architecture.

How Are Monolithic and Microservices Architectures Different?

With a monolithic architecture, the solution is built as one large system, often with a single codebase. It is extremely difficult to change a monolith's technology, language, or framework because all components are tightly coupled and dependent on each other. As a result, even relatively small changes can require lengthy development and deployment times.

With a microservices architecture, the solution is built as a set of independent modules based on business functionality. Each module, or service, is small (*"micro"*), which decreases overall build and development time and makes it easy to create CI/CD pipelines. Smaller functional units also make it easy to change technology and frameworks or use different languages for different services. It's easier to isolate faults since they are usually limited to a specific service. Services can be scaled independently, letting you scale out subsystems that require more resources without scaling out the entire application.

Microservices Use Cases

Let's consider a scenario in which you are migrating a monolithic web application or developing a new one with a microservices architecture. Microservices architectures are often event-driven with the pub/sub model, where one service publishes events and other services subscribe to the events and take action on them.

In this example scenario there are four services: Order, Packaging, Shipping, and Notification:

- When a user places an order on the website, the Order service receives the order, does some preliminary processing, and sends the event to Google Pub/Sub.

- The Packaging and Notification services, which are subscribed to the events from the Order service, start the packaging process for the order and send an email notification to the customer.

- The Packaging service sends an order packaging event to Pub/Sub. The Shipping service, which has subscribed to these events, processes shipping and sends an event to Pub/Sub. The Notification service consumes this event and sends another message to the customer with order shipment info.

Of course, there are multiple ways of deploying a website like this. Choosing the best option will depend on your team's specific requirements and preferences. Notice that in the example the Notification service uses Cloud Functions to run the logic for sending notifications and uses a Firestore database to look up user email addresses. The Shipping and Order services are deployed on Cloud Run while the Packaging service is deployed on GKE. They all are connecting to a Cloud SQL database.

Some other microservices use cases are:

- Media content: Using a microservices architecture, images, and video assets can be stored in a scalable object storage system and served directly to web or mobile apps.

- Transactions and invoices: Payment processing and ordering can be separated as independent services, so payments continue to be accepted even if there is a service disruption with invoicing.

- Data processing: A microservices platform can extend cloud support for existing modular data processing.

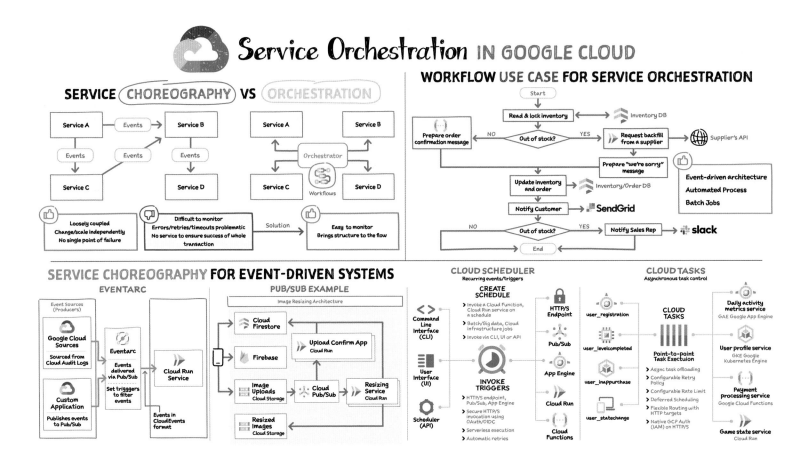

Service Orchestration IN GOOGLE CLOUD

SERVICE (CHOREOGRAPHY) VS (ORCHESTRATION)

Service A — Events → Service B
Events, Events
Service C
Service D

Orchestrator
Workflows

Loosely coupled
Change/scale independently
No single point of failure

Difficult to monitor
Errors/retries/timeouts problematic
No service to ensure success of whole transaction

Solution →

Easy to monitor
Brings structure to the flow

WORKFLOW USE CASE FOR SERVICE ORCHESTRATION

Start
Read & lock inventory ↔ Inventory DB
Prepare order confirmation message ← NO — Out of stock? — YES → Request backfill from a supplier → Supplier's API
Prepare "we're sorry" message
Update inventory and order → Inventory/Order DB
Notify Customer → SendGrid
NO — Out of stock? — YES → Notify Sales Rep → slack
End

👍 **Event-driven architecture**
Automated Process
Batch Jobs

SERVICE CHOREOGRAPHY FOR EVENT-DRIVEN SYSTEMS

EVENTARC

Event Sources (Producers)

Google Cloud Sources
Sourced from Cloud Audit Logs

Custom Application
Publishes events to Pub/Sub

Eventarc
Events delivered via Pub/Sub
Set triggers to filter events

Cloud Run Service
Events in CloudEvents format

PUB/SUB EXAMPLE

Image Resizing Architecture

Cloud Firestore
Firebase
Upload Confirm App Cloud Run
Image Uploads Cloud Storage
Cloud Pub/Sub
Resizing Service Cloud Run
Resized Images Cloud Storage

CLOUD SCHEDULER
Recurring events/triggers

CREATE SCHEDULE
➤ Invoke a Cloud Function, Cloud Run service on a schedule
➤ Batch/Big data, Cloud infrastructure jobs
➤ Invoke via CLI, UI or API

Command Line Interface (CLI)
User Interface (UI)
Scheduler (API)

INVOKE TRIGGERS
➤ HTTP/S endpoint, Pub/Sub, App Engine
➤ Secure HTTP/S invocation using OAuth/OIDC
➤ Serverless execution
➤ Automatic retries

HTTP/S Endpoint
Pub/Sub
App Engine
Cloud Run
Cloud Functions

CLOUD TASKS
Asynchronous task control

user_registration
user_levelcompleted
user_inappurchase
user_statechange

CLOUD TASKS

Point-to-point Task Exectuion
➤ Async task offloading
➤ Configurable Retry Policy
➤ Configurable Rate Limit
➤ Deferred Scheduling
➤ Flexible Routing with HTTP targets
➤ Native GCP Auth (IAM) on HTTP/S

Daily activity metrics service GAE Google App Engine
User profile service GKE Google Kubernetes Engine
Payment processing service Google Cloud Functions
Game state service Cloud Run

Going from a monolithic architecture to microservices has clear benefits, including reusability, scalability, and ease of change. Most of the time, business problems are solved by coordinating multiple microservices. This coordination is based on event-driven architectures, which can be implemented via two approaches: choreography and orchestration.

Service Choreography and Service Orchestration

- **Service Choreography** — With service choreography, each service works independently and interacts with other services in a loosely coupled way through events. Loosely coupled events can be changed and scaled independently, which means there is no single point of failure. But, so many events flying around between services makes it quite hard to monitor. Business logic is distributed and spans across multiple services, so there is no single, central place to go for troubleshooting. There's no central source of truth to understand the system. Understanding, updating, and troubleshooting are all distributed.

- **Service Orchestration** — To handle the monitoring challenges of choreography, developers need to bring structure to the flow of events, while retaining the loosely coupled nature of event-driven services. Using service orchestration, the services interact with each other via a central orchestrator that controls all interactions between the services. This orchestrator provides a high-level view of the business processes to track execution and troubleshoot issues. In Google Cloud, Workflows is the service orchestration service.

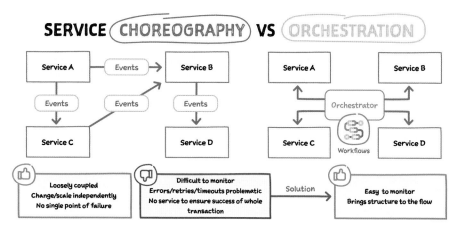

Once you have decided between the two approaches for your application, design questions are largely about the characteristics of the services and the use case. You should prefer orchestration within the bounded context of a microservice, but prefer choreography between bounded contexts. That is, you'll likely have choreography at a higher level, with orchestration at lower levels, both in the same system.

Google Cloud provides services supporting both orchestration and choreography approaches. Pub/Sub and Eventarc are both suited for choreography of event-driven services, whereas Workflows is suited for centrally orchestrated services.

Google Cloud Support for Service Orchestration

Workflows

You use Workflows to orchestrate and automate Google Cloud and HTTP-based API services with serverless workflows. It is a fully managed, scalable, and observable way to define a business process and orchestrate calls to several services. Workflows calls those services as simple web APIs. Using Workflows you can define the flow of your business logic in a YAML-based workflow definition language and use the UI or API to trigger the workflow. You can use Workflows to automate complex processes, including event-driven and batch jobs, error handling logic, sequences of operations, and more. Workflows is particularly helpful with Google Cloud services that perform long-running operations; Workflows will wait for them to complete, even if they take hours. With callbacks, Workflows can wait for external events for days or months.

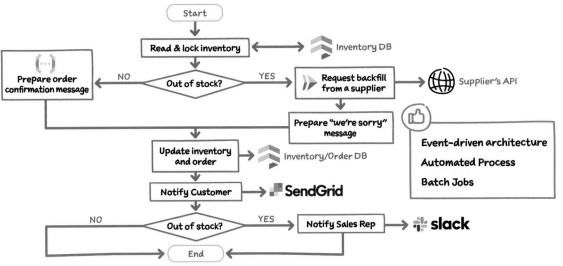

WORKFLOW USE CASE FOR SERVICE ORCHESTRATION

Google Cloud Support for Service Choreography

Pub/Sub

Pub/Sub enables services to communicate asynchronously, with latencies on the order of 100 milliseconds. Pub/Sub is used for messaging-oriented middleware for service integration or as a queue to parallelize tasks. Publishers send events to the Pub/Sub service, without regard to how or when these events will be processed. Pub/Sub then delivers events to all services that need to react to them (Subscribers). Pub/Sub is also used for streaming analytics and data integration pipelines to ingest and distribute data (as covered in Chapter 4, "Data Analytics").

Eventarc

Eventarc enables you to build event-driven architectures without having to implement, customize, or maintain the underlying infrastructure. It offers a standardized solution to manage the flow of state changes, also known as *events*, between decoupled microservices. Eventarc routes these events to Cloud Run while managing delivery, security, authorization, observability, and error-handling for you. Eventarc provides an easy way to receive events not only from Pub/Sub topics but from a number of Google Cloud sources with its Audit Log and Pub/Sub integration. Any service with Audit Log integration or any application that can send a message to a Pub/Sub topic can be event sources for Eventarc.

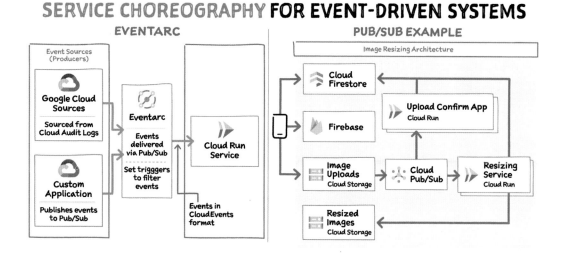

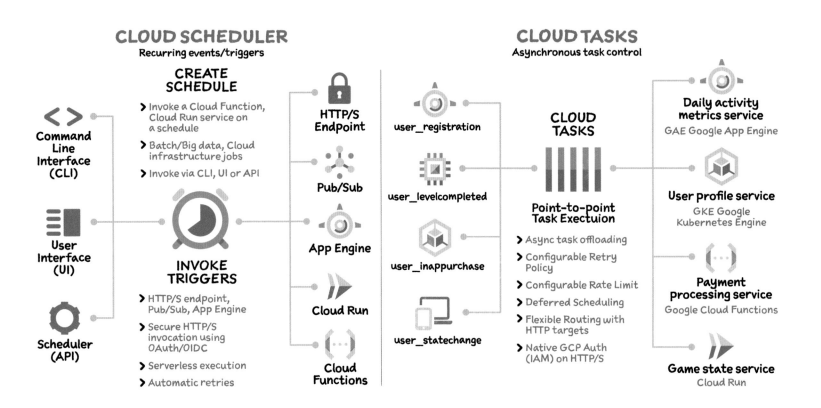

CLOUD SCHEDULER
Recurring events/triggers

CREATE SCHEDULE
- Invoke a Cloud Function, Cloud Run service on a schedule
- Batch/Big data, Cloud infrastructure jobs
- Invoke via CLI, UI or API

INVOKE TRIGGERS
- HTTP/S endpoint, Pub/Sub, App Engine
- Secure HTTP/S invocation using OAuth/OIDC
- Serverless execution
- Automatic retries

Command Line Interface (CLI)

User Interface (UI)

Scheduler (API)

HTTP/S Endpoint

Pub/Sub

App Engine

Cloud Run

Cloud Functions

user_registration

user_levelcompleted

user_inappurchase

user_statechange

CLOUD TASKS
Asynchronous task control

CLOUD TASKS

Point-to-point Task Exectuion
- Async task offloading
- Configurable Retry Policy
- Configurable Rate Limit
- Deferred Scheduling
- Flexible Routing with HTTP targets
- Native GCP Auth (IAM) on HTTP/S

Daily activity metrics service
GAE Google App Engine

User profile service
GKE Google Kubernetes Engine

Payment processing service
Google Cloud Functions

Game state service
Cloud Run

Additional Services That Help with Both Choreography and Orchestration

Cloud Tasks

Cloud Tasks lets you separate pieces of work that can be performed independently, outside of your main application flow, and send them off to be processed asynchronously using handlers that you create. These independent pieces of work are called *tasks*. Cloud Tasks helps speed user response times by delegating potentially slow background operations like database updates to a worker. It can also help smooth traffic spikes by removing non-user-facing tasks from the main user flow.

Difference between Pub/Sub and Cloud Tasks Pub/Sub supports *implicit invocation*: a publisher implicitly causes the subscribers to execute by publishing an event. Cloud Tasks is aimed at *explicit invocation* where the publisher retains full control of execution, including specifying an endpoint where each message is to be delivered. Unlike Pub/Sub, Cloud Tasks provides tools for queue and task management, including scheduling specific delivery times, rate controls, retries, and deduplication.

Cloud Scheduler

With Cloud Scheduler, you set up scheduled units of work to be executed at defined times or regular intervals, commonly known as cron jobs. Cloud Scheduler can trigger a workflow (orchestration) or generate a Pub/Sub message (choreography). Typical use cases include sending out a report email on a daily basis, updating some cached data every x minutes, or updating summary information once an hour.

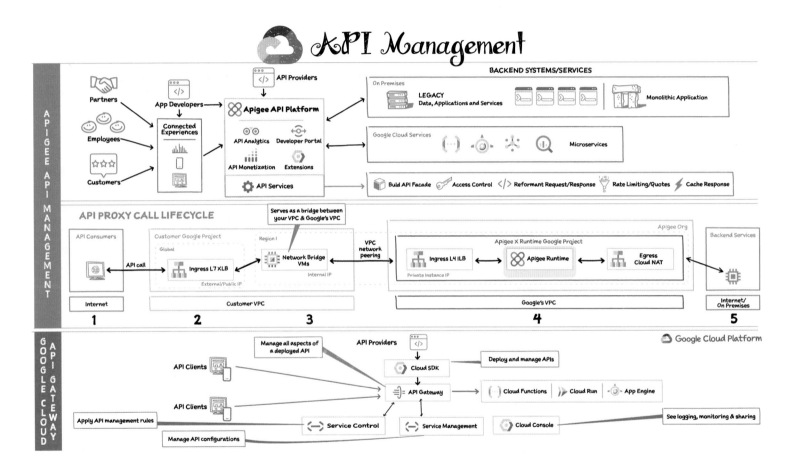

APIs are the de facto standard for building and sharing the modern applications that power today's enterprises. All modern businesses leverage APIs to move fast and stay competitive. But securely delivering, managing, and analyzing APIs, data, and services is complex and critical — and it's getting more challenging as enterprise ecosystems expand beyond on-premises data centers to include private and public clouds, SaaS, and other IT endpoints. To navigate this complexity, businesses need API management.

What Is API Management?

Let's consider a scenario. Suppose you have some backend services, including REST/SOAP services, microservices, a service bus, and maybe some more third-party services. You've got some consumers of these services on the other side: partners, employees, and customers. They have applications that need to get data from your backend services or trigger an action with an API.

Developers are composing new and compelling applications using APIs to build and participate in ecosystems. Productizing those APIs underscores all of the compelling new business applications we see in the Internet economy. All of those things it takes to productize APIs — developer portal, API packaging, flexible security options, and turning operational metrics into business analytics — are what API management is about and what Apigee offers.

What Is Apigee?

Apigee API management helps modernize your applications and monetize your APIs. It helps control an application's access to the backend data and services. It also offers application developers tools they need to access the API and helps API providers with tools they need to manage and provision the APIs.

- **API Services:** This is the part that routes traffic from the applications to the backend services and acts as an enterprise gateway orchestrating those backend services and preventing people from abusing them. This is where an API provider can enforce throttling and quotas on the services to protect the backend. You can build a facade over the backend services and present a set of interfaces to those external applications compared to what's inside. You can even control access so different applications might have access to different services and they might get different results when they call them. You could reformat the request as it comes in and make it appropriate for your backend services. You could change the response that comes from the backend services around before sending it back to the applications. You can add caching to improve performance by responding directly from cache, avoiding a call to the backend.

- **Developer Portal:** Apigee offers a developer portal to serve the API consumer or the application developer. They can sign up to use the API, get credentials to access the service, and access documentation to learn how to use the API. If there's a need to serve the APIs as products, API providers can take all the services and bundle them together into different packages that provide different access. You can even brand the portal to match the branding of your website.

- **API Monetization:** You can create a variety of monetization plans that charge developers (or pay them through revenue sharing) for the use of your APIs.

- **API Analytics:** API Analytics helps your API team measure everything from developer engagement metrics to business and operational metrics. These analytics help API teams improve their APIs and app developers improve their apps. They also help answer questions about traffic patterns, top developers, which API methods are popular, API response times, and other such metrics needed to improve the service.

Apigee gives you a choice between configuration or coding; there are a number of out-of-the-box policies that do basic things. You can drop in these policies to request a token or add response caching if you want to do code-driven development. You can build your own policies, and you can drop those in and mix them with the out-of-the-box policies; that can be done with JavaScript, Java, or Python.

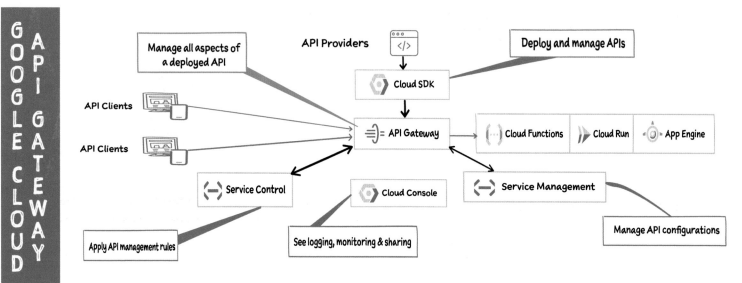

What is API Gateway?

API Gateway is an API management system that provides management, monitoring, and authentication for your APIs. It enables you to provide secure access to your services through a well-defined REST API that is consistent across all of your services, regardless of service implementation. A consistent API:

- Makes it easy for app developers to consume your services
- Enables you to change the backend service implementation without affecting the public API
- Enables you to take advantage of the scaling, monitoring, and security features built into Google Cloud

API Gateway Architecture

The API provider is responsible for creating and deploying an API on API Gateway. Each API is defined by a file written as an OpenAPI 2.0 spec. The OpenAPI spec defines the publicly facing URL of the REST endpoint for the API, the backend service accessed by the API, and any other characteristics of the API such as authentication, data format, and response options.

The API client makes a REST request to an API hosted on API Gateway to access backend services. An API client can be any app capable of making a REST call, such as a browser, mobile app, or web app. The API client only needs to know the URL of the API, the request verb (such as GET, PUT, POST, DELETE), any authentication requirements, and the format of any data sent to or received from the API. The API client does not need to know anything about the backend implementation. In fact, a single API hosted on API Gateway can be configured to access different backends based on information passed in the request.

What's the Difference Between API Gateway and Apigee API Management Platform?

API Gateway is a small subset of an API management platform. It enables you to provide secure access to and exposure of your services in Google Cloud (Cloud Functions, App Engine, Cloud Run, Compute Engine, GKE), through a well-defined REST API that is consistent across all of your services, regardless of service implementation. A consistent API:

- Makes it easy for app developers to consume your services
- Enables you to change the backend service implementation without affecting the public API
- Enables you to take advantage of the scaling, monitoring, and security features built into the Google Cloud Platform (GCP)

Apigee, on the other hand, includes a gateway, but it helps drive API consumption because it also includes a developer portal, monitoring, monetization, advanced API operations, and other extension possibilities. The gateway itself is more capable, with built-in policies. Apigee can connect to arbitrary backends, including but not limited to upstreams hosted in Google Cloud.

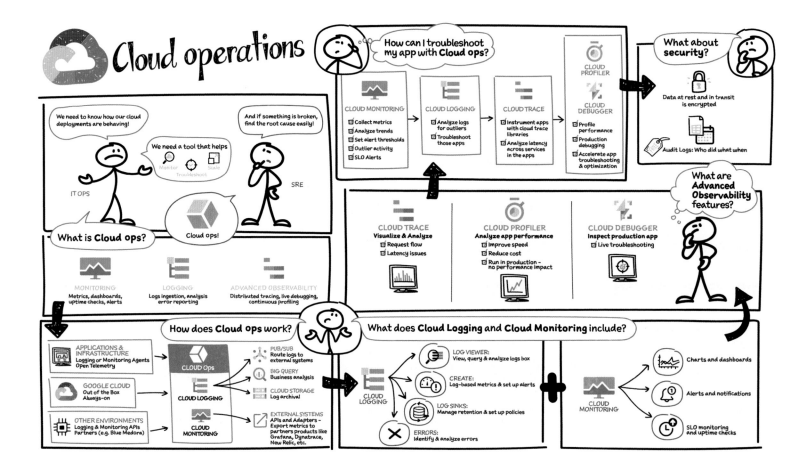

You know the time when you want to see how your cloud deployment is behaving or if something is broken in production and your users might be impacted. You are scrambling because there are too many tools to look through to find and resolve the issue. That's where Google Cloud's operations suite comes in.

What Is the Operations Suite?

Google Cloud's operations suite is made up of products to monitor, troubleshoot, and operate your services at scale, enabling your DevOps, SREs, or ITOps teams to utilize the Google SRE best practices. It offers integrated capabilities for monitoring, logging, and advanced observability services like trace, debugger, and profiler. The end-to-end operations solution includes built-in telemetry, out-of-box dashboards, recommendations, alerts, and more: It helps you capture signals, monitor systems, manage incidents, and troubleshoot issues.

What Does Cloud Operations Include?

Cloud Logging is a fully managed and highly scalable service that aggregates log data from all your infrastructure and applications across Google Cloud into a single location. Cloud Logging collects log data from Google Cloud services automatically, and any custom log source, such as applications, on-premises sources, or other clouds, through the Ops Agent, open source fluentd, or an API. It provides complete control to decide how and where to store the logs, including keeping the logs in Cloud Logging, exporting them to Cloud Storage, or streaming the logs via Cloud Pub/Sub to custom third-party destinations. Logs Explorer gives you powerful capabilities to filter the logs and convert them to log-based metrics for monitoring, alerting, analyzing, and visualizing.

Cloud Monitoring provides observability across your apps and infrastructure, regardless of where it is — Google Cloud, on-premises, or in other clouds. It supports a variety of metrics integrations and allows you to define custom metrics unique to your use cases and even send those metrics to external systems. Using the Metrics Explorer and Monitoring Query Language, you can analyze these metrics on the fly, identify correlations, and easily add the corresponding charts to a dashboard. You can use out-of-box or custom-built dashboards to get a consolidated view of the health of your infrastructure, service, or application and easily spot anomalies. But we cannot sit around all day looking at dashboards. Cloud Monitoring provides alerting, which lets you create policies to alert on performance metrics, uptime checks, and service level indicators.

Application Performance Management (APM) combines monitoring and troubleshooting capabilities of Cloud Logging and Cloud Monitoring with Cloud Trace, Cloud Debugger, and Cloud Profiler, to help you reduce latency and cost so that you can run more efficient applications.

- **Cloud Trace** provides visualization and analysis to understand request flow, service topology, and latency issues in your app.
- **Cloud Debugger** allows you to inspect the state of running applications after deployment, without needing to stop or slow it down.
- **Cloud Profiler** continually analyzes your code's performance on each service so that you can improve its speed and reduce your costs. And it is designed to run in production with effectively no performance impact.

While Cloud Trace is used to track relationships and latency between services, Cloud Profiler tracks this across the individual functions in your codebase and Cloud Debugger helps find the root cause from the method to the problematic piece of code.

How Does Cloud Operations Work?

You can use the tools directly in the cloud console or via APIs. Cloud Logging automatically ingests Google Cloud audit and platform logs. You can also ingest logs and metrics from other environments and on-premises using the API. You can then: Use Log Viewer to view, query, and analyze logs; Create log-based metrics to set up alerts; and Create log sinks to manage retention and set up policies

Cloud Monitoring provides a view of all system metrics created by Google Cloud services, at no cost. Cloud Monitoring also integrates with a variety of third-party providers and supports custom metrics ingested from non-Google Cloud sources via agents or API.

From the security perspective, all your data is encrypted at rest and in transit. All your security-focused audit logs are automatically available in Cloud Logging, telling you who did what, where, and when. With Access Transparency logs, you can always stay in compliance because it captures the actions Google personnel take while offering you support.

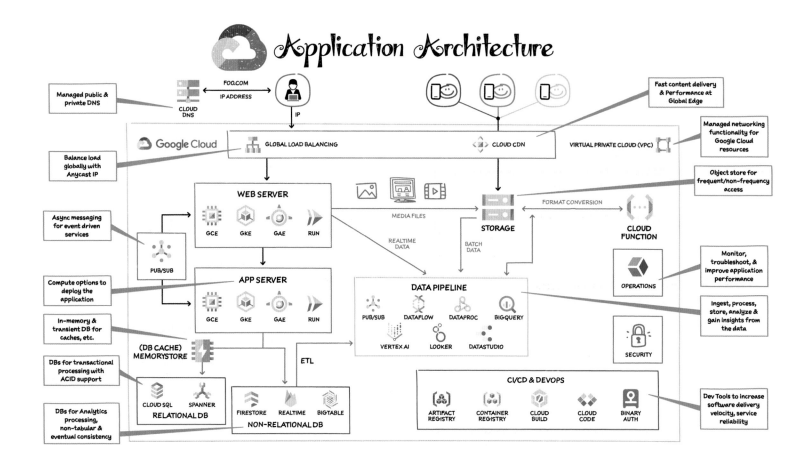

The critical pieces of a typical web application include the web server, application server, databases, and load balancer, among other components. Let's consider one such application to see how it would be deployed on Google Cloud.

Sample Application Architecture

Imagine you are a Google Cloud Architect for foo.com, an internet accessible application. There are many different ways to architect such an application on Google Cloud; no one way is right or wrong. Let's examine one approach, from the perspective of a generic request flow for when a user opens the browser and types **foo.com** in the address bar.

Domain Name System (DNS)

The request goes to the DNS server, which responds with an IP address. Cloud DNS is Google's infrastructure for high-volume authoritative DNS serving that offers 100% SLA (which means it never goes down). It uses Google's global network of anycast name servers to serve DNS zones from redundant locations around the world, providing high availability and low latency for your users.

Web and Application Servers

The IP address obtained from the DNS is used by the user's computer to make a connection to the web server where the code for the foo.com front-end is deployed. The application's business logic is deployed on the application server. This includes functionalities such as authentication service, inventory, and payment service. Requests to this application server are usually limited to only web servers and internal services. The web and application servers are housed inside VPC, which provides managed networking functionality for all Google Cloud resources.

For web and application servers, you have multiple options across Cloud Run, App Engine, GKE, and Compute Engine. Check out "Where I should run my stuff" for more details.

- **Serverless:** If you have a small team of developers, you want them to focus on coding and not worry about infrastructure and scaling tasks. Cloud Run or App Engine would be great picks. Both are serverless and scale from low to high traffic as needed. If you want to run serverless containers serving web and event-driven microservice architectures, then Cloud Run is recommended. Cloud Run should work for most use cases, but you should also check out App Engine if you are developing websites with built-in static file hosting.

- **GKE:** If you want to run containerized apps with more configuration options and flexibility, you can use GKE. It helps you easily deploy containerized apps with Kubernetes while giving you control over the configuration of nodes. Scaling is also easy; you can define the number of nodes to scale to as traffic grows.

- **Compute Engine:** Your other maximum-control option is Compute Engine. It is straight-up virtual machines (VMs), so you can precisely define the configuration of your machines depending on the amount of memory and CPU you need. This level of control, however, means you have more responsibility to scale, manage, patch, and maintain the VMs as needed. Compute Engine works well for legacy applications with specific needs and in situations that truly require full control.

Database

Of course, foo.com needs one or more databases to store information. These could be relational or nonrelational databases depending on the type of data and the use case. (For more detailed guidance on picking the right database for your use case, see "Your Google Cloud database options, explained.")

Google Cloud relational databases include Cloud SQL and Cloud Spanner, which are both managed.

- Cloud SQL is perfect for generic SQL needs — MySQL, PostgreSQL, and SQL Server.

- Spanner is best for massive scale relational databases that need horizontal scalability. (*Massive* here means thousands of writes per second and tens of thousands of reads per second, while supporting ACID transactions.)

For nonrelational databases, Google Cloud has three major options: Firestore, Bigtable, and Memorystore.

- Firestore is a serverless document database that provides strong consistency, supports ACID transactions, and delivers fast results to complex queries. It also supports offline data and syncs, which makes it a great choice for mobile use cases along with web, IoT, and gaming.
- Bigtable is a wide-column NoSQL database that supports heavy reads and writes with extremely low latency. This makes it a perfect choice for events, time series data from IoT devices, click stream data, ad events, fraud detection, recommendations, and other personalization-related use cases.
- Memorystore is a fully managed in-memory data store service for Redis and Memcached. It's best for transient stores and database caches.

Load Balancing and Scale

As your traffic grows, you will need to scale the web and application servers with it. And as the number of servers grows, you will need a load balancer to route traffic to the web and application servers. Cloud Load Balancing is a fully distributed and software-defined system based on anycast IP addresses, which means you can set up your frontend with a single IP address. It is also global, so it can serve content as close as possible to your users and respond to over a million queries per second. You can set up content-based routing decisions based on attributes, such as the HTTP header and uniform resource identifier. It also offers internal load balancing for internal application servers so that you can route traffic among them as needed.

Content Delivery Network (CDN)

Static files don't change often, so CDN is used to cache these files and serve them from a location closest to the user, which helps reduce latency. Right at the load balancer you also have the option to enable Cloud CDN to cache frequently requested media and web content at the edge location closest to your users. This reduces latency and optimizes for last-mile performance. It also saves cost by fielding requests right at the edge, so they don't have to be handled by the backend.

Object Store

All static files for foo.com such as media files and images as well as CSS and JavaScript can be stored in an object store. In Google Cloud, Cloud Storage is your object store for both long- and short-term storage needs.

Serverless Functions

Let's say foo.com is also available on mobile devices, which need images rendered in smaller mobile formats. You can decouple functionality like this from the web server and make it a function-as-a-service with Cloud Functions. This approach enables you to apply your image resizing logic to other applications as well. You can trigger the serverless function as soon as a file is added to Cloud Storage and convert the file into multiple formats and put them back into storage, where they are used by the web server. You could also use serverless functions for other use cases such as address lookups, chatbots, machine learning, and more.

Events

In certain situations, foo.com might need to send messages, notifications to the user, or events between various microservices. This is where an asynchronous messaging service such as Cloud Pub/Sub can be used to push notifications to a topic and have other services subscribe to the topic and take appropriate action on it asynchronously.

Data Analytics

Applications like foo.com generate real-time data (e.g., clickstream data) and batch data (e.g., logs). This data needs to be ingested, processed, and made ready for downstream systems in a data warehouse. From there it can be analyzed further by data analysts, data scientists, and ML engineers to gain insights and make predictions. You can ingest batch data from Cloud Storage or BigQuery and real-time data from the application using Pub/Sub, and scale to ingesting millions of events per second. Dataflow, based on open source Apache Beam, can then be used to process and enrich the batch and streaming data. If you are in the Hadoop ecosystem, you can use Dataproc for processing; it is a managed Hadoop and Spark platform that lets you focus on analysis instead of worrying about managing and standing up your Hadoop cluster.

To store the processed data, you need a data warehouse. BigQuery is a serverless data warehouse that supports SQL queries and can scale to petabytes of storage. It can also act as long-term storage and a data lake along with Cloud Storage. You can use data from BigQuery to create a dashboard in Looker and Data Studio. With BigQuery ML, you can create ML models and make predictions using standard SQL queries.

Machine Learning

For ML/AI projects, you can use the data in BigQuery to train models in Vertex AI. Your media, image, and other static file datasets from Cloud Storage can be directly imported into Vertex AI. You can create your own custom model or use the pretrained models. It's a good idea to start with a pretrained model and see if it works for you. Most common use cases are covered (including image, text, video, and tabular data). If a pretrained model does not work for your use case, then use the AutoML model in Vertex AI to train a custom model on your own dataset. AutoML supports all the common use cases and requires no code. If you have lots of ML and data science expertise in house, you may decide to write your own custom model code in the framework of your choice.

Operations

foo.com needs to be holistically monitored to make sure the servers and every part of its architecture is healthy. Google Cloud's operations suite offers all the tools needed for logging, monitoring, debugging, and troubleshooting your application and infrastructure.

DevOps

You also need to make sure the foo.com development and operations teams have the right access and the right tools to build the application and deploy it. As developers write the code for the app, they can use Cloud Code within the IDE to push the code to Cloud Build, which then packages and tests it, runs vulnerability scans on the code, and invokes Binary Authorization to check for trusted container images, and once the tests are passed, deploys the package to staging. From there you can create a process to review and promote to production. Container images are stored in Artifact Registry from which they can be deployed to GKE or Cloud Run. Compute Engine images are stored in your project.

Security

foo.com needs to be secured at the data, application, user/identity, infrastructure, and compliance levels. This topic will be covered in detail in Chapter 8, "Security."

CHAPTER SIX

Networking

Networking is a necessary foundational component of any cloud application and its ability to connect to data stores, other applications, and available cloud resources. Google Cloud's networking is based on the highly scalable Jupiter network fabric and the high-performance, flexible Andromeda virtual network stack, which are the same technologies that power Google's internal infrastructure and services.

Jupiter provides Google with tremendous bandwidth and scale. For example, Jupiter fabrics can deliver more than 1 petabit per second of total bisection bandwidth. To put this in perspective, that is enough capacity for 100,000 servers to exchange information at a rate of 10 Gbps each, or enough to read the entire scanned contents of the Library of Congress in less than 1/10th of a second.

Andromeda is a software-defined networking (SDN) substrate for Google's network virtualization platform, acting as the orchestration point for provisioning, configuring, and managing virtual networks and in-network packet processing. Andromeda lets Google share Jupiter network fabric for Google Cloud services.

This chapter covers the Google Cloud networking infrastructure and the networking services available to you as you connect, scale, secure, modernize, and optimize your applications in Google Cloud.

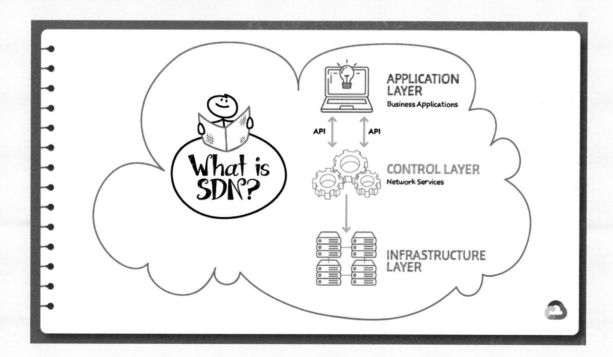

Introduction to Cloud Networking

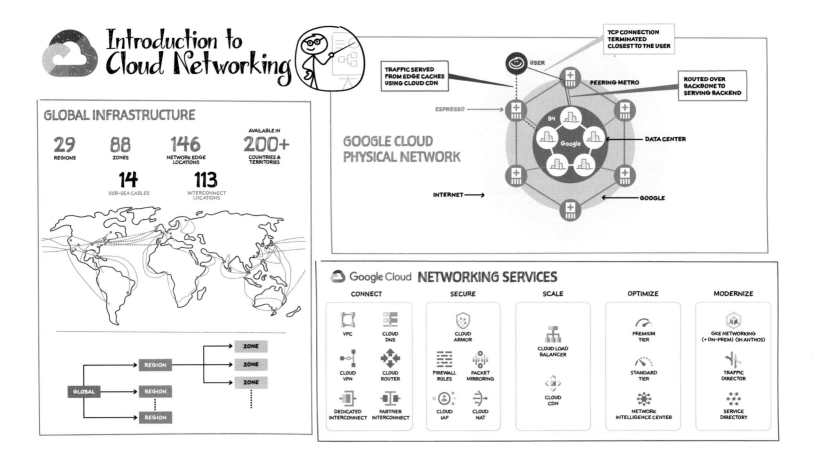

GLOBAL INFRASTRUCTURE

29 REGIONS

88 ZONES

146 NETWORK EDGE LOCATIONS

200+ AVAILABLE IN COUNTRIES & TERRITORIES

14 SUB-SEA CABLES

113 INTERCONNECT LOCATIONS

GLOBAL → REGION → ZONE / ZONE / ZONE
REGION
REGION
REGION

GOOGLE CLOUD PHYSICAL NETWORK

TRAFFIC SERVED FROM EDGE CACHES USING CLOUD CDN

TCP CONNECTION TERMINATED CLOSEST TO THE USER

USER

PEERING METRO

ROUTED OVER BACKBONE TO SERVING BACKEND

ESPRESSO

B4 · Google

DATA CENTER

INTERNET →

GOOGLE

Google Cloud NETWORKING SERVICES

CONNECT	SECURE	SCALE	OPTIMIZE	MODERNIZE
VPC / CLOUD DNS	CLOUD ARMOR	CLOUD LOAD BALANCER	PREMIUM TIER	GKE NETWORKING (+ ON-PREM) (IN ANTHOS)
CLOUD VPN / CLOUD ROUTER	FIREWALL RULES / PACKET MIRRORING	CLOUD CDN	STANDARD TIER	TRAFFIC DIRECTOR
DEDICATED INTERCONNECT / PARTNER INTERCONNECT	CLOUD IAP / CLOUD NAT		NETWORK INTELLIGENCE CENTER	SERVICE DIRECTORY

How Is the Google Cloud Physical Network Organized?

Google Cloud is divided into regions, which are further subdivided into zones:

- A *region* is a geographic area where the round-trip time (RTT) from one VM to another is typically under 1 ms.
- A *zone* is a deployment area within a region that has its own fully isolated and independent failure domain.

This means that no two machines in different zones or in different regions share the same fate in the event of a single failure.

As of this writing, Google has 29 regions and 88 zones across 200+ countries. This includes 146 network edge locations and CDN to deliver the content. This is the same network that also powers Google Search, Maps, Gmail, and YouTube.

Google Network Infrastructure

Google network infrastructure consists of three main types of networks:

- A data center network, which connects all the machines in the network together. This includes hundreds of thousands of miles of fiber-optic cables, including more than a dozen subsea cables.
- A software-based private network WAN connects all data centers together.
- A software-defined public WAN for user-facing traffic entering the Google network.

A machine gets connected from the Internet via the public WAN and gets connected to other machines on the network via the private WAN. For example, when you send a packet from your virtual machine running in the cloud in one region to a GCS bucket in another, the packet does not leave the Google network backbone. In addition, network load balancers and layer 7 reverse proxies are deployed at the network edge, which terminates the TCP/SSL connection at a location closest to the user, eliminating the two network round-trips needed to establish an HTTPS connection.

Cloud Networking Services

The Google physical network infrastructure powers the global virtual network that you use to run your applications in the cloud. It offers virtual network capabilities and tools you need to lift-and-shift, expand, and/or modernize your applications:

- **Connect** — Get started by provisioning the virtual network, connecting to it from other clouds or on-premises, and isolating your resources so that unauthorized projects or resources cannot access the network.
- **Secure** — Use network security tools for defense against infrastructure distributed denial-of-service (DdoS) attacks, mitigation of data exfiltration risks when connecting with services within Google Cloud, and network address translation to allow controlled internet access for resources without public IP addresses.
- **Scale** — Quickly scale applications, enable real-time distribution of load across resources in single or multiple regions, and accelerate content delivery to optimize last-mile performance.
- **Optimize** — Keep an eye on network performance to make sure the infrastructure is meeting your performance needs. This includes visualizing and monitoring network topology, performing diagnostic tests, and visualizing real-time performance metrics.
- **Modernize** — As you modernize your infrastructure, adopt microservices-based architectures, and employ containerization, make use of tools to help manage the inventory of your heterogeneous services, and route traffic among them.

This chapter covers the major services within the Google Cloud networking toolkit that help with connectivity, scale, security, optimization, and modernization.

Network Service Tiers

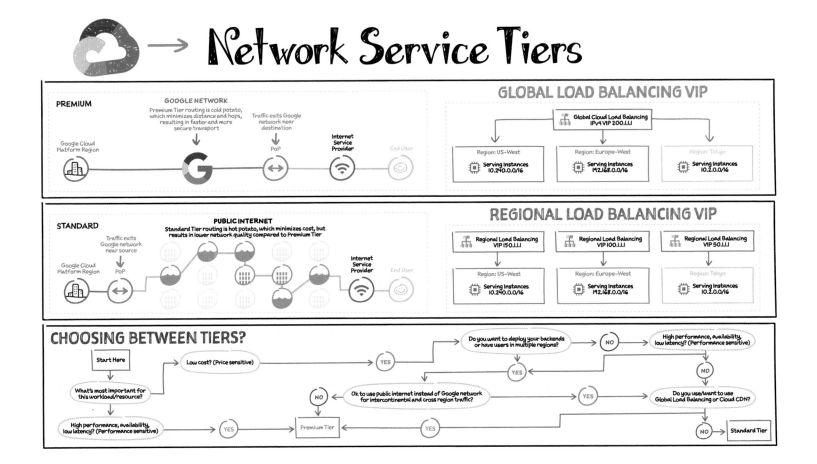

PREMIUM

GOOGLE NETWORK

Premium Tier routing is cold potato, which minimizes distance and hops, resulting in faster and more secure transport

Traffic exits Google network near destination

Google Cloud Platform Region

PoP

Internet Service Provider

End User

GLOBAL LOAD BALANCING VIP

Global Cloud Load Balancing IPv4 VIP 200.1.1.1

Region: US-West — Serving Instances 10.240.0.0/16

Region: Europe-West — Serving Instances 192.168.0.0/16

Region: Tokyo — Serving Instances 10.2.0.0/16

STANDARD

PUBLIC INTERNET

Standard Tier routing is hot potato, which minimizes cost, but results in lower network quality compared to Premium Tier

Traffic exits Google network near source

Google Cloud Platform Region

PoP

Internet Service Provider

End User

REGIONAL LOAD BALANCING VIP

Regional Load Balancing VIP 150.1.1.1

Regional Load Balancing VIP 100.1.1.1

Regional Load Balancing VIP 50.1.1.1

Region: US-West — Serving Instances 10.240.0.0/16

Region: Europe-West — Serving Instances 192.168.0.0/16

Region: Tokyo — Serving Instances 10.2.0.0/16

CHOOSING BETWEEN TIERS?

Start Here

What's most important for this workload/resource?

Low cost? (Price sensitive) — YES

Do you want to deploy your backends or have users in multiple regions? — NO → High performance, availability, low latency? (Performance sensitive)

YES

High performance, availability, low latency? (Performance sensitive) — YES

Ok to use public internet instead of Google network for intercontinental and cross region traffic? — YES → Do you use/want to use Global Load Balancing or Cloud CDN?

NO → Premium Tier ← YES

NO → Standard Tier

With Network Service Tiers, Google Cloud is the first major public cloud to offer a tiered cloud network. Two tiers are available: Premium Tier and Standard Tier.

Premium Tier

Premium Tier delivers traffic from external systems to Google Cloud resources by using Google's highly reliable, low-latency global network. This network consists of an extensive private fiber network with over 100 points of presence (PoPs) around the globe. This network is designed to tolerate multiple failures and disruptions while still delivering traffic.

Premium Tier supports both regional external IP addresses and global external IP addresses for VM instances and load balancers. All global external IP addresses must use Premium Tier. Applications that require high performance and availability, such as those that use HTTP(S), TCP proxy, or SSL proxy load balancers with backends in more than one region, require Premium Tier. Premium Tier is ideal for customers with users in multiple locations worldwide who need the best network performance and reliability.

With Premium Tier, incoming traffic from the Internet enters Google's high-performance network at the PoP closest to the sending system. Within the Google network, traffic is routed from that PoP to the VM in your Virtual Private Cloud (VPC) network or closest Cloud Storage bucket. Outbound traffic is sent through the network, exiting at the PoP closest to its destination. This routing method minimizes congestion and maximizes performance by reducing the number of hops between end users and the PoPs closest to them.

Standard Tier

Standard Tier delivers traffic from external systems to Google Cloud resources by routing it over the Internet. It leverages the double redundancy of Google's network only up to the point where a Google data center connects to a peering PoP. Packets that leave the Google network are delivered using the public Internet and are subject to the reliability of intervening transit providers and ISPs. Standard Tier provides network quality and reliability comparable to that of other cloud providers.

Regional external IP addresses can use either Premium Tier or Standard Tier. Standard Tier is priced lower than Premium Tier because traffic from systems on the Internet is routed over transit (ISP) networks before being sent to VMs in your VPC network or regional Cloud Storage buckets. Standard Tier outbound traffic normally exits Google's network from the same region used by the sending VM or Cloud Storage bucket, regardless of its destination. In rare cases, such as during a network event, traffic might not be able to travel out the closest exit and might be sent out another exit, perhaps in another region.

Standard Tier offers a lower-cost alternative for applications that are not latency or performance sensitive. It is also good for use cases where deploying VM instances or using Cloud Storage in a single region can work.

Choosing a Tier

It is important to choose the tier that best meets your needs. The decision tree can help you decide if Standard Tier or Premium Tier is right for your use case. Because you choose a tier at the resource level — such as the external IP address for a load balancer or VM — you can use Standard Tier for some resources and Premium Tier for others. If you are not sure which tier to use, choose the default Premium Tier and then consider a switch to Standard Tier if you later determine that it's a better fit for your use case.

Network Connectivity Options

DECISION TREE →

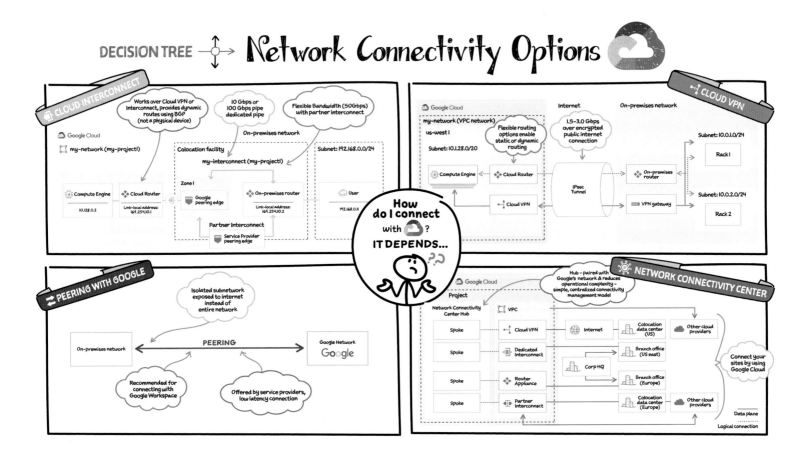

CLOUD INTERCONNECT

Works over Cloud VPN or Interconnect, provides dynamic routes using BGP (not a physical device)

10 Gbps or 100 Gbps pipe dedicated pipe

Flexible Bandwidth (50Gbps) with partner interconnect

Google Cloud
my-network (my-project1)

Compute Engine — Cloud Router
10.128.0.2 — Link-local address: 169.254.10.1

On-premises network

Colocation facility
my-interconnect (my-project1)

Zone 1
Google peering edge — On-premises router
Link-local address: 169.254.10.2

Partner Interconnect
Service Provider peering edge

Subnet: 192.168.0.0/24
User
192.168.0.11

CLOUD VPN

Google Cloud
my-network (VPC network)
us-west 1
Subnet: 10.128.0.0/20

Compute Engine — Cloud Router
Flexible routing options enable static or dynamic routing

Cloud VPN

Internet
1.5–3.0 Gbps over encrypted public internet connection
IPsec Tunnel

On-premises network
On-premises router
VPN gateway

Subnet: 10.0.1.0/24
Rack 1

Subnet: 10.0.2.0/24
Rack 2

How do I connect with ☁? IT DEPENDS...

PEERING WITH GOOGLE

Isolated subnetwork exposed to internet instead of entire network

On-premises network ←PEERING→ Google Network Google

Recommended for connecting with Google Workspace

Offered by service providers, low latency connection

NETWORK CONNECTIVITY CENTER

Hub – paired with Google's network & reduces operational complexity – simple, centralized connectivity management model

Google Cloud
Project
Network Connectivity Center Hub

Spoke — Cloud VPN — Internet — Colocation data center (US) — Other cloud providers

Spoke — Dedicated Interconnect — Branch office (US east)

Corp HQ

Spoke — Router Appliance — Branch office (Europe)

Spoke — Partner Interconnect — Colocation data center (Europe) — Other cloud providers

Connect your sites by using Google Cloud

Data plane
Logical connection

The cloud is an incredible resource, but you can't get the most out of it if you can't interact with it efficiently. And because network connectivity is not a one-size-fits-all situation, you need options for connecting your on-premises network or another cloud provider to Google's network.

When you need to connect to Google's network, you have a few options, let's explore them.

Cloud Interconnect and Cloud VPN

If you want to encrypt traffic to Google Cloud, you need a lower-throughput solution, or if you are experimenting with migrating your workloads to Google Cloud, you can choose Cloud VPN. If you need an enterprise-grade connection to Google Cloud that has higher throughput, you can choose Dedicated Interconnect or Partner Interconnect.

Cloud Interconnect

Cloud Interconnect provides two options: you can create a dedicated connection (Dedicated Interconnect) or use a service provider (Partner Interconnect) to connect to Virtual Private Cloud (VPC) networks. If your bandwidth needs are high (10 Gpbs to 100 Gbps) and you can reach Google's network in a colocation facility, then Dedicated Interconnect is a cost-effective option. If you don't require as much bandwidth (50 Mbps to 50 Gbps) or can't physically meet Google's network in a colocation facility to reach your VPC networks, you can use Partner Interconnect to connect to service providers that connect directly to Google.

Cloud VPN

Cloud VPN lets you securely connect your on-premises network to your VPC network through an IPsec VPN connection in a single region. Traffic traveling between the two networks is encrypted by one VPN gateway and then decrypted by the other VPN gateway. This action protects your data as it travels over the Internet. You can also connect two instances of Cloud VPN to each other. HA VPN provides an SLA of 99.99 percent service availability.

Network Connectivity Center

Network Connectivity Center (in preview) supports connecting different enterprise sites outside of Google Cloud by using Google's network as a wide area network (WAN). On-premises networks can consist of on-premises data centers and branch or remote offices.

Network Connectivity Center is a hub-and-spoke model for network connectivity management in Google Cloud. The hub resource reduces operational complexity through a simple, centralized connectivity management model. Your on-premises networks connect to the hub via one of the following spoke types: HA VPN tunnels, VLAN attachments, or router appliance instances that you or select partners deploy within Google Cloud.

Peering

If you need access to only Google Workspace or supported Google APIs, you have two options:

- Direct Peering to directly connect (peer) with Google Cloud at a Google edge location.
- Carrier Peering to peer with Google by connecting through an ISP (support provider), which in turn peers with Google.

Direct Peering exists outside of Google Cloud. Unless you need to access Google Workspace applications, the recommended methods of access to Google Cloud are Dedicated Interconnect, Partner Interconnect, or Cloud VPN.

CDN Interconnect

CDN Interconnect (not shown in the image) enables select third-party Content Delivery Network (CDN) providers to establish direct peering links with Google's edge network at various locations, which enables you to direct your traffic from your VPC networks to a provider's network. Your network traffic egressing from Google Cloud through one of these links benefits from the direct connectivity to supported CDN providers and is billed automatically with reduced pricing. This option is recommended for high-volume egress and frequent content updates in the CDN.

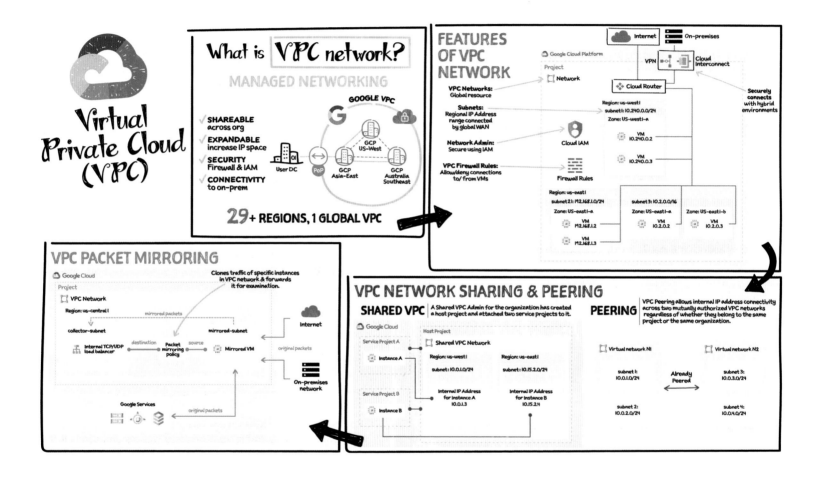

Virtual Private Cloud (VPC)

What is VPC network?

MANAGED NETWORKING

- √ **SHAREABLE** across org
- √ **EXPANDABLE** increase IP space
- √ **SECURITY** Firewall & IAM
- √ **CONNECTIVITY** to on-prem

GOOGLE VPC

User DC — PoP — GCP US-West / GCP Asia-East / GCP Australia Southeast

29+ REGIONS, 1 GLOBAL VPC

FEATURES OF VPC NETWORK

VPC Networks: Global resource

Subnets: Regional IP Address range connected by global WAN

Network Admin: Secure using IAM

VPC Firewall Rules: Allow/deny connections to/ from VMs

Google Cloud Platform

Project — Network

Internet — On-premises — VPN — Cloud Interconnect — Cloud Router — Securely connects with hybrid environments

Cloud IAM

Firewall Rules

Region: us-west1 — subnet: 10.240.0.0/24 — Zone: US-west1-a — VM 10.240.0.2 — VM 10.240.0.3

Region: us-east1 — subnet2: 192.168.1.0/24 — Zone: US-east1-a — VM 192.168.1.2 — VM 192.168.1.3

subnet 3: 10.2.0.0/16 — Zone: US-east1-a — VM 10.2.0.2 — Zone: US-east1-b — VM 10.2.0.3

VPC PACKET MIRRORING

Google Cloud

Project

VPC Network

Region: us-central1

collector-subnet — mirrored packets — mirrored-subnet

Internal TCP/UDP load balancer — destination — Packet mirroring policy — source — Mirrored VM

Clones traffic of specific instances in VPC network & forwards it for examination.

Internet — original packets — On-premises network

Google Services — original packets

VPC NETWORK SHARING & PEERING

SHARED VPC | A Shared VPC Admin for the organization has created a host project and attached two service projects to it.

Google Cloud

Service Project A — Instance A

Service Project B — Instance B

Host Project — Shared VPC Network

Region: us-west1 — subnet: 10.0.1.0/24 — Internal IP Address for Instance A 10.0.1.3

Region: us-east1 — subnet: 10.15.2.0/24 — Internal IP Address for Instance B 10.15.2.4

PEERING | VPC Peering allows internal IP address connectivity across two mutually authorized VPC networks regardless of whether they belong to the same project or the same organization.

Virtual network N1 — subnet 1: 10.0.1.0/24 — subnet 2: 10.0.2.0/24

Already Peered

Virtual network N2 — subnet 3: 10.0.3.0/24 — subnet 4: 10.0.4.0/24

Virtual Private Cloud (VPC) provides networking functionality for your cloud-based resources. You can think of a VPC network the same way you'd think of a physical network, except that it is virtualized within Google Cloud and logically isolated from other networks. A VPC network is a global resource that consists of regional virtual subnetworks (subnets) in data centers, all connected by a global wide area network (Google's SDN).

Features of VPC Networks

A VPC network:

- Provides connectivity for Compute Engine virtual machine (VM) instances, including Google Kubernetes Engine (GKE) clusters, App Engine flexible environment instances, and other Google Cloud products built on Compute Engine VMs.
- Offers built-in Internal TCP/UDP load balancing and proxy systems for internal HTTP(S) Load Balancing.
- Connects to on-premises networks using Cloud VPN tunnels and Cloud Interconnect attachments.
- Distributes traffic from Google Cloud external load balancers to backends.
- VPC firewall rules let you allow or deny connections to or from your VM instances based on a configuration that you specify. Every VPC network functions as a distributed firewall. While firewall rules are defined at the network level, connections are allowed or denied on a per-instance basis. You can think of the VPC firewall rules as existing not only between your instances and other networks, but also between individual instances within the same network.

Shared VPC

Shared VPC enables an organization to connect resources from multiple projects to a common Virtual Private Cloud (VPC) network so that they can communicate with each other securely and efficiently using internal IPs from that network. When you use Shared VPC, you designate a project as a *host project* and attach one or more other *service projects* to it. The VPC networks in the host project are called *Shared VPC networks*. Eligible resources from service projects can use subnets in the Shared VPC network.

VPC Network Peering

Google Cloud VPC Network Peering enables internal IP address connectivity across two VPC networks regardless of whether they belong to the same project or the same organization. Traffic stays within Google's network and doesn't traverse the public Internet.

VPC Network Peering is useful in organizations that have several network administrative domains that need to communicate using internal IP addresses. The benefits of using VPC Network Peering over using external IP addresses or VPNs are lower network latency, added security, and cost savings due to less egress traffic.

VPC Packet Mirroring

Packet Mirroring is useful when you need to monitor and analyze your security status. VPC Packet Mirroring clones the traffic of specific instances in your VPC network and forwards it for examination. It captures all traffic (ingress and egress) and packet data, including payloads and headers. The mirroring happens on the VM instances, not on the network, which means it consumes additional bandwidth on the VMs.

Packet Mirroring copies traffic from *mirrored sources* and sends it to a *collector destination*. To configure Packet Mirroring, you create a *packet mirroring policy* that specifies the source and destination. Mirrored sources are Compute Engine VM instances that you select. A *collector destination* is an instance group behind an internal load balancer.

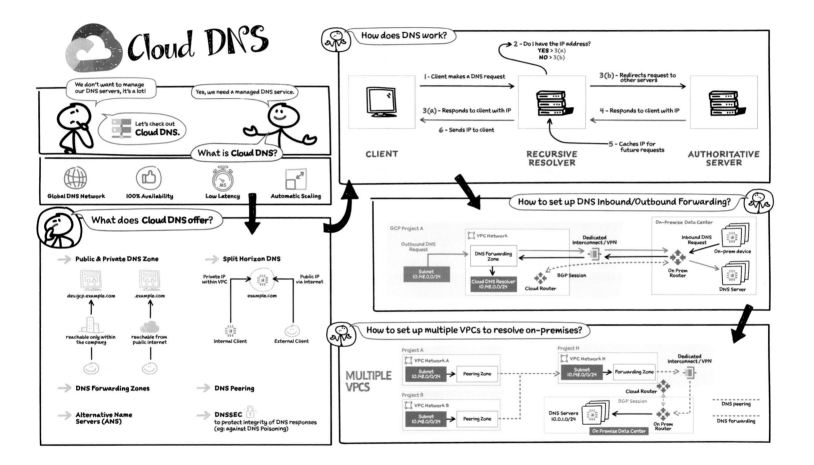

Cloud DNS

We don't want to manage our DNS servers, it's a lot!

Yes, we need a managed DNS service.

Let's check out **Cloud DNS.**

What is **Cloud DNS?**

- Global DNS Network
- 100% Availability
- Low Latency
- Automatic Scaling

What does **Cloud DNS offer?**

Public & Private DNS Zone

dev.gcp.example.com — reachable only within the company

.example.com — reachable from public internet

Split Horizon DNS

Private IP within VPC — example.com — Public IP via internet

Internal Client   External Client

DNS Forwarding Zones

DNS Peering

Alternative Name Servers (ANS)

DNSSEC
to protect integrity of DNS responses
(eg: against DNS Poisoning)

How does DNS work?

2 – Do I have the IP address?
YES > 3(a)
NO > 3(b)

1 – Client makes a DNS request

3(b) – Redirects request to other servers

3(a) – Responds to client with IP

4 – Responds to client with IP

6 – Sends IP to client

5 – Caches IP for future requests

CLIENT   **RECURSIVE RESOLVER**   **AUTHORITATIVE SERVER**

How to set up DNS Inbound/Outbound Forwarding?

GCP Project A

VPC Network

Outbound DNS Request

DNS Forwarding Zone

Subnet 10.148.0.0/24

Cloud DNS Resolver 10.148.0.0/24

Dedicated Interconnect / VPN

BGP Session

Cloud Router

On-Premise Data Center

Inbound DNS Request

On-prem device

On Prem Router

DNS Server

How to set up multiple VPCs to resolve on-premises?

MULTIPLE VPCS

Project A

VPC Network A
Subnet 10.148.0.0/24 → Peering Zone

Project B

VPC Network B
Subnet 10.148.0.0/24 → Peering Zone

Project H

VPC Network H
Subnet 10.148.0.0/24 → Forwarding Zone

Dedicated Interconnect / VPN

Cloud Router

BGP Session

DNS Servers 10.0.1.0/24

On Premise Data Center

On Prem Router

DNS peering

DNS forwarding

How many times have you heard this:

It's not DNS
NO way it is DNS
It was the DNS!

When you are building and managing cloud -native or hybrid cloud appli- cations, you don't want to add more stuff to your plate, especially not DNS. DNS is one of the necessary services for your application to function, but you can rely on a managed service to take care of DNS requirements. Cloud DNS is a managed, low-latency DNS service running on the same infrastructure as Google, which allows you to easily publish and manage millions of DNS zones and records.

How Does DNS Work?

When a client requests a service, the first thing that happens is DNS reso- lution, which means hostname-to–IP address translation. Here is how the request flow works:

Step 1 — A client makes a DNS request.

Step 2 — The request is received by a recursive resolver, which checks if it already knows the response to the request.

Step 3 (a) — If yes, the recursive resolver responds to the request if it already has it stored in cache.

Step 3 (b) — If no, the recursive resolver redirects the request to other servers.

Step 4 — The authoritative server then responds to requests.

Step 5 — The recursive resolver caches the result for future queries.

Step 6 — The recursive resolver finally sends the information to the client.

What Does Cloud DNS Offer?

- **Global DNS Network:** The Managed Authoritative Domain Name Sys- tem (DNS) service running on the same infrastructure as Google. You don't have to manage your DNS server — Google does it for you.

- **100 Percent Availability and Automatic Scaling:** Cloud DNS uses Google's global network of anycast name servers to serve your DNS zones from redundant locations around the world, providing high avail- ability and lower latency for users. Allows customers to create, update, and serve millions of DNS records.

- **Private DNS Zones:** Used for providing a namespace that is only visible inside the VPC or hybrid network environment. Example: A business organization has a domain dev.gcp.example.com, reachable only from within the company intranet.

- **Public DNS Zones:** Used for providing authoritative DNS resolution to clients on the public Internet. Example: A business has an external website, example.com, accessible directly from the Internet. Not to be confused with Google Public DNS (8.8.8.8), which is just a public recur- sive resolver.

- **Split Horizon DNS:** Used to serve different answers (different resource record sets) for the same name depending on who is asking — internal or external network resource.

- **DNS Peering:** DNS peering makes available a second method of sharing DNS data. All or a portion of the DNS namespace can be configured to be sent from one network to another and, once there, will respect all DNS configuration defined in the peered network.

- **Security:** Domain Name System Security Extensions (DNSSEC) is a fea- ture of the Domain Name System (DNS) that authenticates responses to domain name lookups. It prevents attackers from manipulating or poi- soning the responses to DNS requests.

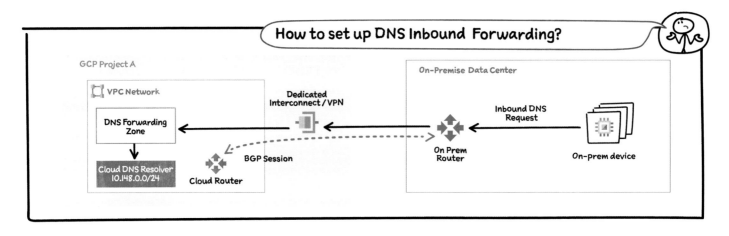

Hybrid Deployments: DNS Forwarding

Google Cloud offers inbound and outbound DNS forwarding for private zones. You can configure DNS forwarding by creating a forwarding zone or a Cloud DNS server policy. The two methods are inbound and outbound. You can simultaneously configure inbound and outbound DNS forwarding for a VPC network.

Inbound:

Create an inbound server policy to enable an on-premises DNS client or server to send DNS requests to Cloud DNS. The DNS client or server can then resolve records according to a VPC network's name resolution order. On-premises clients use Cloud VPN or Cloud Interconnect to connect to the VPC network.

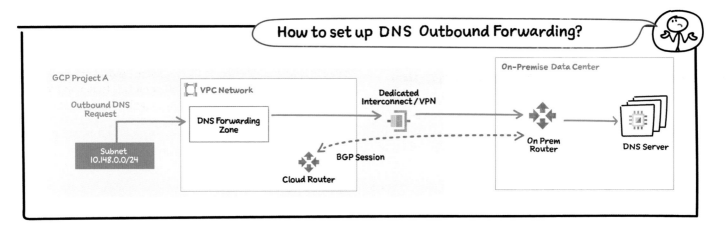

Outbound

You can configure VMs in a VPC network to do the following:

- Send DNS requests to DNS name servers of your choice. The name servers can be located in the same VPC network, in an on-premises network, or on the Internet.

- Resolve records hosted on name servers configured as forwarding targets of a forwarding zone authorized for use by your VPC network.

- Create an outbound server policy for the VPC network to send all DNS requests an alternative name server.

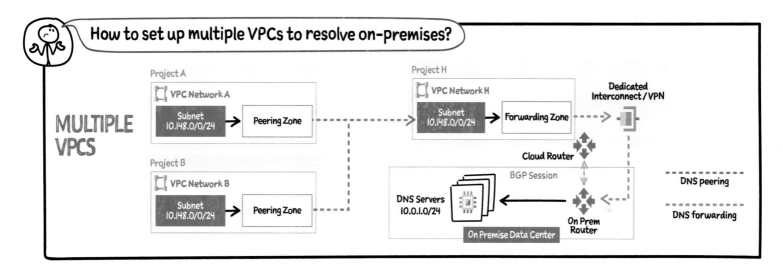

Hybrid Deployments: Hub and Spoke

If you have multiple VPCs that connect to multiple on-premises locations, it's recommended that you utilize a hub-and-spoke model, which helps get around reverse routing challenges due to the usage of the Google DNS proxy range. For redundancy, consider a model where the DNS-forwarding VPC network spans multiple Google Cloud regions, and where each region has a separate path (via interconnect or other means) to the on-premises network. This model allows the VPC to egress queries out of either interconnect path, and allows return queries to return via either interconnect path. The outbound request path always leaves Google Cloud via the nearest interconnect location to where the request originated.

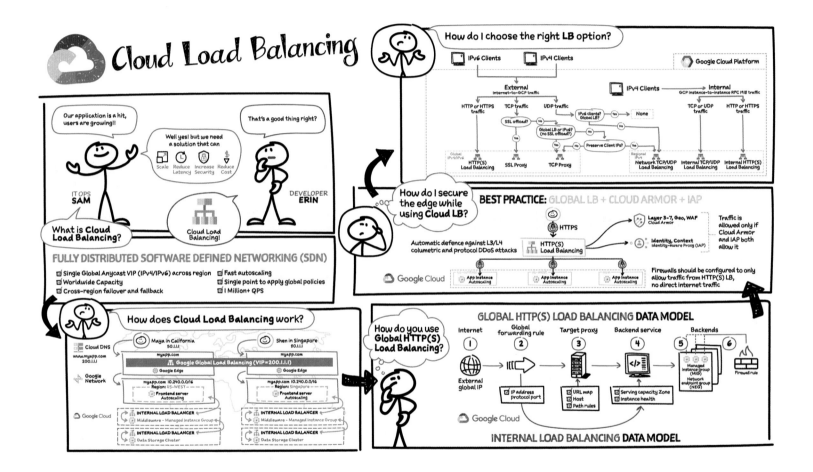

Let's say your new application has been a hit. Usage is growing across the world and you now need to figure out how to scale, optimize, and secure the app while keeping your costs down and your users happy. That's where Cloud Load Balancing comes in.

What Is Cloud Load Balancing?

Cloud Load Balancing is a fully distributed load-balancing solution that balances user traffic — HTTP(s), HTTPS/2 with gRPC, TCP/SSL, UDP, and QUIC — to multiple backends to avoid congestion, reduce latency, increase security, and reduce costs. It is built on the same frontend-serving infrastructure that powers Google, supporting 1 million+ queries per second with consistent high performance and low latency.

- **Software-defined network** (SDN) — Cloud Load Balancing is not an instance- or a device-based solution, which means you won't be locked into physical infrastructure or face HA, scale, and management challenges.
- **Single global anycast IP and autoscaling** — Cloud Load Balancing frontends all your backend instances in regions around the world. It provides cross-region load balancing, including automatic multiregion failover, which gradually moves traffic in fractions if backends become unhealthy or scales automatically if more resources are needed.

How Does Cloud Load Balancing Work?

External Load Balancing

Consider the following scenario. You have a user, Shen, in California. You deploy your frontend instances in that region and configure a load-balancing virtual IP (VIP). When your user base expands to another region, all you need to do is create instances in additional regions. There is no change in the VIP or the DNS server settings. As your app goes global, the same patterns follow: Maya from India is routed to the instance closer to her in India. If the instances in India are overloaded and are autoscaling to handle the load, Maya will seamlessly be redirected to the other instances in the meantime and routed back to India when instances have scaled sufficiently to handle the load. This is an example of external load balancing at Layer 7.

Internal Load Balancing

In any three-tier app, after the frontend you have the middleware and the data sources to interact with, in order to fulfill a user request. That's where you need Layer 4 internal load balancing between the frontend and the other internal tiers. Layer 4 internal load balancing is for TCP/UDP traffic behind RFC 1918 VIP, where the client IP is preserved.

You get automatic heath checks and there is no middle proxy; it uses the SDN control and data plane for load balancing.

How to Use Global HTTP(S) Load Balancing

- For global HTTP(s) load balancing, the Global Anycast VIP (IPv4 or IPv6) is associated with a forwarding rule, which directs traffic to a target proxy.
- The target proxy terminates the client session, and for HTTPs you deploy your certificates at this stage, define the backend host, and define the path rules. The URL map provides Layer 7 routing and directs the client request to the appropriate backend service.
- The backend services can be managed instance groups (MIGs) for compute instances, or network endpoint groups (NEGs) for your containerized workloads. This is also where service instance capacity and health is determined.
- Cloud CDN is enabled to cache content for improved performance. You can set up firewall rules to control traffic to and from your backend.
- The internal load balancing setup works the same way; you still have a forwarding rule but it points directly to a backend service. The forwarding rule has the virtual IP address, the protocol, and up to five ports.

How to Secure Your Application with Cloud Load Balancing

As a best practice, run SSL everywhere. With HTTPS and SSL proxy load balancing, you can use managed certs — Google takes care of the provisioning and managing of the SSL certificate life cycle.

- Cloud Load Balancing supports multiple SSL certificates, enabling you to serve multiple domains using the same load balancer IP address and port.

- It absorbs and dissipates Layer 3 and Layer 4 volumetric attacks across Google's global load-balancing infrastructure.

- Additionally, with Cloud Armor, you can protect against Layer 3–Layer 7 application-level attacks.

- By using Identity-Aware Proxy and firewalls, you can authenticate and authorize access to backend services.

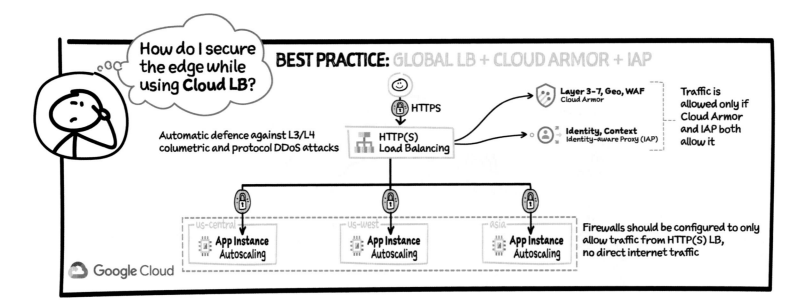

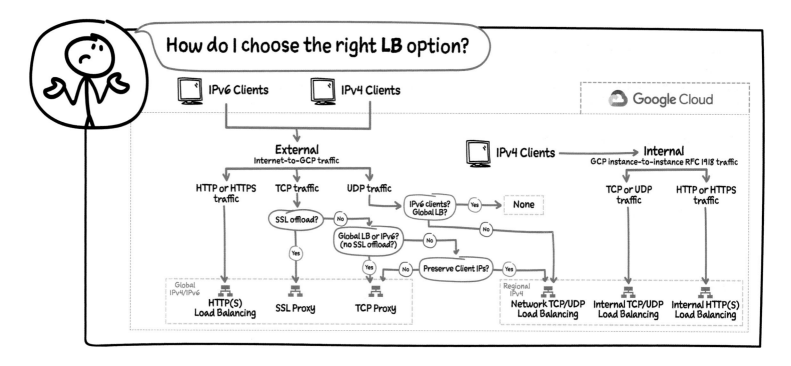

How to Choose the Right Load-Balancing Option

When deciding which load-balancing option is right for your use case, consider factors such as internal vs. external, global vs. regional, and type of traffic (HTTPs, TLS, or UDP).

If you are looking to reduce latency, improve performance, enhance security, and lower costs for your backend systems. then check out Cloud Load Balancing. It is easy to deploy in just a few clicks; simply set up the frontend and backends associated with global VIP, and you are good to go.

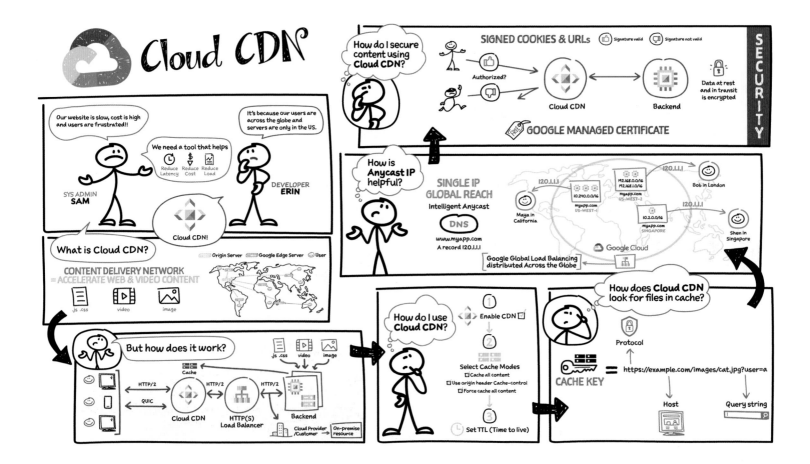

No matter what your app or website does, chances are that your users are distributed across various locations and are not necessarily close to your servers. This means the requests travel long distances across the public Internet, leading to inconsistent and sometimes frustrating user experiences. That's where Cloud CDN comes in!

What Is Cloud CDN?

Cloud CDN is a content delivery network that accelerates your web and video content delivery by using Google's global edge network to bring content as close to your users as possible. As a result, latency, cost, and load on your backend servers is reduced, making it easier to scale to millions of users. Global anycast IP provides a single IP for global reach. It enables Google Cloud to route users to the nearest edge cache automatically and avoid DNS propagation delays that can impact availability. It supports HTTP/2 end-to-end and the QUIC protocol from client to cache. QUIC is a multiplexed stream transport over UDP, which reduces latency and makes it ideal for lossy mobile networks.

How Does Cloud CDN Work?

Let's consider an example to understand how Cloud CDN works:

- When a user makes a request to your website or app, the request is routed to the closest Google edge node (we have over 120 of these!) for fast and reliable traffic flow. From there the request gets routed to the global HTTPS Load Balancer to the backend or origin.

- With Cloud CDN enabled, the content gets directly served from the cache — a group of servers that store and manage cacheable content so that future requests for that content can be served faster.

- The cached content is a copy of cacheable web assets (JavaScript, CSS), images, video, and other content that is stored on your origin servers.

- Cloud CDN automatically caches this content when you use the recommended "cache mode" to cache all static content. If you need more control, you can direct Cloud CDN by setting HTTP headers on your responses. You can also force all content to be cached; just know that this ignores the "private," "no-store," or "no-cache" directives in Cache-Control response headers.

- When the request is received by Cloud CDN, it looks for the cached content using a cache key. This is typically the URI, but you can customize the cache key to remove protocol, hosts, or query strings.

- If a cached response is found in the Cloud CDN cache, the response is retrieved from the cache and sent to the user. This is called a *cache hit*. When a cache hit occurs, Cloud CDN looks up the content by its cache key and responds directly to the user, shortening the round-trip time and reducing the load on the origin server.

- The first time that a piece of content is requested, Cloud CDN can't fulfill the request from the cache because it does not have it in cache. This is called a cache miss. When a cache miss occurs, Cloud CDN might attempt to get the content from a nearby cache. If the nearby cache has the content, it sends it to the first cache by using cache-to-cache fill. Otherwise, it just sends the request to the origin server.

- The maximum lifetime of the object in a cache is defined by the TTLs, or time-to-live values, set by the cache directives for each HTTP response or cache mode. When the TTL expires, the content is evicted from cache.

How to Use Cloud CDN

You can set up Cloud CDN through gCloud CLI, Cloud Console, or the APIs. Since Cloud CDN uses Cloud Load Balancing to provide routing, health checking, and anycast IP support, it can be enabled easily by selecting a checkbox while setting up your backends or origins.

Cloud CDN makes it easy to serve web and media content using Cloud Storage. You just upload your content to a Cloud Storage bucket, set up your load balancer, and enable caching. To enable hybrid architectures spanning across clouds and on-premises, Cloud CDN and HTTP(S) Load Balancing also support external backends.

Security

- Data is encrypted at rest and in transit from Cloud Load Balancing to the backend for end-to-end encryption.

- You can programmatically sign URLs and cookies to limit video segment access to authorized users only. The signature is validated at the CDN edge and unauthorized requests are blocked right there!

- On a broader level, you can enable SSL for free using Google managed certs.

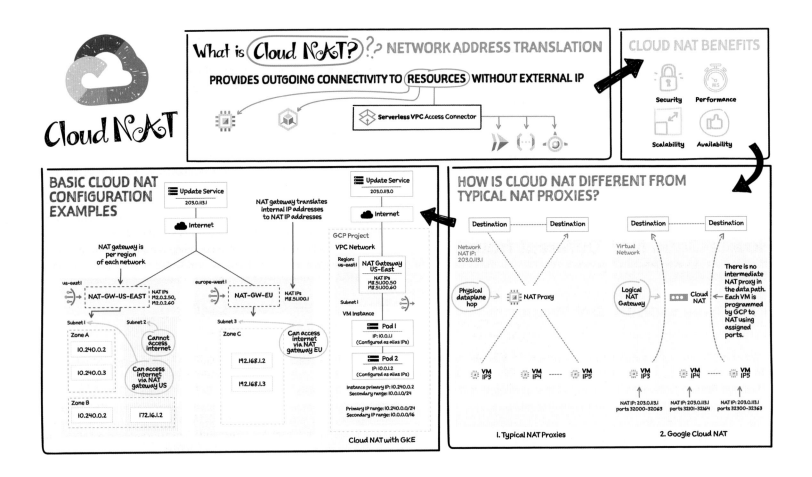

What is Cloud NAT? ?? NETWORK ADDRESS TRANSLATION

PROVIDES OUTGOING CONNECTIVITY TO RESOURCES WITHOUT EXTERNAL IP

Serverless VPC Access Connector

Cloud NAT

CLOUD NAT BENEFITS

Security   Performance

Scalability   Availability

BASIC CLOUD NAT CONFIGURATION EXAMPLES

Update Service
203.0.113.1

Internet

NAT gateway is per region of each network

NAT gateway translates internal IP addresses to NAT IP addresses

Update Service
203.0.113.0

Internet

us-east1
NAT-GW-US-EAST
NAT IPs 112.0.2.50, 112.0.2.60

europe-west1
NAT-GW-EU
NAT IPs 118.51.100.1

Subnet 1   Subnet 2

Subnet 3

Zone A
10.240.0.2
10.240.0.3

Cannot access internet

Can access internet via NAT gateway US

Zone C
192.168.1.2
192.168.1.3

Can access internet via NAT gateway EU

Zone B
10.240.0.2   172.16.1.2

GCP Project

VPC Network

Region: us-east1
NAT Gateway US-East
NAT IPs 118.51.100.50 118.51.100.60

Subnet 1

VM Instance

Pod 1
IP: 10.0.1.1
(Configured as alias IPs)

Pod 2
IP: 10.0.1.2
(Configured as alias IPs)

Instance primary IP: 10.240.0.2
Secondary range: 10.0.1.0/24

Primary IP range: 10.240.0.0/24
Secondary IP range: 10.0.0.0/16

Cloud NAT with GKE

HOW IS CLOUD NAT DIFFERENT FROM TYPICAL NAT PROXIES?

Destination ----- Destination

Destination ----- Destination

Network
NAT IP:
203.0.113.1

Physical dataplane hop

NAT Proxy

Virtual Network

Logical NAT Gateway

Cloud NAT

There is no intermediate NAT proxy in the data path. Each VM is programmed by GCP to NAT using assigned ports.

VM IP3   VM IP4 ---- VM IP5

VM IP3   VM IP4 ---- VM IP5

NAT IP: 203.0.113.1 ports 32000–32063

NAT IP: 203.0.113.1 ports 32101–32164

NAT IP: 203.0.113.1 ports 32300–32363

1. Typical NAT Proxies

2. Google Cloud NAT

For security, it is a best practice to limit the number of public IP addresses in your network. In Google Cloud, Cloud NAT (network address translation) lets certain resources without external IP addresses create outbound connections to the Internet.

Cloud NAT provides outgoing connectivity for the following resources:

- Compute Engine virtual machine (VM) instances without external IP addresses

- Private Google Kubernetes Engine (GKE) clusters

- Cloud Run instances through Serverless VPC Access

- Cloud Functions instances through Serverless VPC Access

- App Engine standard environment instances through Serverless VPC Access

How Is Cloud NAT Different from Typical NAT Proxies?

Cloud NAT is a distributed, software-defined managed service, not based on proxy VMs or appliances. This proxy-less architecture means higher scalability (no single choke point) and lower latency. Cloud NAT configures the Andromeda software that powers your Virtual Private Cloud (VPC) network so that it provides *source network address translation (SNAT)* for VMs without external IP addresses. It also provides *destination network address translation (DNAT)* for established inbound response packets only.

Benefits of Using Cloud NAT

- **Security:** Helps you reduce the need for individual VMs to each have external IP addresses. Subject to egress firewall rules, VMs without external IP addresses can access destinations on the Internet.

- **Availability:** Since Cloud NAT is a distributed software-defined managed service, it doesn't depend on any VMs in your project or on a single physical gateway device. You configure a NAT gateway on a Cloud Router, which provides the control plane for NAT, holding configuration parameters that you specify.

- **Scalability:** Cloud NAT can be configured to automatically scale the number of NAT IP addresses that it uses, and it supports VMs that belong to managed instance groups, including those with autoscaling enabled.

- **Performance:** Cloud NAT does not reduce network bandwidth per VM because it is implemented by Google's Andromeda software-defined networking.

NAT Rules

In Cloud NAT, the NAT rules feature lets you create access rules that define how Cloud NAT is used to connect to the Internet. NAT rules support source NAT based on destination address. When you configure a NAT gateway without NAT rules, the VMs using that NAT gateway use the same set of NAT IP addresses to reach all Internet addresses. If you need more control over packets that pass through Cloud NAT, you can add NAT rules. A NAT rule defines a match condition and a corresponding action. After you specify NAT rules, each packet is matched with each NAT rule. If a packet matches the condition set in a rule, then the action corresponding to that match occurs.

Basic Cloud NAT Configuration Examples

In the example pictured in Sketchnote, the NAT gateway in the east is configured to support the VMs with no external IPs in subnet-1 to access the Internet. These VMs can send traffic to the Internet by using either gateway's primary internal IP address or an alias IP range from the primary IP address range of subnet-1, 10.240.0.0/16. A VM whose network interface does not have an external IP address and whose primary internal IP address is located in subnet-2 cannot access the Internet.

Similarly, the NAT gateway Europe is configured to apply to the primary IP address range of subnet-3 in the west region, allowing the VM whose network interface does not have an external IP address to send traffic to the Internet by using either its primary internal IP address or an alias IP range from the primary IP address range of subnet-3, 192.168.1.0/24.

To enable NAT for all the containers and the GKE node, you must choose all the IP address ranges of a subnet as the NAT candidates. It is not possible to enable NAT for specific containers in a subnet.

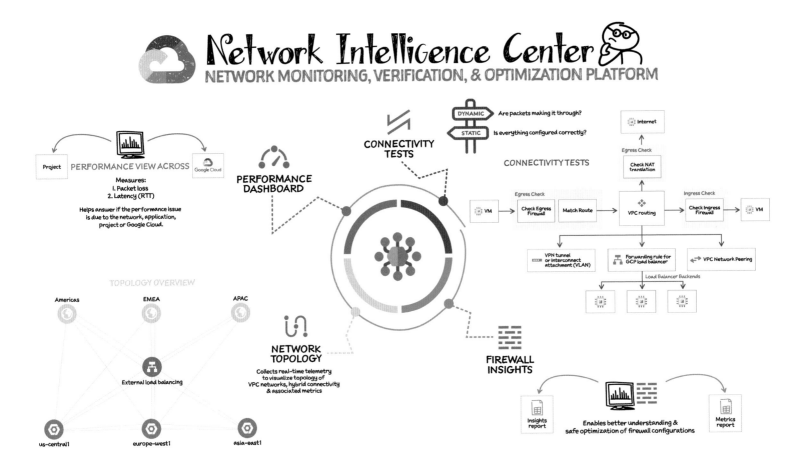

Network Intelligence Center

NETWORK MONITORING, VERIFICATION, & OPTIMIZATION PLATFORM

PERFORMANCE VIEW ACROSS

Project — Google Cloud

Measures:
1. Packet loss
2. Latency (RTT)

Helps answer if the performance issue is due to the network, application, project or Google Cloud.

PERFORMANCE DASHBOARD

CONNECTIVITY TESTS

DYNAMIC — Are packets making it through?
STATIC — Is everything configured correctly?

CONNECTIVITY TESTS

Egress Check — Check NAT translation — Internet

VM → Check Egress Firewall → Match Route → VPC routing → Check Ingress Firewall → VM

Egress Check / Ingress Check

VPN tunnel or interconnect attachment (VLAN) — Forwarding rule for GCP load balancer — VPC Network Peering

Load Balancer Backends

TOPOLOGY OVERVIEW

Americas — EMEA — APAC

External load balancing

us-central1 — europe-west1 — asia-east1

NETWORK TOPOLOGY

Collects real-time telemetry to visualize topology of VPC networks, hybrid connectivity & associated metrics

FIREWALL INSIGHTS

Insights report — Enables better understanding & safe optimization of firewall configurations — Metrics report

You need visibility into your cloud platform in order to monitor and troubleshoot it. Network Intelligence Center provides that visibility with a single console for Google Cloud network observability, monitoring, and troubleshooting. Currently Network Intelligence Center has four modules:

- **Network Topology:** Helps you visualize your network topology, including VPC connectivity to on-premises, Internet, and the associated metrics.
- **Connectivity Tests:** Provides both static and dynamic network connectivity tests for configuration and data plane reachability, to verify that packets are actually getting through.
- **Performance Dashboard:** Shows packet loss and latency between zones and regions that you are using.
- **Firewall Insights:** Shows usage for your VPC firewall rules and enables you to optimize their configuration.

Network Topology

Network Topology collects real-time telemetry and configuration data from Google infrastructure and uses it to help you visualize your resources. It captures elements such as configuration information, metrics, and logs to infer relationships between resources in a project or across multiple projects. After collecting each element, Network Topology combines them to generate a graph that represents your deployment. Using this graph, you can quickly view the topology and analyze the performance of your deployment without configuring any agents, sorting through multiple logs, or using third-party tools.

Connectivity Tests

The Connectivity Tests diagnostics tool lets you check connectivity between endpoints in your network. It analyzes your configuration and in some cases performs runtime verification.

To analyze network configurations, Connectivity Tests simulates the expected inbound and outbound forwarding path of a packet to and from your Virtual Private Cloud (VPC) network, Cloud VPN tunnels, or VLAN attachments.

For some connectivity scenarios, Connectivity Tests also performs runtime verification, where it sends packets over the data plane to validate connectivity and provides baseline diagnostics of latency and packet loss.

Performance Dashboard

Performance Dashboard gives you visibility into the network performance of the entire Google Cloud network, as well as the performance of your project's resources. It collects and shows packet loss and latency metrics. With these performance-monitoring capabilities, you can distinguish between a problem in your application and a problem in the underlying Google Cloud network. You can also debug historical network performance problems.

Firewall Insights

Firewall Insights enables you to better understand and safely optimize your firewall configurations. It provides reports that contain information about firewall usage and the impact of various firewall rules on your VPC network.

Traffic Director

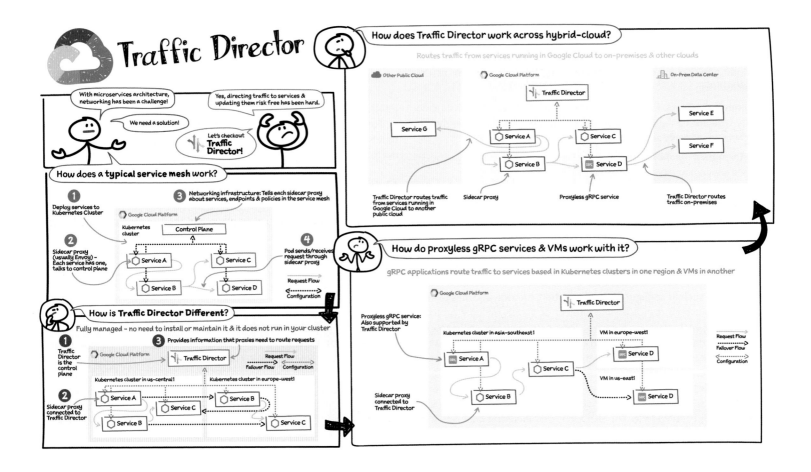

With microservices architecture, networking has been a challenge!

We need a solution!

Yes, directing traffic to services & updating them risk free has been hard.

Let's checkout **Traffic Director!**

How does a typical service mesh work?

① Deploy services to Kubernetes Cluster

③ Networking infrastructure: Tells each sidecar proxy about services, endpoints & policies in the service mesh

Kubernetes cluster

Control Plane

Google Cloud Platform

② Sidecar proxy (usually Envoy) – Each service has one, talks to control plane

Service A
Service B
Service C
Service D

④ Pod sends/receives request through sidecar proxy

Request Flow
Configuration

How is **Traffic Director Different?**

Fully managed – no need to install or maintain it & it does not run in your cluster

① Traffic Director is the control plane

③ Provides information that proxies need to route requests

Google Cloud Platform

Traffic Director

Request Flow
Failover Flow
Configuration

Kubernetes cluster in us-central1

② Sidecar proxy connected to Traffic Director

Service A
Service B
Service C

Kubernetes cluster in europe-west1

Service B
Service C

How does Traffic Director work across hybrid-cloud?

Routes traffic from services running in Google Cloud to on-premises & other clouds

Other Public Cloud

Google Cloud Platform

On-Prem Data Center

Traffic Director

Service G

Service A
Service B

Service C
Service D

Service E
Service F

Traffic Director routes traffic from services running in Google Cloud to another public cloud

Sidecar proxy

Proxyless gRPC service

Traffic Director routes traffic on-premises

How do proxyless gRPC services & VMs work with it?

gRPC applications route traffic to services based in Kubernetes clusters in one region & VMs in another

Proxyless gRPC service: Also supported by Traffic Director

Google Cloud Platform

Traffic Director

Kubernetes cluster in asia-southeast1

VM in europe-west1

Service A
Service C
Service B

Service D

VM in us-east1

Service D

Sidecar proxy connected to Traffic Director

Request Flow
Failover Flow
Configuration

If your application is deployed in a microservices architecture, then you are likely familiar with the networking challenges that come with it. Traffic Director helps you run microservices in a global service mesh. The mesh handles networking for your microservices so that you can focus on your business logic and application code. This separation of application logic from networking logic helps you improve your development velocity, increase service availability, and introduce modern DevOps practices in your organization.

How Does a Typical Service Mesh Work in Kubernetes?

In a typical service mesh, you deploy your services to a Kubernetes cluster.

- Each of the services' Pods has a dedicated proxy (usually Envoy) running as a sidecar container alongside the application container(s).
- Each sidecar proxy talks to the networking infrastructure (a control plane) that is installed in your cluster. The control plane tells the sidecar proxies about services, endpoints, and policies in your service mesh.
- When a Pod sends or receives a request, the request is intercepted by the Pod's sidecar proxy. The sidecar proxy handles the request, for example, by sending it to its intended destination.

The control plane is connected to each proxy and provides information that the proxies need to handle requests. To clarify the flow, if application code in Service A sends a request, the proxy handles the request and forwards it to Service B. This model enables you to move networking logic out of your application code. You can focus on delivering business value while letting the service mesh infrastructure take care of application networking.

How Is Traffic Director Different?

Traffic Director works similarly to the typical service mesh model, but it's different in a few, very crucial ways. Traffic Director provides:

- A fully managed and highly available control plane. You don't install it, it doesn't run in your cluster, and you don't need to maintain it. Google Cloud manages all this for you with production-level service-level objectives (SLOs).
- Global load balancing with capacity and health awareness and failovers.
- Integrated security features to enable a zero-trust security posture.
- Rich control plane and data plane observability features.
- Support for multi-environment service meshes spanning across multi-cluster Kubernetes, hybrid cloud, VMs, gRPC services, and more.

Traffic Director is the control plane and the services in the Kubernetes cluster, each with sidecar proxies, connect to Traffic Director. Traffic Director provides the information that the proxies need to route requests. For example, application code on a Pod that belongs to Service A sends a request. The sidecar proxy running alongside this Pod handles the request and routes it to a Pod that belongs to Service B.

Multicluster Kubernetes: Traffic Director supports application networking across Kubernetes clusters. In this example, it provides a managed and global control plane for Kubernetes clusters in the United States and Europe. Services in one cluster can talk to services in another cluster. You can even have services that consist of Pods in multiple clusters. With Traffic Director's proximity-based global load balancing, requests destined for Service B go to the geographically nearest Pod that can serve the request. You also get seamless failover; if a Pod is down, the request automatically fails over to another Pod that can serve the request, even if this Pod is in a different Kubernetes cluster.

How Does Traffic Director Support Proxy-less gRPC and VMs?

Virtual machines: Traffic Director solves application networking for VM-based workloads alongside Kubernetes-based workloads. You simply add a flag to your Compute Engine VM instance template, and Google seamlessly handles the infrastructure set up, which includes installing and configuring the proxies that deliver application networking capabilities.

As an example, traffic enters your deployment through External HTTP(S) Load Balancing to a service in the Kubernetes cluster in one region and can then be routed to another service on a VM in a totally different region.

gRPC: With Traffic Director, you can easily bring application networking capabilities such as service discovery, load balancing, and traffic management directly to your gRPC applications. This functionality happens natively in gRPC, so service proxies are not required — that's why they're called proxy-less gRPC applications. For more information, refer to Traffic Director and gRPC — proxyless services for your service mesh.

How Does Traffic Director Work Across Hybrid and Multicloud Environments?

Whether you have services in Google Cloud, on-premises, in other clouds, or all of these, your fundamental application networking challenges remain

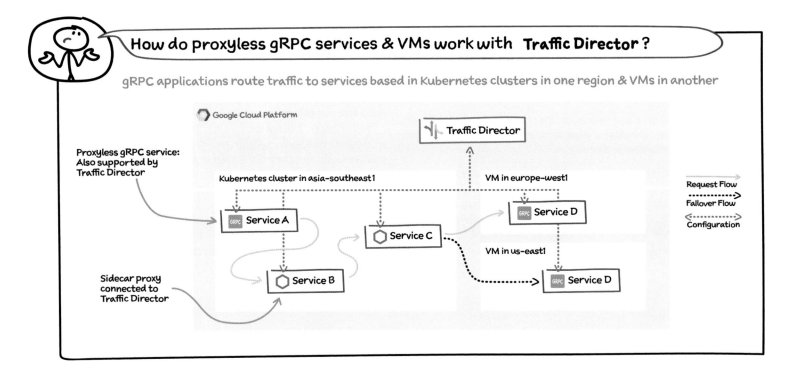

the same. How do you get traffic to these services? How do these services communicate with each other?

Traffic Director can route traffic from services running in Google Cloud to services running in another public cloud and to services running in an on-premises data center. Services can use Envoy as a sidecar proxy or a proxy-less gRPC service. When you use Traffic Director, you can send requests to destinations outside of Google Cloud. This enables you to use Cloud Inter-connect or Cloud VPN to privately route traffic from services inside Google Cloud to services or gateways in other environments. You can also route requests to external services reachable over the public Internet.

Ingress and gateways

For many use cases, you need to handle traffic that originates from clients that aren't configured by Traffic Director. For example, you might need to ingress public internet traffic to your microservices. You might

also want to configure a load balancer as a reverse proxy that handles traffic from a client before sending it on to a destination. In such cases Traffic Director works with Cloud Load Balancing to provide a managed ingress experience. You set up an external or internal load balancer, and then configure that load balancer to send traffic to your microservices. Public internet clients reach your services through External HTTP(S) Load Balancing. Clients, such as microservices that reside on your Virtual Private Cloud (VPC) network, use Internal HTTP(S) Load Balancing to reach your services.

For some use cases, you might want to set up Traffic Director to config-ure a gateway. This gateway is essentially a reverse proxy, typically Envoy running on one or more VMs, that listens for inbound requests, handles them, and sends them to a destination. The destination can be in any Google Cloud region or Google Kubernetes Engine (GKE) cluster. It can even be a destination outside of Google Cloud that is reachable from Google Cloud by using hybrid connectivity.

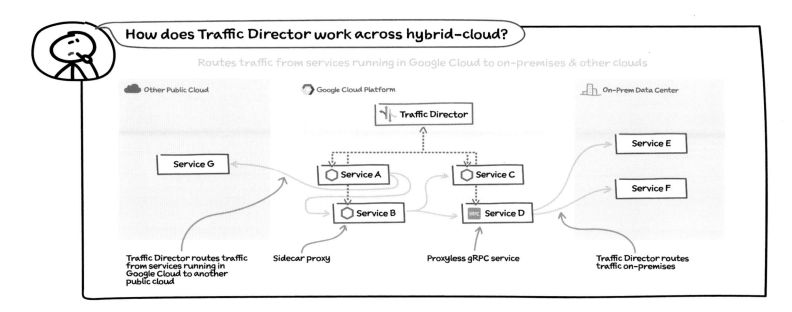

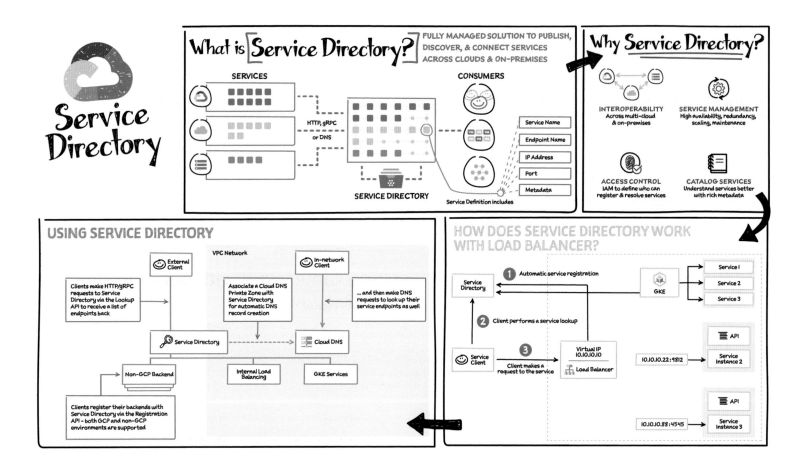

Service Directory

What is [Service Directory?]

FULLY MANAGED SOLUTION TO PUBLISH, DISCOVER, & CONNECT SERVICES ACROSS CLOUDS & ON-PREMISES

SERVICES

CONSUMERS

HTTP, gRPC or DNS

SERVICE DIRECTORY

Service Definition includes:
- Service Name
- Endpoint Name
- IP Address
- Port
- Metadata

Why Service Directory?

INTEROPERABILITY
Across multi-cloud & on-premises

SERVICE MANAGEMENT
High availability, redundancy, scaling, maintenance

ACCESS CONTROL
IAM to define who can register & resolve services

CATALOG SERVICES
Understand services better with rich metadata

USING SERVICE DIRECTORY

VPC Network

External Client

Clients make HTTP/gRPC requests to Service Directory via the Lookup API to receive a list of endpoints back

In-network Client

Associate a Cloud DNS Private Zone with Service Directory for automatic DNS record creation

...and then make DNS requests to look up their service endpoints as well

Service Directory

Cloud DNS

Non-GCP Backend

Internal Load Balancing

GKE Services

Clients register their backends with Service Directory via the Registration API - both GCP and non-GCP environments are supported

HOW DOES SERVICE DIRECTORY WORK WITH LOAD BALANCER?

Service Directory

① Automatic service registration

GKE
- Service 1
- Service 2
- Service 3

② Client performs a service lookup

Service Client

③ Client makes a request to the service

Virtual IP 10.10.10.10

Load Balancer

10.10.10.22:9812 → **API** Service Instance 2

10.10.10.88:4545 → **API** Service Instance 3

Most enterprises have a large number of heterogeneous services deployed across different clouds and on-premises environments. It is complex to look up, publish, and connect these services, but it is necessary to do so for deployment velocity, security, and scalability. That's where Service Directory comes in!

Service Directory is a fully managed platform for discovering, publishing, and connecting services, regardless of the environment. It provides real-time information about all your services in a single place, enabling you to perform service inventory management at scale, whether you have a few service endpoints or thousands.

Why Service Directory?

Imagine that you are building a simple API and that your code needs to call some other application. When endpoint information remains static, you can hard-code these locations into your code or store them in a small configuration file. However, with microservices and multicloud, this problem becomes much harder to handle as instances, services, and environments can all change.

Service Directory solves this! Each service instance is registered with Service Directory, where it is immediately reflected in Domain Name System (DNS) and can be queried by using HTTP/gRPC regardless of its implementation and environment. You can create a universal service name that works across environments, make services available over DNS, and apply access controls to services based on network, project, and IAM roles of service accounts.

Service Directory solves the following problems:

- **Interoperability:** Service Directory is a universal naming service that works across Google Cloud, multicloud, and on-premises. You can migrate services between these environments and still use the same service name to register and resolve endpoints.

- **Service management:** Service Directory is a managed service. Your organization does not have to worry about the high availability, redundancy, scaling, or maintenance concerns of maintaining your own service registry.

- **Access control:** With Service Directory, you can control who can register and resolve your services using IAM. Assign Service Directory roles to teams, service accounts, and organizations.

- **Limitations of pure DNS:** DNS resolvers can be unreliable in terms of respecting TTLs and caching, cannot handle larger record sizes, and do not offer an easy way to serve metadata to users. In addition to DNS support, Service Directory offers HTTP and gRPC APIs to query and resolve services.

How Service Directory Works with Load Balancer

Here's how Service Directory works with Load Balancer:

- In Service Directory, Load Balancer is registered as a provider of each service.

- The client performs a service lookup via Service Directory.

- Service Directory returns the Load Balancer address.

- The client makes a call to the service via Load Balancer.

Using Cloud DNS with Service Directory

Cloud DNS is a fast, scalable, and reliable DNS service running on Google's infrastructure. In addition to public DNS zones, Cloud DNS also provides a managed internal DNS solution for private networks on Google Cloud. Private DNS zones enable you to internally name your virtual machine (VM) instances, load balancers, or other resources. DNS queries for those private DNS zones are restricted to your private networks. Here is how you can use Service Directory zones to make service names available using DNS lookups:

- The endpoints are registered directly with Service Directory using the Service Directory API. This can be done for both Google Cloud and non-Google Cloud services.

- Both external and internal clients can look up those services.

- To enable DNS requests, create a Service Directory zone in Cloud DNS that is associated with a Service Directory namespace.

- Internal clients can resolve this service via DNS, HTTP, or gRPC. External clients (clients not on the private network) must use HTTP or gRPC to resolve service names.

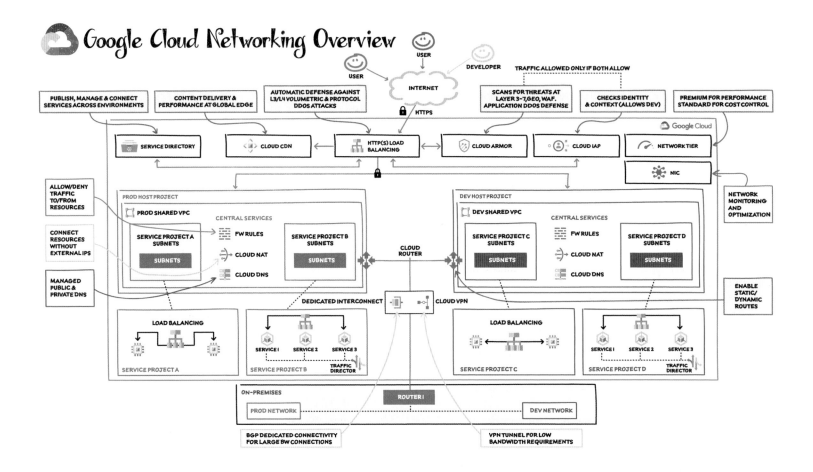

Google Cloud Networking Overview

USER

DEVELOPER

USER

INTERNET

HTTPS

TRAFFIC ALLOWED ONLY IF BOTH ALLOW

PUBLISH, MANAGE & CONNECT SERVICES ACROSS ENVIRONMENTS

CONTENT DELIVERY & PERFORMANCE AT GLOBAL EDGE

AUTOMATIC DEFENSE AGAINST L3/L4 VOLUMETRIC & PROTOCOL DDOS ATTACKS

SCANS FOR THREATS AT LAYER 3-7, GEO, WAF. APPLICATION DDOS DEFENSE

CHECKS IDENTITY & CONTEXT (ALLOWS DEV)

PREMIUM FOR PERFORMANCE STANDARD FOR COST CONTROL

Google Cloud

SERVICE DIRECTORY

CLOUD CDN

HTTP(S) LOAD BALANCING

CLOUD ARMOR

CLOUD IAP

NETWORK TIER

NIC

ALLOW/DENY TRAFFIC TO/FROM RESOURCES

CONNECT RESOURCES WITHOUT EXTERNAL IPS

MANAGED PUBLIC & PRIVATE DNS

NETWORK MONITORING AND OPTIMIZATION

PROD HOST PROJECT

PROD SHARED VPC

CENTRAL SERVICES

SERVICE PROJECT A SUBNETS

SUBNETS

FW RULES

CLOUD NAT

CLOUD DNS

SERVICE PROJECT B SUBNETS

SUBNETS

CLOUD ROUTER

DEV HOST PROJECT

DEV SHARED VPC

CENTRAL SERVICES

SERVICE PROJECT C SUBNETS

SUBNETS

FW RULES

CLOUD NAT

CLOUD DNS

SERVICE PROJECT D SUBNETS

SUBNETS

ENABLE STATIC/ DYNAMIC ROUTES

DEDICATED INTERCONNECT

CLOUD VPN

LOAD BALANCING

SERVICE PROJECT A

SERVICE 1 SERVICE 2 SERVICE 3

SERVICE PROJECT B

TRAFFIC DIRECTOR

LOAD BALANCING

SERVICE PROJECT C

SERVICE 1 SERVICE 2 SERVICE 3

SERVICE PROJECT D

TRAFFIC DIRECTOR

ON-PREMISES

PROD NETWORK

ROUTER 1

DEV NETWORK

BGP DEDICATED CONNECTIVITY FOR LARGE BW CONNECTIONS

VPN TUNNEL FOR LOW BANDWIDTH REQUIREMENTS

Google's physical network infrastructure powers the global virtual network that you need to run your applications in the cloud. It offers virtual networking and tools needed to lift-and-shift, expand, and/or modernize your applications. Let's check out an example of how services help you connect, scale, secure, optimize, and modernize your applications and infrastructure.

Connect

The first thing you need is to provision the virtual network, connect to it from other clouds or on-premises, and isolate your resources so that other projects and resources cannot inadvertently access the network.

- **Hybrid Connectivity:** Consider Company X, which has an on-premises environment with a production and a development network. They would like to connect their on-premises environment with Google Cloud so that the resources and services can easily connect between the two environments. They can use either Cloud Interconnect for dedicated connection or Cloud VPN for connection via an IPsec secure tunnel. Both work, but the choice would depend on how much bandwidth they need; for higher bandwidth and more data, dedicated interconnect is recommended. Cloud Router would help enable the dynamic routes between the on-premises environment and Google Cloud VPC. If they have multiple networks/locations, they could also use Network Connectivity Center to connect their different enterprise sites outside of Google Cloud by using the Google network as a wide area network (WAN).

- **Virtual Private Cloud (VPC):** They deploy all their resources in VPC, but one of the requirements is to keep the Prod and Dev environments separate. For this, the team needs to use Shared VPC, which allows them to connect resources from multiple projects to a common Virtual Private Cloud (VPC) network so that they can communicate with each other securely and efficiently using internal IPs from that network.

- **Cloud DNS:** They use Cloud DNS to manage:
  - Public and private DNS zones
  - Public/private IPs within the VPC and over the Internet

- DNS peering
- Forwarding
- Split horizons
- DNSSEC for DNS security

Scale

Scaling includes not only quickly scaling applications, but also enabling real-time distribution of load across resources in single or multiple regions, and accelerating content delivery to optimize last-mile performance.

- **Cloud Load Balancing:** Quickly scale applications on Compute Engine — no pre-warming needed. Distribute load-balanced compute resources in single or multiple regions (and near users) while meeting high-availability requirements. Cloud Load Balancing can put resources behind a single anycast IP, scale up or down with intelligent autoscaling, and integrate with Cloud CDN.

- **Cloud CDN:** Accelerate content delivery for websites and applications served out of Compute Engine with Google's globally distributed edge caches. Cloud CDN lowers network latency, offloads origin traffic, and reduces serving costs. Once you've set up HTTP(S) load balancing, you can enable Cloud CDN with a single checkbox.

Secure

Networking security tools allow you to defend against infrastructure DDoS attacks, mitigate data exfiltration risks when connecting with services within Google Cloud, and use network address translation to enable controlled Internet access for resources without public IP addresses.

- **Firewall Rules:** Lets you allow or deny connections to or from your virtual machine (VM) instances based on a configuration that you specify. Every VPC network functions as a distributed firewall. While firewall rules are defined at the network level, connections are allowed or denied on a per-instance basis. You can think of the VPC firewall rules as existing not only between your instances and other networks, but also between individual instances within the same network.

- **Cloud Armor:** It works alongside an HTTP(S) load balancer to provide built-in defenses against infrastructure DDoS attacks. Features include IP-based and geo-based access control, support for hybrid and multicloud deployments, preconfigured WAF rules, and named IP lists.

- **Packet Mirroring:** Packet Mirroring is useful when you need to monitor and analyze your security status. VPC Packet Mirroring clones the traffic of specific instances in your Virtual Private Cloud (VPC) network and forwards it for examination. It captures all traffic (ingress and egress) and packet data, including payloads and headers. The mirroring happens on the virtual machine (VM) instances, not on the network, which means it consumes additional bandwidth only on the VMs.

- **Cloud NAT:** Lets certain resources without external IP addresses create outbound connections to the Internet.

- **Cloud IAP:** Helps work from untrusted networks without the use of a VPN. Verifies user identity and uses context to determine if a user should be granted access. Uses identity and context to guard access to your on-premises and cloud-based applications.

Optimize

It's important to keep a watchful eye on network performance to make sure the infrastructure is meeting your performance needs. This includes visualizing and monitoring network topology, performing diagnostic tests, and assessing real-time performance metrics.

- **Network Service Tiers:** The Premium Tier delivers traffic from external systems to Google Cloud resources by using Google's low-latency, highly reliable global network. Standard Tier is used for routing traffic over the Internet. Choose Premium Tier for performance and Standard Tier as a low-cost alternative.

- **Network Intelligence Center:** Provides a single console for Google Cloud network observability, monitoring, and troubleshooting.

Modernize

As you modernize your infrastructure, adopt microservices-based architectures, and expand your use of containerization, you will need access to tools that can help you manage the inventory of your heterogeneous services and route traffic among them.

- **GKE Networking** (+ on-premises in Anthos)**:** When you use GKE, Kubernetes and Google Cloud dynamically configure IP filtering rules, routing tables, and firewall rules on each node, depending on the declarative model of your Kubernetes deployments and your cluster configuration on Google Cloud.

- **Traffic Director:** Helps you run microservices in a global service mesh (outside of your cluster). This separation of application logic from networking logic helps you improve your development velocity, increase service availability, and introduce modern DevOps practices in your organization.

- **Service Directory:** A platform for discovering, publishing, and connecting services, regardless of the environment. It provides real-time information about all your services in a single place, enabling you to perform service inventory management at scale, whether you have a few service endpoints or thousands.

CHAPTER SEVEN

Data Science, Machine Learning, and Artificial Intelligence

The purpose of data science is to enable better decision making. Data scientists develop techniques to systematically derive insights from data. As a data scientist, you want to quickly and interactively analyze large datasets, and then share your work, communicate your insights, and operationalize your models. This process involves several key steps that are performed by different functions in companies but that can be performed by one person end-to-end. The role depends on the size and maturity of the team.

- Data Engineering — Ingest, process, and analyze real-time or batch data from a variety of sources to make data more useful and accessible. For this step, data lakes and data warehouses empower teams to securely and cost-effectively ingest, store, and analyze large volumes of diverse, full-fidelity data.

- Data Analysis — Perform data exploration, processing, and analysis in a consistent and shareable way.

- Model Development — After feature engineering, train your model and then evaluate it to see how well it is performing.

- ML Engineering — Deploy the model, serve it, and then monitor it continuously to make sure it consistently performs the way it needs to.

- Insights Activation — Use insights derived from your data to make better business decisions, influence consumer decisions, and power applications.

- Orchestration — Apply pipelines, scheduling, and CI/CD to your ML models.

In addition to offering solutions for these fundamental steps, Google Cloud offers prebuilt AI services for complex tasks (such as item matching and document form parsing) because you don't want to have to build absolutely everything from scratch. This chapter covers the Google Cloud ML and AI services that will help make your data science journey easier.

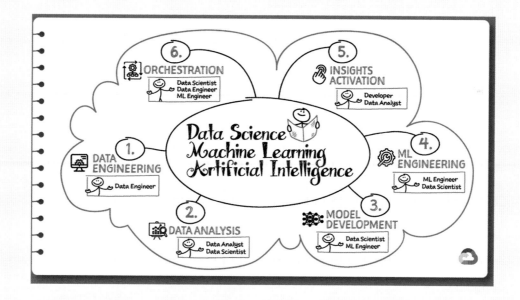

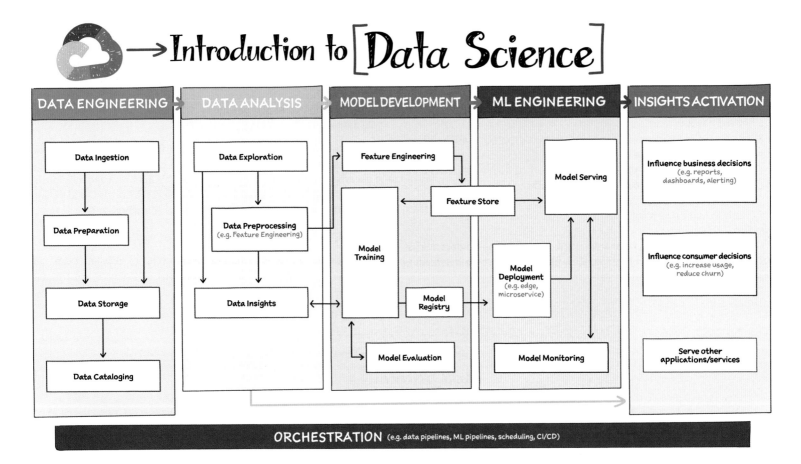

Data science is the practice of making data useful. Let's look at the most common stages in the data science workflow.

Data Engineering

The greatest missed opportunities in data science stem from data that hasn't been made accessible for use in further analysis. Laying the critical foundation for downstream systems, data engineering involves the transporting, shaping, and enriching of data for of making it available and accessible.

Data ingestion is moving data from one place to another, and data preparation is the process of transformation, augmentation, or enrichment before consumption. Global scalability, high throughput, real-time access, and robustness are common challenges in this stage.

Data engineering typically falls under the responsibility of data engineers is such a critical stage in the overall practice of making data useful.

Data Analysis

This step includes data exploration, processing, and analysis. From descriptive statistics to visualizations, data analysis is where the value of data starts to appear. Data exploration, a highly iterative process, involves slicing and dicing data via data preprocessing before data insights can start to manifest through visualizations or simple group-by, order-by operations.

One hallmark of this phase is that the data scientist may not yet know which questions to ask about the data. In this somewhat ephemeral phase, a data analyst or scientist has likely uncovered some aha moments but hasn't shared them yet. Once insights are shared, the flow enters the Insights Activation stage.

Typically, data analysis falls under the responsibility of the data analyst and data scientist, who are charged with the first phase of understanding the data and the potential insights to be gained.

Model Development

This stage is where machine learning (ML) starts to provide new ways of unlocking value from your data. Experimentation is a strong theme here, with data scientists looking to accelerate iteration speed between models without worrying about infrastructure overhead or context-switching between tools for data analysis and tools for productionizing models with MLOps.

MLOps is the industry term for modern, well-engineered ML services, with scalability, monitoring, reliability, automated CI/CD, and many other characteristics and functions. While model training is a big step in this stage, feature engineering, feature store, ML metadata, model registry, and model evaluation are the supplementary steps needed for an effective and continuous ML development.

Data scientists are typically responsible for this step, along with ML engineers.

ML Engineering

Once a satisfactory model is developed, the next step is to incorporate all the activities of a well-engineered application life cycle, including testing, deployment, and monitoring. All of those activities should be as automated and robust as possible. This is where ML engineers come in to deploy and scale the model, making sure the model can scale as the consumption increases.

Continuously monitoring the model becomes critical because after you deploy a model in production, the input data provided to the model for predictions often changes. When the prediction input data deviates from the data that the model was trained on, the performance of the model can deteriorate, even though the model itself hasn't changed.

Insights Activation

This is the step where your data becomes useful to different teams and processes. It can influence business decisions with charts, reports, and alerts. It can also influence customer decisions such as increasing usage, decreasing churn, and other such metrics. Other apps and API can also use this data for users.

Developers, business intelligence, and data analysts are all typically involved in insights activation depending on the use case.

Orchestration

All of the capabilities we have discussed provide the key building blocks to a modern data science solution, but a practical application of those capabilities requires orchestration to automatically manage the flow of data from one service to another. This is where a combination of data pipelines, ML pipelines, and MLOps comes into play. Effective orchestration reduces the amount of time that it takes to reliably go from data ingestion to deploying your model in production, in a way that lets you monitor and understand your ML system.

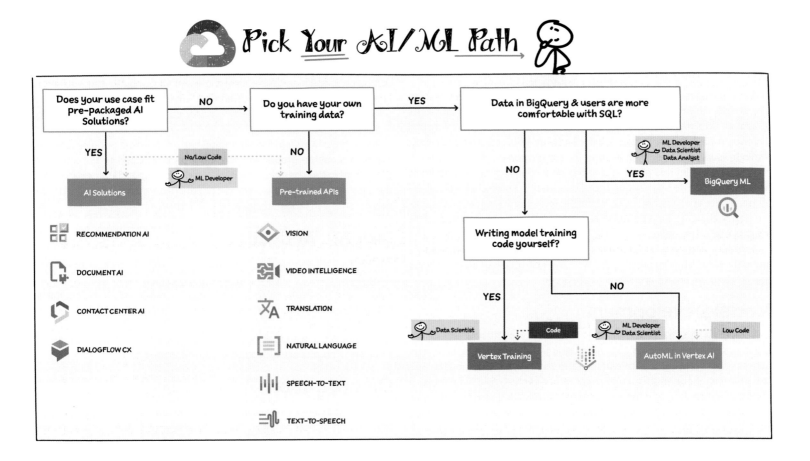

Many users within an organization play important roles in the machine learning (ML) life cycle. There are *product managers*, who can simply type natural language queries to pull necessary insights from BigQuery; *data scientists,* who work on different aspects of building and validating models; and *ML engineers,* who are responsible for keeping the models working well in production systems. Each of these roles involves different needs; this section covers the Google Cloud ML/AI services that are available to help meet those needs.

The services that will work best for you will depend on your specific use case and your team's level of expertise. Because it takes a lot of effort and ML expertise to build and maintain high-quality ML models, a general rule of thumb is to use pretrained models or AI solutions whenever possible — that is, when they fit your use case. If your data is structured, and it's in BigQuery, and your users are already comfortable with SQL, then choose **BigQuery ML**. If you realize that your use case requires writing your own model code, then use custom training options in Vertex AI. Let's look at your options in more detail.

Prepackaged AI Solutions

Both pretrained APIs and prepackaged AI solutions can be used without prior ML expertise. Here are some prepackaged solutions that can be used directly:

Contact Center AI — Create rich and natural conversational experiences.

Document AI — Tap into your unstructured data (such as images and PDFs) and make it accessible using Google computer vision (including OCR) and natural language processing (NLP).

Recommendations AI — Use machine learning to deliver recommendations personalized for each customer's tendencies and preferences.

Pretrained APIs

If you don't have any training data to train a model and you have a generic unstructured data use case such as video, images, text, or natural language, then a pretrained API would be a great choice for your AI/ML project. Pretrained APIs are trained on a huge corpus of generic unstructured data that is built, tuned, and maintained by Google. This means you don't have to worry about creating and managing the models behind them.

BigQuery ML

If your training data is in BigQuery and your users are most comfortable with SQL, then it likely will make sense for your data analysts and data scientists to build ML models in BigQuery using BigQuery ML. You will have to make sure that the set of models available in BigQuery ML matches the problem you're trying to solve. BigQuery ML offers simple SQL statements to build, train, and make predictions within the BigQuery interface or via the API.

Vertex AI

Vertex AI offers a fully managed, end-to-end platform for data science and machine learning. If you need to create your own custom models with your own data, then use Vertex AI. Vertex AI offers two options to train models: AutoML and custom training. Here is how to choose between these two options:

- **Use case:** If your use case fits a supported AutoML offering, then starting with AutoML is a good choice. This includes use cases involving data types such as image, video, text, and tabular. But if your model takes a mixed input type such as images and tabular metadata, then it makes sense to use a custom model.

- **Requirements:** If you need control over your model architecture, framework, or exported model assets (for example, if your model needs to be built with TensorFlow or PyTorch), then use a custom model.

- **Team expertise:** How experienced is your team with ML/AI? If you have a team with limited experience in building custom models, then explore AutoML before you look into custom model development.

- **Team size:** If you have a small data science and ML team, then it may make more sense to work with AutoML because custom model code requires more time to develop and maintain.

- **Prototyping:** Use AutoML if you want to develop a quick initial model to use as a baseline. You can then decide if you want to use this baseline as your production model or look to improve upon it by developing your own custom model.

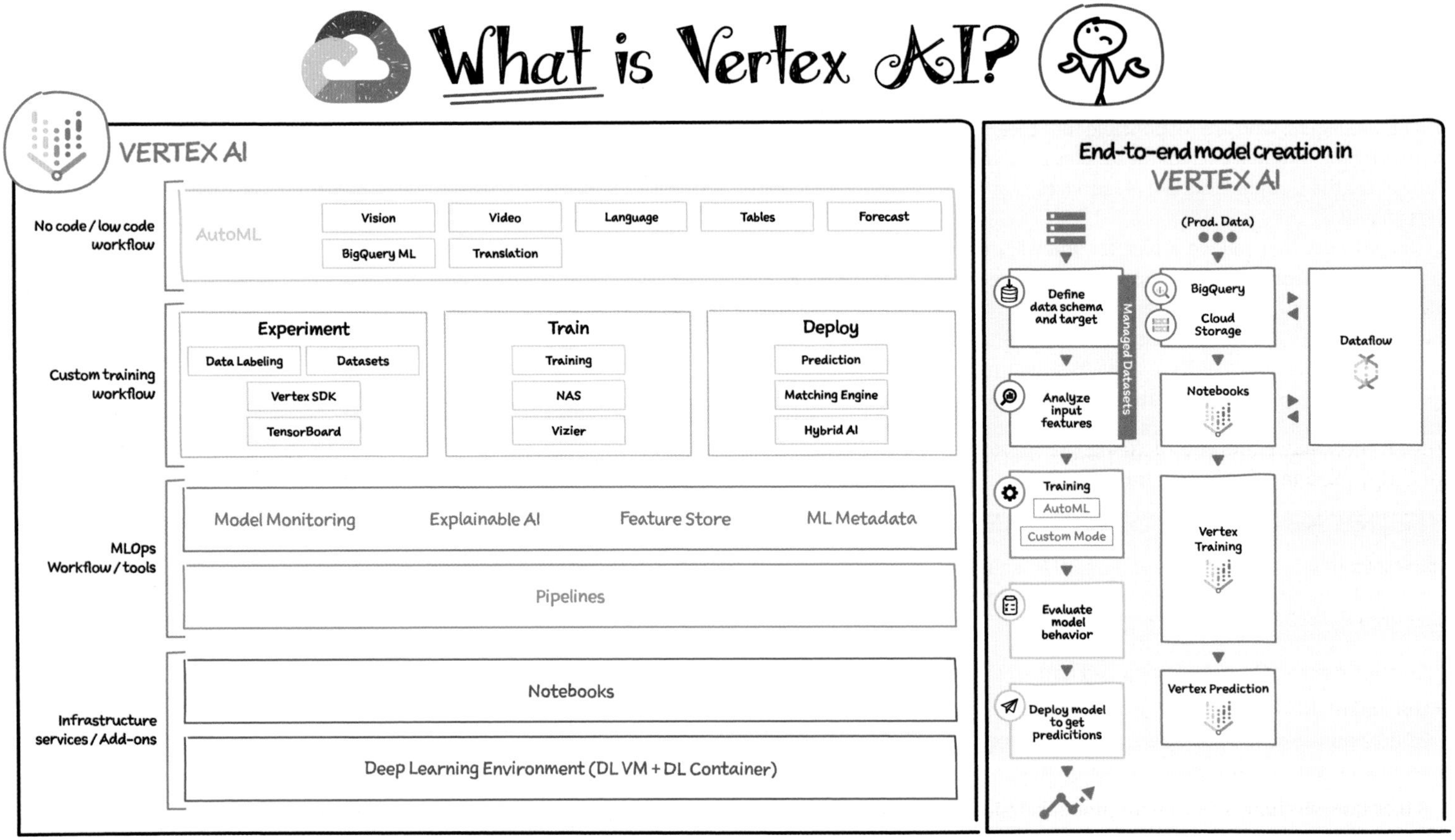

What is Vertex AI?

VERTEX AI

No code / low code workflow	AutoML	Vision	Video	Language	Tables	Forecast
		BigQuery ML	Translation			

Custom training workflow

Experiment	Train	Deploy
Data Labeling · Datasets	Training	Prediction
Vertex SDK	NAS	Matching Engine
TensorBoard	Vizier	Hybrid AI

MLOps Workflow / tools

Model Monitoring · Explainable AI · Feature Store · ML Metadata

Pipelines

Infrastructure services / Add-ons

Notebooks

Deep Learning Environment (DL VM + DL Container)

End-to-end model creation in VERTEX AI

(Prod. Data)

Managed Datasets

- Define data schema and target → BigQuery / Cloud Storage
- Analyze input features → Notebooks
- Training — AutoML / Custom Mode → Vertex Training
- Evaluate model behavior
- Deploy model to get predicitions → Vertex Prediction

Dataflow

Many organizations have varying levels of machine learning (ML) expertise, ranging from novice to expert, so a platform that can help build expertise for the novice users while providing a seamless and flexible environment for the experts is a great way to accelerate AI innovation. This is where Vertex AI comes in! It provides tools for every step of the ML workflow across different model types for varying levels of ML expertise.

ML is an inherently experimental discipline. It's called *data science* for a reason — done properly, there's quite a bit of experimental method, hypothesis testing, and trial-and-error. As a science, then, experimental rigor should be baked into the processes (and therefore tools) that data scientists use. That is the fundamental principle that Vertex AI is built on.

End-to-End Model Creation in Vertex AI

The ML workflow starts with defining your prediction task, followed by ingesting data, analyzing it, and transforming it. Then you create and train a model, evaluate that model for efficiency, optimize it, and finally deploy it to make predictions. With Vertex AI you get a simplified ML workflow for all of these activities in one central place.

- Managed datasets — Helps streamline data preparation, including ingestion, analysis, and transformation. You can upload data from your own computer, Cloud Storage, or BigQuery. After uploading, you can label and annotate the data right from within the console.

- Model training — Vertex AI offers two options, AutoML and custom training. More on this in the next section.

- Model evaluation — Once your model is trained, you have the ability to assess it, optimize it, and even understand the signals behind your model's predictions with Explainable AI.

- Model deployment — When you're happy with the model, you can deploy it to an endpoint to serve online predictions and offline predictions in case of tabular and image models. This deployment includes all the physical resources needed by the model to serve with low latency and scale with increasing traffic. You can use the undeployed model for batch predictions on massive batch datasets and serve online endpoints for low-latency predictions.

- Predictions — After you've deployed the model, you can get predictions using the UI, CLI, or the SDK.

What Does Vertex AI Include?

No-code/low-code ML workflow: The easiest way to create a custom model is by using **AutoML** in Vertex AI. If your use case falls under a supported prediction category (such as translation, vision, video, language, tables, and forecast), then use AutoML before writing your own custom model code. Simply upload your data and Vertex AI automatically finds the best model for the use case.

Custom training ML workflow: If your team of ML experts and data scientists prefers to write custom training code, Vertex AI offers a set of tools for doing just that. Vertex AI supports both custom and prebuilt containers for running training code. Prebuilt containers support common ML frameworks such as PyTorch, TensorFlow, scikit-learn, and XGBoost. For use cases that are based on other dependencies, libraries, and binaries, Vertex AI supports custom containers. You provide the path to the training package in Artifact Registry and your model output artifacts are stored in the Cloud Storage bucket of your choice.

When running custom training jobs on Vertex AI, you can also make use of Vertex's hyperparameter tuning service. Hyperparameters are variables that govern the process of training a model, such as batch size or the number of hidden layers in a deep neural network. In a hyperparameter tuning job, Vertex AI creates trials of your training job with different sets of hyperparameters and searches for the best combination of hyperparameters across the series of trials.

To run the training you need compute resources — either a single node or multiple worker pools for distributed training. To do this with Vertex AI training, you select the machine types, CPU, disk type, disk size, and accelerators you want to use for your training job.

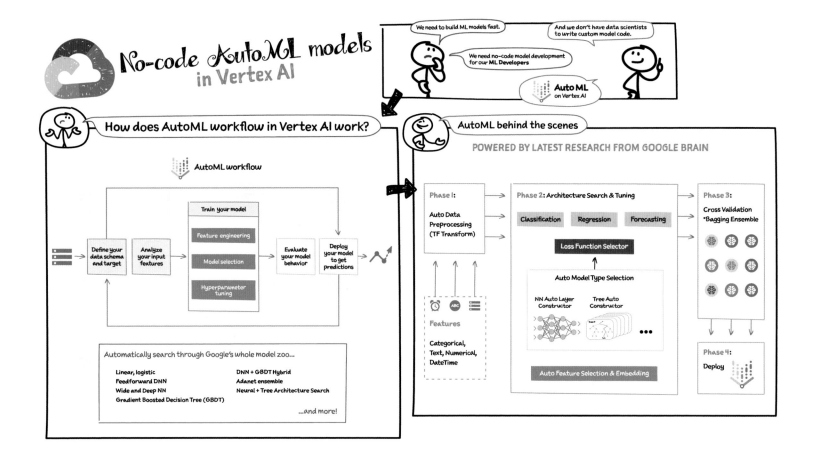

Once the training is done, you need the trained model as an endpoint to be served for prediction. In Vertex AI you can serve models for prediction using prebuilt containers for supported runtimes, or you can build your own custom container stored in the Artifact Registry.

MLOps workflow and tools: ML workflows are complex, where each step in a multistage pipeline may execute in a different environment and pipelines vary considerably between use cases.

- Model Monitoring: Model Moderating enables proactive monitoring of model performance and lets you visualize drift over time, compare latest feature distributions with a baseline, and set alerting thresholds.

- ML Metadata: Maintaining a consistent, flexible approach to manage the life cycle of artifacts generated by all the various steps across these workloads is a considerable challenge. Vertex ML Metadata provides artifact, lineage, and execution tracking for your ML workflow.

- Explainable AI: Explainable AI is a fully managed service on Vertex AI that enables you to generate "feature attributions" or "feature importance" values for your model's predictions. Feature attributions are an explainability method that shows you how much each input feature contributed to your model's predictions, which can help improve confidence that your models are performing as expected.

- Feature Store: Reduce the cycle time of AI/ML development by building and organizing ML features for an entire organization, and making it easy to efficiently share, discover, and serve them at scale.

Infrastructure services: Vertex AI offers preconfigured VMs for deep learning applications. Deep Learning VM images deliver a seamless notebook experience with integrated support for JupyterLab.

Deep Learning VMs are optimized for performance, accelerated model development, and training, enabling fast prototyping with common ML frameworks such as TensorFlow, PyTorch, and scikit-learn preinstalled. You can also easily add Cloud GPUs and Cloud TPU as needed.

AutoML in Vertex AI: AutoML enables developers — even those with limited machine learning (ML) expertise — to train high-quality models specific to their own data and business needs with minimal effort. AutoML in Vertex AI supports common data types such as image, tabular, text, and video. It provides a graphical interface that guides you through the end-to-end ML life cycle. Once your model is built and deployed, you can use it to make predictions using the API or client libraries.

AutoML Behind the Scenes

AutoML ensures that the model development and training tasks that used to take months can now be completed in weeks or even days. With significant automation, as well as guardrails at each step, AutoML helps you:

- Easily define your model's features and target label
- Generate statistics on your input data
- Automatically train your model with automated feature engineering, model selection, and hyperparameter tuning
- Evaluate your model's behavior before deploying to production
- Deploy your model with one click

AutoML automatically searches through Google's model zoo to find the best model to fit your use case. Vertex AI choreographs supervised learning tasks to achieve a desired outcome. The specifics of the algorithm and training methods change based on the data type and use case. There are many different subcategories of machine learning, all of which solve different problems and work within different constraints. For smaller/simpler datasets, it applies linear, logistic models, and for larger ones it selects advanced deep, ensemble methods.

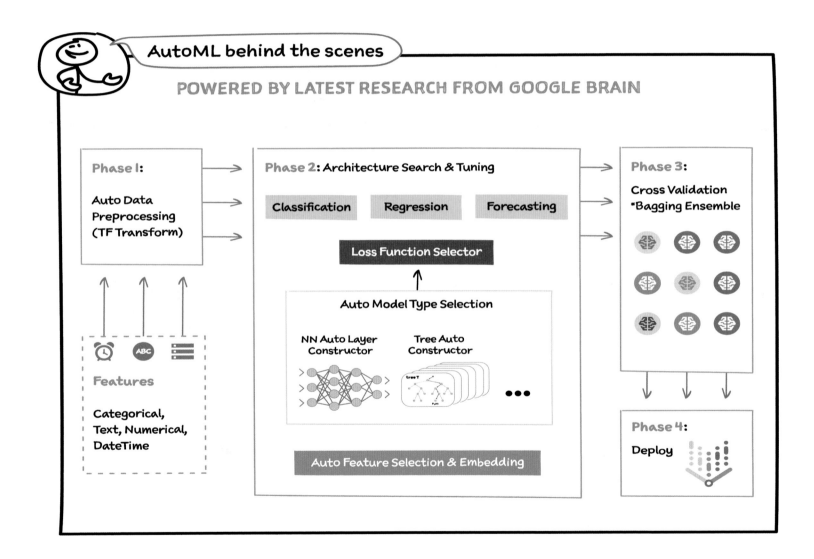

How Do I Work with AutoML in Vertex AI?

Assess your use case: What is the outcome you want to achieve? What type of data are you working with: text, video, tabular, image? How much data do you have? What is your prediction task: classification, regression, forecasting, object detection?

Gather your data: Determine what data you need for training and testing your model based on the outcome you want to achieve.

- Include enough data. Although AutoML enables you to train models with less data, in general, more training data is always better for the accuracy of your resulting model.

- Your dataset should capture the diversity of your problem space. For example, if you're trying to classify photos of consumer electronics into categories, the wider a variety of consumer electronics the model is exposed to in training, the more likely it will be able to distinguish between a novel model of tablet, phone, or laptop, even if it's never seen that specific model before.

- Select relevant features. Features are how your model identifies patterns to make predictions, so they need to be relevant to your problem. For example, to build a model that predicts whether or not a credit card transaction is fraudulent, you'll need to build a dataset that contains transaction details like the buyer, seller, amount, date and time, and items purchased.

Prepare your data: Make sure your data is properly formatted and labeled.

- You can add data in Vertex AI by either importing from your computer or from Cloud Storage in an available format (CSV or JSONL) with the labels inline.

- If your image or text data hasn't been annotated, you can upload unlabeled data and use the Google Cloud Console to apply annotations.

Train: Set parameters and build your model. Your dataset contains training, validation, and testing sets. If you do not specify the splits, then Vertex AI automatically uses 80 percent of your data for training, 10 percent for validation, and 10 percent for testing. You can also define splits manually.

Evaluate and test: In Vertex AI you can assess your custom model's performance using the model's output on test examples and common machine learning metrics. These metrics include:

- **Model output:** For image, text, and video classification datasets, the model outputs a series of numbers that communicate how strongly it associates each label with that example. For a regression dataset, the model output is a new predicted value, and for a tabular forecasting dataset, the model output is a new column with forecasted values.

- **Performance metrics:** Performance metrics also differ depending on the type of model you create.

Classification models show prediction outcomes in the form of true positives, true negatives, false positives, and false negatives.

Precision and recall refer to how well your model is capturing information. *Precision* tells you, from all the test examples that were assigned a label, how many actually were supposed to be categorized with that label. *Recall* tells you, from all the test examples that should have had the label assigned, how many were actually assigned the label. Depending on your use case, you may want to optimize for either precision or recall.

Regression and forecasting models show mean absolute error (MAE), which is the average of absolute differences between observed and predicted values. They also show root mean square error (RMSE), mean absolute percentage error (MAPE), root mean squared log error (RMSLE), and R squared (R^2), which is the square of the Pearson correlation coefficient between the observed and predicted values.

There's no one-size-fits-all answer on how to evaluate your model; consider evaluation metrics in context with your problem type and what you want to achieve with your model.

Deploy and predict: When you're satisfied with your model's performance, it's time to get predictions. Perhaps that means production-scale usage, or maybe it's a one-time prediction request. Depending on your use case, you can use your model for batch or online predictions.

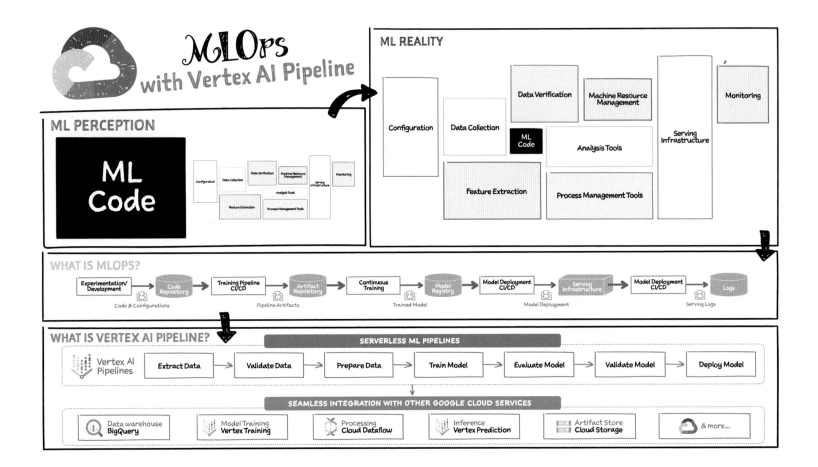

Many people think that the main challenge in building a machine learning (ML) application is getting the model working, but in practice that is only a small part of a much bigger picture. After you collect your data, verify it, analyze it, extract features, secure machine resources to train the model, and finally train your model, you face the challenge of moving to production, where you'll need the ability to scale the serving infrastructure, and monitor and manage all your models continuously. That's where the growing discipline of MLOps comes in!

What Is MLOps?

MLOps has a fairly straightforward goal: unify machine learning system development and operations, to guide teams through the challenges of doing production machine learning. It takes both its name as well as some of its core principles and tooling from DevOps. However, the development of ML applications comes with its own unique challenges — for example, it's necessary to manage the life cycle of data and models, as well as code — and that has led MLOps to evolve as a domain of its own.

Here are some high-level MLOps patterns and practices that help address the challenges of ML application development and deployment:

- Formalization — As you formalize your ML workflows for production, you can (and should) move away from stitched-together notebooks or monolithic scripts.
- Standardization — Standardized ML workflows behave in the same way across environments.

- Scalability — An efficient MLOps workflow will scale out resources when needed, and scale down when they're not.
- Reproducibility — Designing for composability, modularity, and reuse of ML workflow building blocks will ensure that you can reliably reproduce and rerun your workflows.
- Monitoring, versioning, and caching — Your infrastructure should support workflow monitoring, versioning, and caching. This typically requires making ML workflow metadata explicit.
- Productization — The data scientists on your team will likely prototype ML models in their own notebooks. You need well-defined processes to capture that work and move it out of notebooks for production use.
- Collaboration — Mechanisms for supporting collaboration and role-based access control also become important. Informal methods of providing team members access won't scale.

A typical machine learning workflow might include experimentation and prototyping stages as well as automation of training, model evaluation and deployment, and monitoring and retraining. Many steps and actions need to be coordinated and supported with particular capabilities (such as continuous monitoring). For a production environment, an ad hoc approach won't work. By formalizing and orchestrating these steps with Vertex AI Pipelines, you can automate, track, and reproduce workflows; more easily debug problems; and reuse subcomponents of a workflow elsewhere.

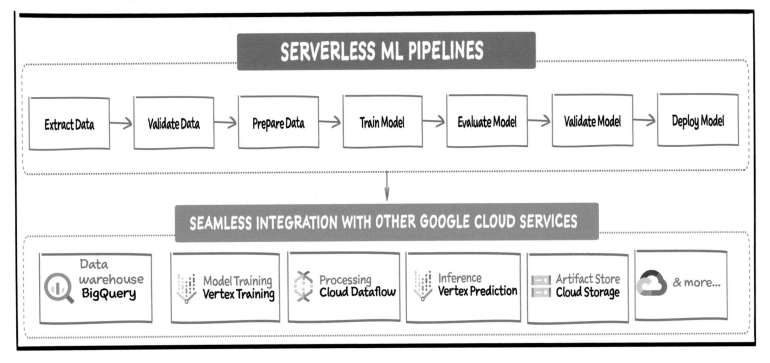

Vertex AI Pipelines

Vertex AI Pipelines is a managed ML service that enables you to increase the pace at which you experiment with and develop machine learning models and the pace at which you transition those models to production. Vertex AI Pipelines is serverless, which means that you don't need to deal with managing an underlying GKE cluster or infrastructure. It scales up when you need it to, and you pay only for what you use. In short, it lets you focus on building your pipelines.

Vertex AI Pipelines features data scientist–friendly Python SDKs that make it easy to build and run pipelines. You can use prebuilt components from the Vertex AI Pipelines SDKs, or use the SDKs to define your own custom components. You can add control flow to your pipelines, and the SDKs make it easy to experiment and prototype right from notebooks.

Vertex AI Pipelines also has a metadata layer that simplifies the process of tracking artifacts generated throughout your ML workflow. Artifact, lineage, and execution information is automatically logged to a metadata server when you run a pipeline, and you can explore all of this information in the UI. You can also query the underlying metadata server directly, which lets you compare run information and group artifacts by projects to track usage of datasets and models across your organization.

Vertex AI Pipelines workflows are secured with Google Cloud Platform standard enterprise security controls, including identity and access management as well as VPC Service Controls.

Vertex AI Pipelines Under the Hood

With Vertex AI Pipelines you don't have to worry about building, scaling, and maintaining your own Kubernetes clusters. Each step within a pipeline is completed either by a call to a Google Cloud managed service or through the execution of user code in a container. In both cases, Vertex AI Pipelines allocates the resources it needs at execution time. When you call a managed service, that service spins up the necessary resources. When the pipeline executes user code in a container, Vertex AI spins up the resources needed for that container.

Vertex AI Pipelines Open Source Support

Vertex AI Pipelines supports two open source Python SDKs: Kubeflow Pipelines (KFP) and TensorFlow Extended (TFX). You can use either of these SDKs with both Vertex AI Pipelines and open source Kubeflow Pipelines. If you use TensorFlow in an ML workflow that processes terabytes of structured data or text data, then it makes sense to build your pipeline using TFX.

For other use cases, you'll likely want to build your pipeline using the Kubeflow Pipelines SDK. With this SDK, you can implement your workflow by building custom components or by reusing prebuilt components, such as Google Cloud pipeline components, which make it easier to use Vertex AI services like AutoML in your pipeline.

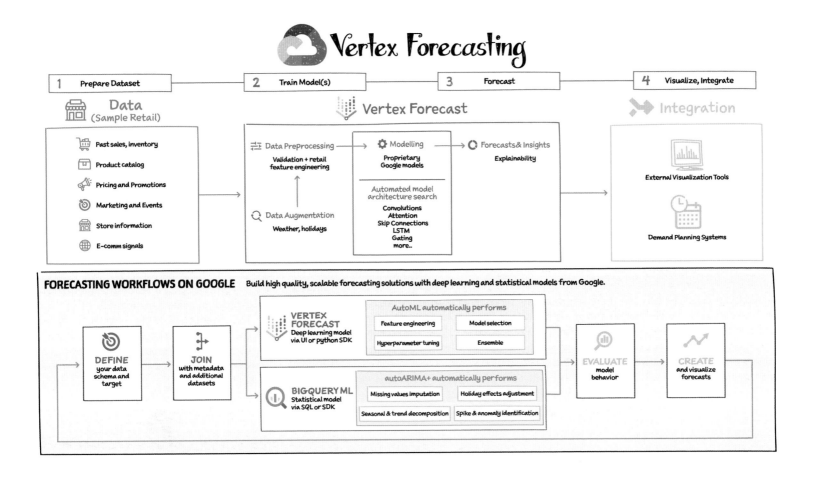

A retailer needs to predict product demand or sales, a call center manager wants to predict the call volume to hire more representatives, a hotel chain requires hotel occupancy predictions for next season, and a hospital needs to forecast bed occupancy. Vertex Forecast provides accurate forecasts for these and many other business forecasting use cases.

Univariate vs. Multivariate Datasets

Forecasting datasets come in many shapes and sizes. In univariate datasets, a single variable is observed over a period of time — for example, in an airline passenger dataset with trend variations and seasonal patterns. More often, business forecasters are faced with the challenge of forecasting large groups of related time series at scale using multivariate datasets. A typical retail or supply chain demand planning team has to forecast demand for thousands of products across hundreds of locations or zip codes, leading to millions of individual forecasts. Similarly, financial planning teams often need to forecast revenue and cash flow from hundreds or thousands of individual customers and lines of business.

Forecasting Algorithms

The most popular forecasting methods today are statistical models. Autoregressive integrated moving average (ARIMA) models, for example, are widely used as a classical method for forecasting, and BigQuery ML offers an advanced ARIMA_PLUS model for univariate forecasting use cases. More recently, deep learning models have been gaining a lot of popularity for forecasting applications. There is ongoing debate on when to apply which methods, but it's becoming increasingly clear that neural networks are here to stay for forecasting applications.

Why Use Deep Learning Models for Forecasting?

Deep learning's recent success in the forecasting space is because they are global forecasting models (GFMs). Unlike univariate (i.e., local) forecasting models, for which a separate model is trained for each individual time series in a dataset, a deep learning time series forecasting model can be trained simultaneously across a large dataset of hundreds or thousands of unique time series. This allows the model to learn from correlations and metadata across related time series, such as demand for groups of related products or traffic to related websites or apps. While many types of ML models can be used as GFMs, deep learning architectures, such as the ones used for Vertex Forecast, are also able to ingest different types of features, such as text data, categorical features, and covariates that are not known in the future. These capabilities make Vertex Forecast ideal for situations where there are very large and varying numbers of time series, short life cycles, and cold-start forecasts.

What Is Vertex Forecast?

You can build forecasting models in Vertex Forecast using advanced AutoML algorithms for neural network architecture search. Vertex Forecast offers automated preprocessing of your time-series data, so instead of fumbling with data types and transformations you can just load your dataset into BigQuery or Vertex AI and AutoML will automatically apply common transformations and even engineer features required for modeling.

Most importantly it searches through a space of multiple deep learning layers and components, such as attention, dilated convolution, gating, and skip connections. It then evaluates hundreds of models in parallel to find the right architecture, or ensemble of architectures, for your particular dataset, using time series–specific cross-validation and hyperparameter tuning techniques (generic automated machine learning tools are not suitable for time series model search and tuning purposes, because they induce leakage into the model selection process, leading to significant overfitting).

This process requires lots of computational resources, but the trials are run in parallel, dramatically reducing the total time needed to find the model architecture for your specific dataset. In fact, it typically takes less time than setting up traditional methods.

Best of all, by integrating Vertex Forecast with Vertex AI Workbench and Vertex AI Pipelines, you can significantly speed up the experimentation and deployment process of GFM forecasting capabilities, reducing the time required from months to just a few weeks, and quickly augmenting your forecasting capabilities from being able to process just basic time series inputs to complex unstructured and multimodal signals.

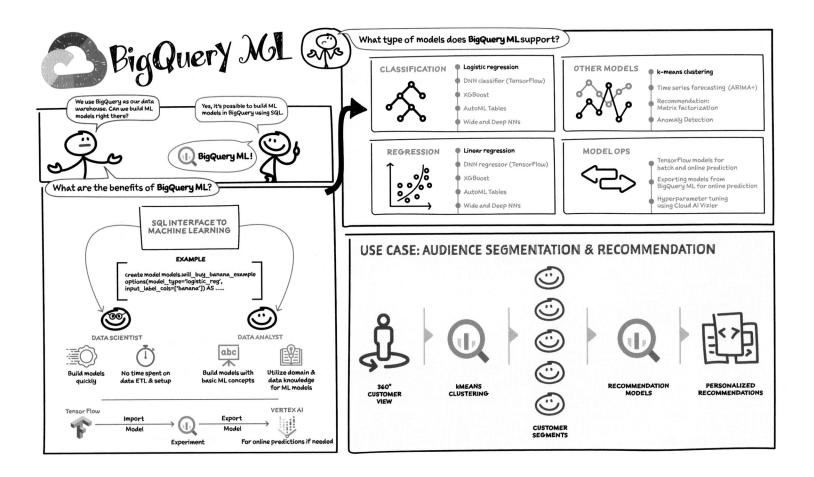

BigQuery is a fully managed data warehouse for storing and running petabyte-scale analytics using SQL, without worrying about the underlying infrastructure. If your data scientist and analysts are already using SQL queries in BigQuery to analyze the data, they might want to go further and create ML models right there too. That's where BigQuery ML comes in!

BigQuery ML lets you create and execute machine learning models in BigQuery using standard SQL queries. BigQuery ML democratizes machine learning by letting SQL practitioners build models using existing SQL tools and skills. BigQuery ML increases development speed by eliminating the need to move data.

Benefits of BigQuery ML

BigQuery ML democratizes the use of ML by empowering data analysts, the primary data warehouse users, to build and run models using existing business intelligence tools and spreadsheets. BigQuery ML increases the speed of model development and innovation by removing the need to export data from the data warehouse. Instead, BigQuery ML brings ML to the data by providing these benefits:

- It is serverless, which means no instances to create and manage.
- In-place data means no data movement and ETL tasks.
- SQL means users don't need specialized skills like Python/Java.
- Governance and compliance is built in.

When You Should Use BigQuery ML over Vertex AI:

- Your data is already in BigQuery.
- You want to model on structured data.
- You want to do some model exploration right where the data is.

Additional Notable Features of BigQuery ML

- Explainable AI for predictive models in BigQuery ML helps make it easy to understand why your models made the predictions they made.
- Hyperparameter tuning helps you automatically optimize your hyperparameters when creating your models.

- Model export lets you export your BigQuery ML models to Cloud Storage, so you can host them anywhere you like, including Vertex AI.

Supported Models in BigQuery ML

In BigQuery ML, you can use a model with data from multiple BigQuery datasets for training and prediction. BigQuery ML supports the following types of models:

- Linear regression for forecasting; for example, the sales of an item on a given day.
- Binary logistic regression for classification; for example, determining whether a customer will make a purchase.
- Multiclass logistic regression for classification. These models can be used to predict multiple possible values such as whether an input is low-value, medium-value, or high-value.
- K-means clustering for data segmentation; for example, identifying customer segments. The models can also be used for anomaly detection.
- Matrix factorization for creating product recommendation systems using historical customer behavior, transactions, and product ratings.
- Time series for performing time-series forecasts. You can use this feature to create millions of time series models and use them for forecasting. The model automatically handles anomalies, seasonality, and holidays.
- Boosted tree for creating XGBoost-based classification and regression models.
- Deep Neural Network (DNN) for creating TensorFlow-based Deep Neural Networks for classification and regression models.
- AutoML Tables to create best-in-class models without feature engineering or model selection.
- TensorFlow model importing lets you create BigQuery ML models from previously trained TensorFlow models, then perform batch predictions on your data in BigQuery.
- Autoencoder for creating TensorFlow-based BigQuery ML models with the support of sparse data representations. The models can be used in BigQuery ML for tasks such as unsupervised anomaly detection and non-linear dimensionality reduction.

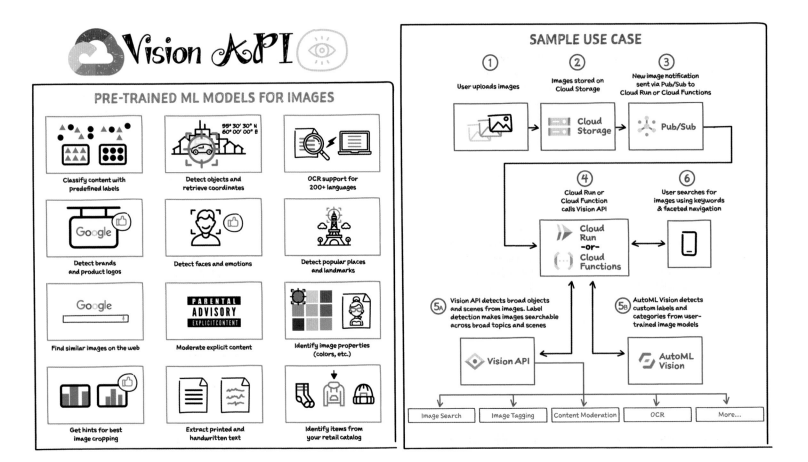

Are you building an application that can benefit from image search; detection of products, logos, and landmarks; text extraction from images; or other image AI-related capabilities? If so, Vision AI may be just what you need. Vision AI enables you to easily integrate computer vision features within your applications to detect emotion, understand text, and much more. It includes image labeling, face and landmark detection, optical character recognition (OCR), and tagging of explicit content.

How to Use Vision AI

You can use Vision AI to derive insights from your images in different ways:

Vision API — As the name suggests, Vision API provides access to a set of pretrained machine learning models for images through REST and RPC APIs. You just need to enable the API in Cloud Console or use the SDK and call the API. It assigns labels to images and quickly classifies them into millions of predefined categories such as landmarks, logos, text, emotions, and so on. It helps build valuable metadata into your image catalog.

AutoML Vision in Vertex AI — You can automate the creation of your own custom machine learning models by simply uploading your image datasets using the graphical interface and training the model. Once you've trained your model, you can evaluate its accuracy, latency, and size, and export it to your application in the cloud. Furthermore, by using the AutoML Vision Edge capabilities, you can train and deploy low-latency, high-accuracy models optimized for edge devices.

What Can I Do with Vision API?

- **Classify content using predefined labels** — Provides a label for the supplied image based on millions of predefined categories.

- **Detect brands and product logos** — Provides a textual description of the logo or product entity identified, a confidence score, and a bounding polygon for the logo in the image.

- **Find similar images on the web** — Infers entities (labels/descriptions) from similar images on the web. Provides a list of URLs for fully matching images or cropped versions.

- **Get crop hints** — Provides a bounding polygon for the cropped image, a confidence score, and an importance fraction of this salient region with respect to the original image.

- **Detect objects and retrieve object coordinates** — Provides general label and bounding box annotations for multiple objects recognized in a single image.

- **Detect faces and emotions** — Locates faces with bounding polygons and identifies specific facial features such as eyes, ears, nose, and mouth along with their corresponding confidence values. Also returns likelihood ratings for emotion (joy, sorrow, anger, surprise) and general image properties (underexposed, blurred, headwear present).

- **Moderate explicit content** — Provides likelihood ratings for explicit content categories such as adult, spoof, medical, violence, and racy.

- **Detect and extract printed and handwritten text** — Performs optical character recognition (OCR) for an image, including text recognition and conversion to machine-coded text. Identifies and extracts UTF-8 text in an image.

- **Detect popular places and landmarks** — Provides the name of the landmark, a confidence score, and a bounding box in the image for the landmark. Gives coordinates for the detected entity.

- **Identify dominant colors and other image properties** — Returns dominant colors in an image.

- **Identify products from your catalog** — Matches entities identified in the image with items (such as a hat or a shirt) in your retail catalog.

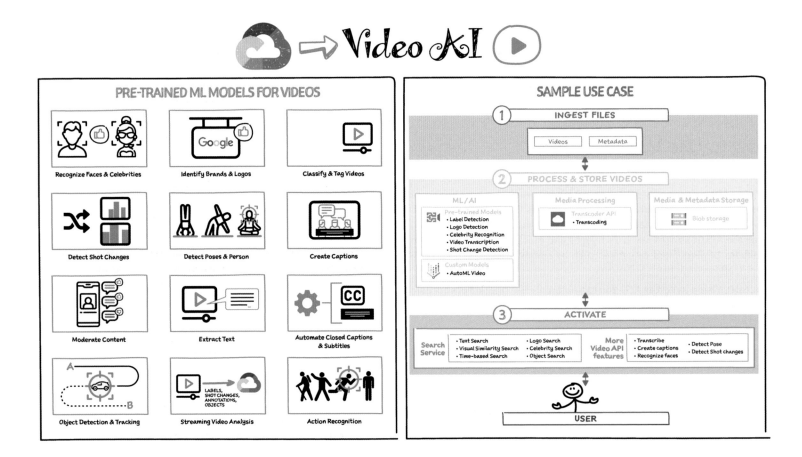

If you deal with lots of video content, you likely have use cases for content moderation, video recommendations, media archiving, or contextual advertising. All such use cases depend on powerful content discovery. That's where Video AI comes in! Video AI offers precise video analysis that recognizes over 20,000 objects, places, and actions in video. You can get near-real-time insights with streaming video annotation and object-based event triggers. Video AI also enables you to extract rich metadata at the video, shot, or frame level, leading to more engaging experiences.

How to Use Video AI

There are a few ways to use Video AI to derive insights from your videos:

Video Intelligence API — Offers pretrained machine learning models that automatically recognize a vast number of objects, places, and actions in stored and streaming video.

AutoML for Video in Vertex AI — Automate the training of your own custom machine learning models by uploading your video datasets using the graphical interface and training the model.

What Can I Do with the Video Intelligence API?

- Explicit content detection: Detects adult content within a video. Annotates a video with explicit content annotations (tags) for entities that are detected in the input video.

- Face detection: Looks for faces in a video and returns segments in which a face is detected across all videos in the given request. It can also return bounding boxes defining the area of the video frame in which the face is detected, or the detected attributes of the face such as mouth, lips, smiling, and so on.

- Analyze videos for labels: Identify entities shown in video footage and annotate these entities with labels (tags). For example, for a video of a train at a crossing, the Video Intelligence API returns labels such as "train," "transportation," and "railroad crossing." Each label includes a time segment with the time offset (timestamp) for the entity's appearance from the beginning of the video.

- Logo recognition: The Video Intelligence API automatically identifies 100,000 logos, tracks the number of appearances of logos, and evaluates brand prominence by measuring how long a particular brand appears on screen.

- Object tracking: Tracks multiple objects detected in an input video or video segments and returns labels (tags) associated with the detected

entities along with the location of the entity in the frame. For example, a video of vehicles crossing an intersection may produce labels such as "car," "truck," "bike," "tires," "lights," "window," and so on. Each label includes a series of bounding boxes showing the location of the object(s) in the frame. Each bounding box also has an associated time segment with a time offset (timestamp) that indicates the duration offset from the beginning of the video.

- Person detection: Detects the presence of humans, poses, and clothing attributes in a video file and tracks the bounding box of individual people across the video or video segment.

- Shot change: Annotates a video with video segments that are generated when detecting abrupt shot changes in the video.

- Speech transcription: Transcribes spoken audio in a video or video segment into text and returns blocks of text.

- Text detection: Performs OCR to detect visible text from frames in a video, or video segments, and returns the detected text along with information about the frame-level location and timestamp in the video for that text.

Use Case Scenarios

- **Content moderation:** You can identify when inappropriate content is being shown in a video and can instantly moderate content to quickly and efficiently filter content.

- **Recommended content:** To simplify content discovery for your users and to guide them to the most relevant content, you can build a content recommendation engine that uses labels generated by the Video Intelligence API and a user's viewing history and preferences.

- **Media archives:** For mass media companies, media archives are crucial. Using the metadata from the Video Intelligence API, you can create an indexed archive of your entire video library.

- **Contextual advertisements:** You can identify appropriate locations in videos to insert ads that are contextually relevant to the video content. This can be done by matching the timeframe-specific labels of your video content with the content of your advertisements.

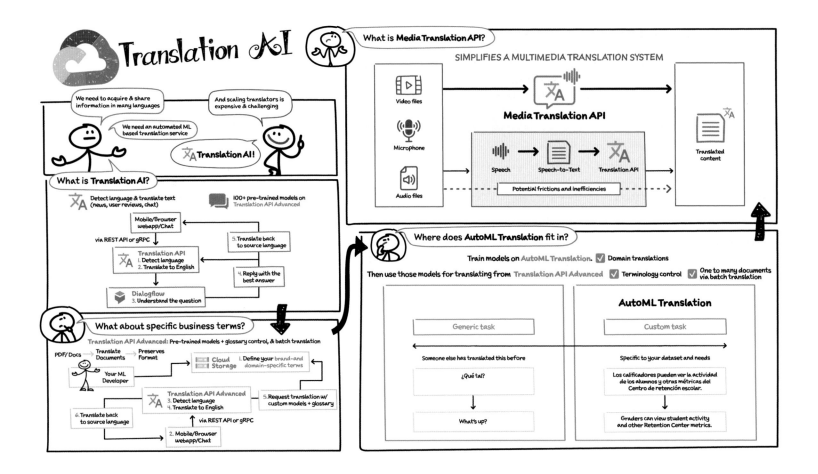

As products and companies become more and more global, there is an increasing need to acquire and share information in many languages. Scaling translators to meet these needs is a challenge, however, and it is also expensive. Translation AI provides a cost-effective way to meet this challenge in the cloud, with machine learning models that enable rapid, efficient translation.

What Is Translation AI?

Translation AI offers real-time on-demand translations so that your end users can get content in their language in seconds. It can be used in three different ways: Translation API (Basic and Advanced), AutoML Translation, and Media Translation API.

Translation API's pretrained model supports more than 100 languages. It's easy to integrate with Google APIs via REST or with your mobile or browser app using gRPC. It scales seamlessly, comes with a generous daily quota, and lets you set lower limits.

Consider a multi-language chat support use case. When a chat request is made from a mobile app or browser to the Translation API, it detects the language and translates it to English, then sends the request to Dialogflow to understand the question. (Dialogflow is a natural language understanding platform that makes it easy to design and integrate conversational user interfaces.) Dialogflow replies back with a best answer and Google Translation API then converts it back to the user's source language.

What If Your Business Has Specific Terms?

Translation API does a great job with general-purpose text, and with its advanced glossary features, you can take it further by providing a dictionary of words or phrases. With Translation API's glossary feature, you can retain your brand names or other specific terms in translated content. Simply define the names and vocabulary in your source and target languages, then save the glossary file to your translation project in Cloud Storage, and those words and phrases will be included in your copy when you include the glossary in your translation request.

Translation API Advanced also offers a Document Translation API for directly translating documents in formats such as PDF and DOCX. Unlike simple plain-text translations, Document Translation preserves the original formatting and layout in your translated documents, helping you retain much of the original context.

AutoML Translation

There are times when you don't know exactly which word translations you want to control but you need the translations to be more relevant to the content domain, like manufacturing or medical. AutoML Translation shines in such use cases, which require a custom model to bridge the "last mile" between generic translation tasks and specific niche vocabularies and linguistic style. AutoML custom models are built on top of the generic Translation API model for domain-specific content that matters to you, which means you are taking advantage of the underlying pretrained model.

What Is the Media Translation API?

Translating audio files and streaming speech has long been a challenge. Because the data and files are not in the form of text, you first had to transcribe the original source into text, and then translate the resulting text into different languages. Friction in this process forced many organizations to make a trade-off between quality, speed, and ease-of-deployment. That's where the Media Translation API comes in!

The Media Translation API simplifies this process by abstracting away the transcription and translation behind a single API call, enabling you to perform real-time translation of video clips and audio data with higher translation accuracy. With the Media Translation API, you can enable real-time engagement for users by streaming translation from a microphone or pre-recorded audio file. Or, you can power an interactive experience on your platform with video chat featuring translated captions or add subtitles to your videos in real time as they are played. You can probably think of numerous other use cases for this capability.

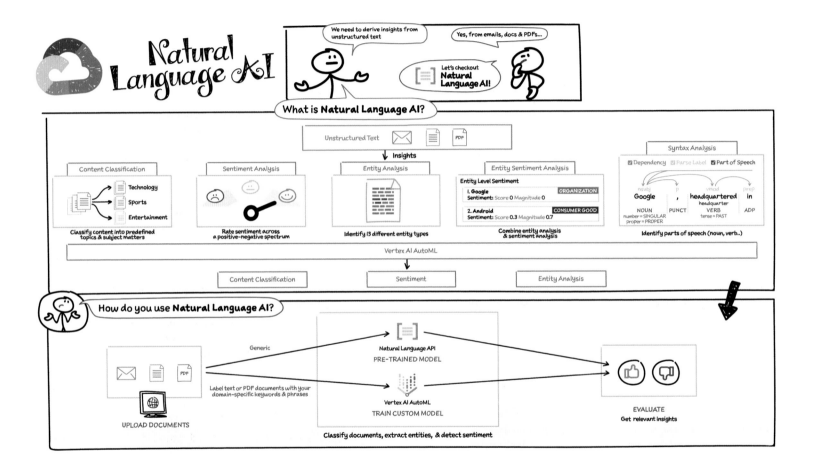

Text is everywhere: in emails, messages, comments, reviews, and documents. The ability to derive insights from unstructured text powers use cases such as sentiment analysis, content classification, moderation, and more. That's where Natural Language AI comes in! It offers insightful text analysis with machine learning for extracting and analyzing text. With Natural Language AI you can incorporate natural language understanding (NLU) into your apps.

How to Use Natural Language AI

There are a few ways to use Natural Language AI to derive insights from your unstructured text:

Natural Language API — Offers pretrained machine learning models that empower developers to easily apply natural language understanding (NLU) to their applications with such features as sentiment analysis, entity analysis, entity sentiment analysis, content classification, and syntax analysis. You can use Natural Language AI to quickly perform analysis and annotation on your text using thousands of predefined labels through REST and RPC APIs. Simply enable the API in Cloud Console or use the SDK and then call the API.

AutoML for Natural Language in Vertex AI — Train your own high-quality, custom machine learning models to classify, extract, and detect sentiment with minimum effort and machine learning expertise using Vertex AI for natural language, powered by AutoML. You can use the AutoML UI to upload your training data and test your custom model without writing a single line of code. Once it is trained, you can assess the model's accuracy, latency, and size, and export it to your application in the cloud. You can also choose to train and deploy low-latency, high-accuracy models optimized for edge devices.

Healthcare Natural Language AI — Enables you to distill machine-readable medical insights from medical documents, while AutoML Entity Extraction for Healthcare makes it easy to build custom knowledge extraction models for healthcare and life sciences apps with no coding skills required.

What Can I Do with the Natural Language API?

The Natural Language API has several methods for performing analysis and annotation on your text:

- Sentiment analysis inspects the text and identifies the prevailing emotional opinion within the text as positive, negative, or neutral. This is useful in customer feedback and satisfaction use cases, where the API would identify "I had a bad experience," for example, as a negative sentiment.

- Entity analysis inspects the given text for known entities (including proper nouns such as public figures, landmarks, and so on as well as common nouns such as "restaurant," "stadium," and so on) and returns information about those entities. You can use this capability to identify mentions of your brand along with other entities in reviews, social media, and other text.

- Entity sentiment analysis inspects the given text for known entities (proper nouns and common nouns), returns information about those entities, and identifies the prevailing emotional opinion of the writer about the entity. For example, an analysis of "I like this new mobile phone, but the battery life is poor" would return a positive sentiment on "phone," but a negative sentiment on "battery."

- Syntactic analysis extracts linguistic information, breaking up the given text into a series of sentences and tokens (generally, word boundaries) and providing further analysis on those tokens.

- Content classification analyzes text and returns a list of content categories found in that text, for example, "Internet & Telecom" or "Computers & Electronics."

Each API call also detects and returns the language of the given text if a language is not specified by the caller in the initial request.

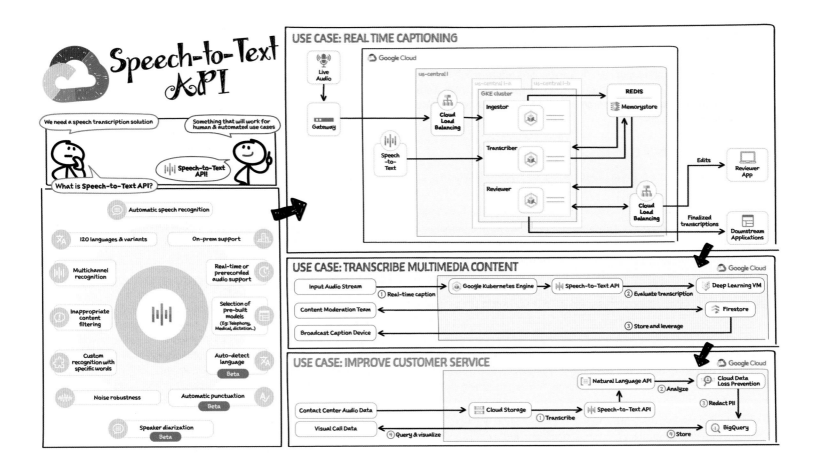

Fortunately Google has spent the last 20 years working on improving speech recognition across Google Assistant, Gboard voice typing on Android, YouTube captions, Google Meet, and more. The Speech-to-Text API, the result of that work, gives you access to Google's most advanced deep learning neural network algorithms for automatic speech recognition (ASR) and transcription. It offers high accuracy with no training or tuning in 73 languages in over 125 locales.

Speech use cases usually fall into one of two categories: human-consumed or machine-consumed for downstream processing. Human-consumed use cases include closed captions and subtitles in videos, whereas machine-consumed use cases include reading audio-based content, summarization, extraction, and customer service improvement. One thing that's common to all speech use cases is the accuracy of transcription. A number of issues can affect accuracy: audio quality, a need for domain-specific terms, multiple speakers/background noise, and speakers. The Speech-to-Text API helps with transcribing your speech content to text with high accuracy in a variety of environments.

What Can I Do with the Speech-to-Text API?

The Speech-to-Text API provides automatic speech recognition for real-time or prerecorded audio and supports a global user base with extensive language support in over 125 languages and variants. It also allows you to evaluate quality by iterating on your configuration. Some additional features are:

- **Inappropriate content filtering:** A profanity filter helps you detect inappropriate or unprofessional content in your audio data and filter out profane words in text results.

- **Speech adaptation, custom recognition with specific words:** Customize speech recognition to transcribe domain-specific terms and rare words by providing hints and boost your transcription accuracy of specific words or phrases. Automatically convert spoken numbers into addresses, years, currencies, and more using classes.

- **Noise robustness:** Speech-to-Text can handle noisy audio from many environments without requiring additional noise cancellation.

- **Selection of prebuilt models:** Choose from a selection of pretrained models for voice control, phone call, dictation, and video transcription optimized for domain-specific quality requirements.

- **Multichannel recognition:** Speech-to-Text can recognize distinct channels in multichannel situations (e.g., video conferences) and annotate the transcripts to preserve the order.

- **Automatic punctuation:** Speech-to-Text accurately punctuates transcriptions (e.g., commas, question marks, and periods).

- **Speaker diarization:** Know who said what by receiving automatic predictions about which of the speakers in a conversation spoke each utterance.

- **Speech-to-Text On-Prem:** Available on Google Cloud Marketplace to be deployed as a container on any Anthos GKE cluster. It provides more accurate, smaller in size models to run on-premises.

How to Use the Speech-to-Text API

- **Synchronous Recognition** (REST and gRPC) sends audio data to the Speech-to-Text API, performs recognition on that data, and returns results after all audio has been processed. Synchronous recognition requests are limited to audio data of one minute or less in duration. Note that a synchronous request is *blocking*, meaning that Speech-to-Text must return a response before processing the next request.

- **Asynchronous Recognition** (REST and gRPC) sends audio data to the Speech-to-Text API and initiates a long-running operation. Using this operation, you can periodically poll for recognition results. Use asynchronous requests for audio data of any duration up to 480 minutes.

- **Streaming Recognition** (gRPC only) performs recognition on audio data provided within a gRPC bi-directional stream. Streaming requests are designed for real-time recognition purposes, such as capturing live audio from a microphone. Streaming recognition provides interim results while audio is being captured, allowing results to appear while a user is still speaking.

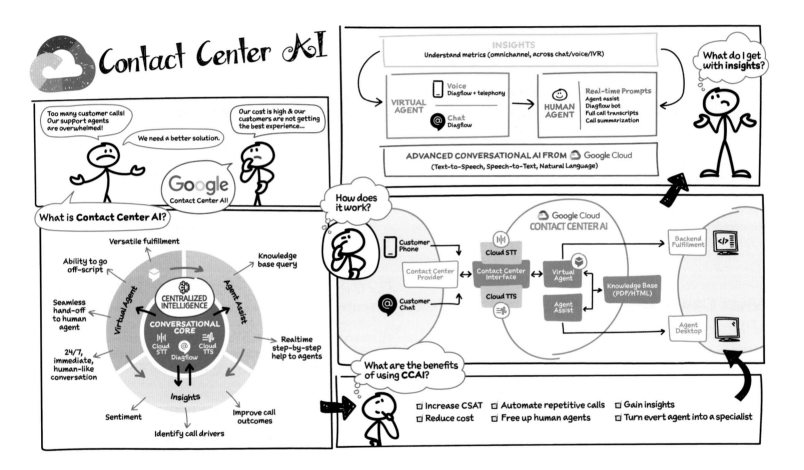

As the volume of customer calls increases, it's becoming even more important to make the most of human agents' time to lower costs and improve customer experiences. Google Cloud Contact Center AI (CCAI) enables you to do just that by freeing human agents to concentrate on more complex calls while providing them with real-time information to better handle those calls.

Single source of intelligence: Contact Center AI provides a consistent, high-quality conversational experience across all channels and platforms, both human and virtual.

Ability to go off-script: Huge cost savings can be realized by having a virtual agent handle voice calls. CCAI has the ability to go "off script" — to let callers go down tangents or side paths to the main conversation, while still tracking toward the main objective of the call. With CCAI, your virtual agents can answer complex questions and complete complicated tasks, including allowing for unexpected stops and starts, unusual word choices, or implied meanings. Developers can define supplemental questions, and CCAI can easily retain the context, answer the supplemental question, and come back to the main flow.

Versatile fulfillment: CCAI has the ability to handle multiple use cases for the customer with the same virtual agent, which enables you to fully automate routine tasks and deflect calls.

What Is Contact Center AI?

Contact Center AI is a conversational AI technology solution that automates simple interactions and enables agents to solve issues quickly, using AI. CCAI has four key components:

- **Conversation Core:** This is the central AI brain that underpins CCAI and its ability to understand, talk, and interact. It enables and orchestrates high-quality conversational experiences at scale, making it possible for customers to have conversations with a virtual agent that are as good as conversations with a human agent.
  - **Understand** — Speech-to-Text speech recognition understands what customers are saying regardless of how they phrase things, what vocabulary they use, what accent they have, and so on.
  - **Talk** — Text-to-Speech enables virtual agents to respond to customers in a natural, human-like manner that pushes the conversation along, rather than frustrate customers.
  - **Interact** — Dialogflow identifies customer intent and determines the appropriate next step. You can build conversational flows in a point-and-click interface, and generate automated ML models for human-like conversational experiences.
- **Virtual agents with Dialogflow:** This component automates interactions with customers, using natural conversation to identify and address their issues. Virtual agents enable customers to get immediate help any time, day or night.
- **Agent Assist:** This component brings AI to human agents to increase the quality of their work, while decreasing their average handling time. Agent Assist shares initial context and provides real-time, turn-by-turn guidance to coach agents through business processes, as well as full call transcriptions that agents can edit and file quickly.
- **CCAI Insights:** CCAI Insights helps your contact center managers in making better data-driven decisions for their business by breaking down conversations using natural language processing and machine learning.

How Does Contact Center AI Work?

When a user initiates a chat or voice call and the contact center provider connects them with CCAI, a virtual agent engages with the user, understands their intent, and fulfills the request by connecting to the backend. If necessary, the call can be handed off to a human agent, who sees the transcript of the interaction with the virtual agent, gets feedback from the knowledge base to respond to queries in real time, and receives a summary of the call at the end. Insights help you understand what happened during the virtual agent and live agent sessions. The result is improved customer experiences and customer satisfaction scores, lower agent handling times, and more time for human agents to spend on more complicated customer issues.

Document AI

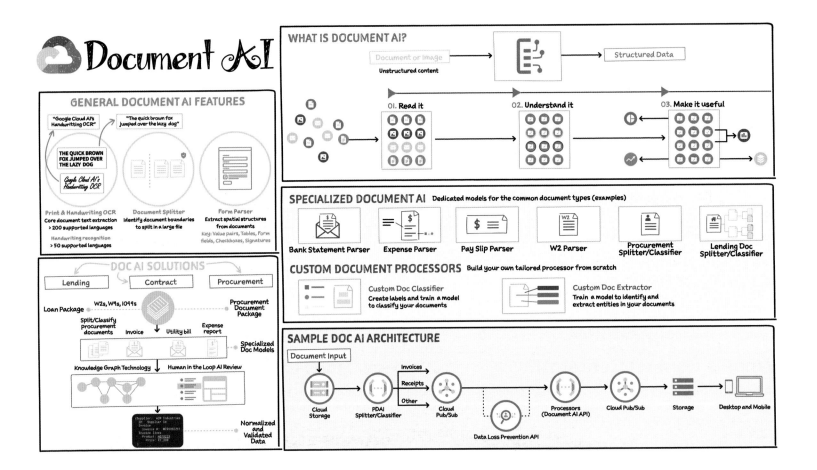

GENERAL DOCUMENT AI FEATURES

Print & Handwriting OCR
Core document text extraction
> 200 supported languages

Handwriting recognition
> 50 supported languages

Document Splitter
Identify document boundaries
to split in a large file

Form Parser
Extract spatial structures
from documents
Key: Value pairs, Tables, Form
fields, Checkboxes, Signatures

WHAT IS DOCUMENT AI?

Document or Image → Structured Data

Unstructured content

01. **Read it**   02. **Understand it**   03. **Make it useful**

SPECIALIZED DOCUMENT AI   Dedicated models for the common document types (examples)

Bank Statement Parser   Expense Parser   Pay Slip Parser   W2 Parser   Procurement Splitter/Classifier   Lending Doc Splitter/Classifier

CUSTOM DOCUMENT PROCESSORS   Build your own tailored processor from scratch

Custom Doc Classifier
Create labels and train a model
to classify your documents

Custom Doc Extractor
Train a model to identify and
extract entities in your documents

DOC AI SOLUTIONS

Lending   Contract   Procurement

Loan Package   W2s, W4s, 1099s   Procurement Document Package

Split/Classify procurement documents   Invoice   Utility bill   Expense report   Specialized Doc Models

Knowledge Graph Technology   Human in the Loop AI Review

Normalized and Validated Data

SAMPLE DOC AI ARCHITECTURE

Document Input

Cloud Storage → PDAI Splitter/Classifier → Invoices / Receipts / Other → Cloud Pub/Sub → Processors (Document AI API) → Cloud Pub/Sub → Storage → Desktop and Mobile

Data Loss Prevention API

Some of the most important data in companies isn't living in databases, but rather in documents. Transforming documents into structured data helps increase the speed of decision making, reduce costs related to manual data entry, and develop better experiences for customers. Documents include everything from PDFs, emails, images, and more. Think about all the contracts, patents, and business attachments you've worked with that are in difficult-to-parse formats. This is what is known as "dark data." Dark data is information assets that organizations collect, process, and store during regular business activities but that is generally not used for other purposes such as analytics or directly monetizing. Document AI can help you safely and securely use this data.

What Is Document AI?

Document AI lets you tackle the end-to-end flow of extracting and classifying information from unstructured documents. Not only does it read and ingest your documents, it understands the spatial structure of the document. For example, if you run a form through a parser, it understands that there are questions and answers in your form, and you'll get those back in key-value pairs. This facilitates a way to incorporate documents into your existing app or service by using the API. If you're working on an on-premises or hybrid system, you can still use this API in your code from where it's running.

How to Use Document AI

There are three flavors of Document AI:

- **General Document AI** offers general models such as optical character recognition (OCR) and structured form parser capabilities. If you upload a multipage PDF that has several different form types present, the splitter can tell you where each individual form actually starts and ends.
- **Specialized Document AI** for several common business form types. These include models for tax forms such as W2s and W9s; high-variance

document types, such as invoices and receipts; U.S. licenses; passports, and bank statements. Google trains and maintains these models so that you don't have to.

- **Custom Document AI** for training the model on your own documents. With the AutoML technology, you can upload your own document and create custom models with a no-code graphical user interface.

You can use the Document AI API synchronously for real-time document processing or asynchronously to batch process bulk documents from Cloud Storage.

Sample Document AI Architecture

You get your data into Cloud Storage, then split/classify it by calling Document AI API using Cloud Functions. You can integrate data loss prevention DLP for de-identification of documents to mask sensitive information. You could use Pub/Sub to effectively stream your data into your storage system of choice. If you are not using Google Cloud services and just using your own SQL or PostgreSQL database on-premises or on another cloud, that's fine! You can still call this API.

Vertical Solutions

In addition to the specialized parsers, the vertical solutions help make it easy to derive value from documents specific to procurement, lending, and contract. These vertical solutions help reduce processing time and streamline data capture so that you can optimize your development and usage. These solutions are enhanced by the Google Knowledge Graph technology to normalize and enrich entity extraction (certain fields are detected). To ensure accuracy, they provide a workflow and user interface for humans to review, validate, and correct the data extracted from documents by Human in the Loop (HITL) processors.

Recommendations AI

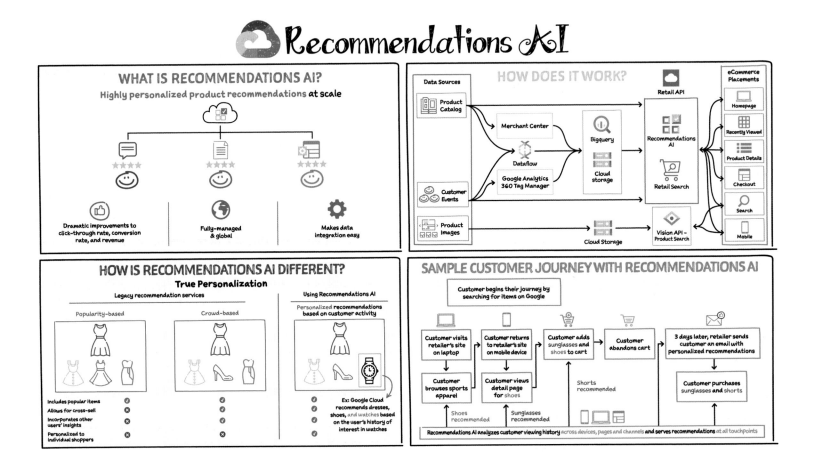

WHAT IS RECOMMENDATIONS AI?
Highly personalized product recommendations at scale

- Dramatic improvements to click-through rate, conversion rate, and revenue
- Fully-managed & global
- Makes data integration easy

HOW DOES IT WORK?

Data Sources → Product Catalog, Customer Events, Product Images

Merchant Center → Dataflow → Google Analytics 360 Tag Manager → BigQuery → Cloud storage → Recommendations AI → Retail Search

Retail API

Product Images → Cloud Storage → Vision API – Product Search

eCommerce Placements
- Homepage
- Recently Viewed
- Product Details
- Checkout
- Search
- Mobile

HOW IS RECOMMENDATIONS AI DIFFERENT?
True Personalization

Legacy recommendation services
- Popularity-based
- Crowd-based

Using Recommendations AI
Personalized recommendations based on customer activity

Ex: Google Cloud recommends dresses, shoes, and watches based on the user's history of interest in watches

	Popularity-based	Crowd-based	Using Recommendations AI
Includes popular items	✓	✓	✓
Allows for cross-sell	✗	✓	✓
Incorporates other users' insights	✗	✓	✓
Personalized to individual shoppers	✗	✗	✓

SAMPLE CUSTOMER JOURNEY WITH RECOMMENDATIONS AI

Customer begins their journey by searching for items on Google

- Customer visits retailer's site on laptop → Customer browses sports apparel (Shoes recommended)
- Customer returns to retailer's site on mobile device → Customer views detail page for shoes (Sunglasses recommended)
- Customer adds sunglasses and shoes to cart
- Customer abandons cart (Shorts recommended)
- 3 days later, retailer sends customer an email with personalized recommendations → Customer purchases sunglasses and shorts

Recommendations AI analyzes customer viewing history across devices, pages and channels and serves recommendations at all touchpoints

Recommendations are a huge part of discovering what your customers are interested in. Effective recommendations improve the customer experience by helping customers discover products that they are likely to need or want. Google has spent years delivering recommended content across Google Shopping, Google Search, and YouTube. Recommendations AI draws on that experience and Google's expertise in machine learning to deliver personalized recommendations in a managed solution that improves individual customer experiences.

What Is Recommendations AI?

Recommendations AI offers true personalization for each individual customer, using the complete history of the customer's shopping journey to serve them with real-time personalized product recommendations. It excels at generating recommendations in scenarios with long-tail products and cold-start users and items. Its context-hungry deep learning models use item and user metadata to draw insights across millions of items at scale and constantly iterate on those insights in real time — a pace that is impossible for manually curated rules to keep up with.

Sample Customer Journey with Recommendations AI

Recommendations AI works throughout the entire buying process, from initial product discovery to consideration, and through to purchase. And it doesn't stop there! It can be used for remarketing as well as email campaigns that deliver personalized recommendations for customers.

Let's meet a user who is browsing on one of her favorite apparel sites. She wants to replace some of her old workout gear, so she starts to browse the activewear section of the site. When she clicks through to the product page of a jacket that she's interested in, she's immediately served a recommendation for a pair of shoes that is often purchased with this jacket.

She checks out the shoes and sees another item recommended for her: sunglasses.

She adds the sunglasses and shoes to the cart. She decides not to complete the purchase right at that moment, so a few days later the retailer sends her a reminder email with additional personalized recommendations, including one for a pair of shorts. She returns to the site to find a customized home page with her personalized recommendations. This sample flow illustrates not only the power of effective recommendations, but also the value of being able to easily re-engage the customer from where they left off and reduce shopping cart abandonments.

How Does Recommendations AI Work?

Recommendations AI uses the Retail API to power three essential functions:

- **Collecting and ingesting the necessary data:** There are two data sources for recommendations: your product catalog and the record of user-generated events on your website. This data can be processed using Dataflow, with the results stored in BigQuery or Cloud Storage. When the data is properly formatted, you can ingest it into the Retail API. Direct imports from data sources into the Retail API are also possible.

- **Processing the data and building models to provide recommendations and search results:** The Retail API supports two types of models: product recommendations and retail search. The API uses the same data for both, so there is no need to ingest data twice. Models are designed to optimize for click-through rate (CTR), revenue per order, and conversion rate (CVR). Recommendation AI offers models for frequently bought together, recently viewed, others you may like, and recommended items.

- **Embedding the models in your website:** The Retail API provides easy-to-integrate REST APIs and client libraries in popular programming languages to supply recommendations and search results.

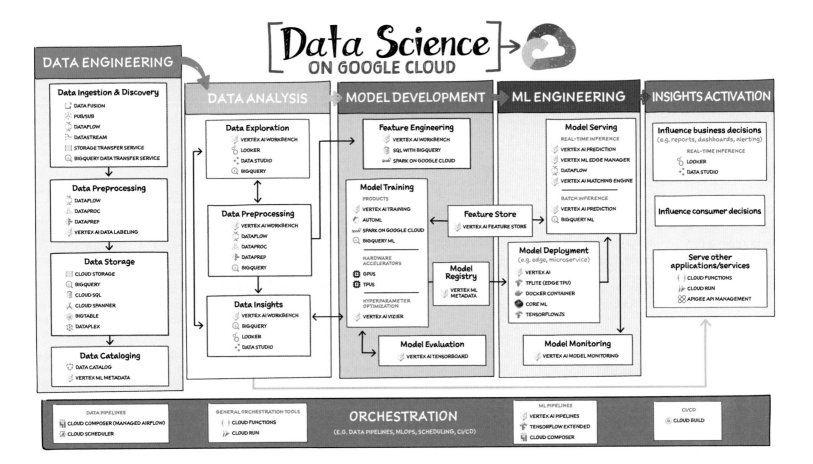

Data Engineering

Data engineering involves the transporting, shaping, and enriching of data to make it available and accessible. Google Cloud offers multiple tools to ingest, prepare, store, and catalog data. We covered this topic in detail in the data analytics section of the book. Refresh the concepts there and continue on here.

Data Analysis

Data analysis is where the value of data starts to appear. On Google Cloud, there are many ways to explore, preprocess, and uncover insights in your data. If you are looking for a notebook-based end-to-end data science environment, use Vertex AI Workbench, which enables you to access, analyze, and visualize your entire data estate, from structured data at the petabyte scale in SQL with BigQuery, to process data with Spark on Google Cloud with serverless, autoscaling, and GPU acceleration capabilities. As a unified data science environment, Vertex AI Workbench also makes it easy to do machine learning.

If your focus is on analyzing structured data from data warehouses and insight activation for business intelligence, use Looker which helps accelerate your time-to-insight.

Model Development

Model development is where ML models are built using the data. Vertex AI Workbench makes it easy as the one-stop-shop for data science, combining analytics and machine learning, including Vertex AI services. It supports Spark, XGBoost, TensorFlow, PyTorch and more. As a Jupyter-based fully managed, scalable, and enterprise-ready environment, Vertex AI Workbench makes managing the underlying compute infrastructure needed for model training easy, with the ability to scale vertically and horizontally, and with idle timeouts and auto shutdown capabilities to reduce unnecessary costs. Notebooks themselves can be used for distributed training and hyperparameter optimization, and they include Git integration for version control.

For low-code model development, data analysts and data scientists can use BigQuery ML to train and deploy models directly using BigQuery's built-in serverless, autoscaling capabilities integrated with Vertex AI. For no-code model development, Vertex AI Training provides a point-and-click interface to train powerful models using AutoML.

ML Engineering

The next step is to incorporate all the activities of a well-engineered application life cycle, including testing, deployment, and monitoring. And all those activities should be as automated and robust as possible.

Vertex AI Managed Datasets and Feature Store provide shared repositories for datasets and engineered features, respectively, which provide a single source of truth for data and promote reuse and collaboration within and across teams. Vertex AI model serving enables deployment of models with multiple versions, automatic capacity scaling, and user-specified load balancing. Finally, Vertex AI Model Monitoring provides the ability to monitor prediction requests flowing into a deployed model and automatically alert model owners whenever the production traffic deviates beyond user-defined thresholds and previous historical prediction requests.

Insights Activation

The insights activation stage is where your data has become useful to other teams and processes. You can use Looker and Data Studio to enable use cases in which data is used to influence business decisions with charts, reports, and alerts.

Finally, the data can also be used by other services to drive insights; these services can run outside Google Cloud, inside Google Cloud on Cloud Run or Cloud Functions, and/or using Apigee API Management as an interface.

Orchestration

Effective orchestration reduces the amount of time that it takes to reliably go from data ingestion to deploying your model in production, in a way that lets you monitor and understand your ML system. For data pipeline orchestration, Cloud Composer and Cloud Scheduler are both used to kick off and maintain the pipeline. For ML pipeline orchestration, Vertex AI Pipeline is a managed machine learning service that enables you to increase the pace at which you experiment with and develop machine learning models and the pace at which you transition those models to production.

CHAPTER EIGHT

Security

Cloud security at its core, cloud security is a combination of hardware, software, application, data, and user security. *Cloud providers* provide services that *you* use to build your applications. Cloud security requires collaboration between both parties; providers are responsible for securing the infrastructure on which the services run and you are responsible for securing your data using the best practices, templates, products, and solutions made available by your cloud provider. Your specific responsibilities vary based on the cloud computing model you choose: infrastructure-as-a-service (IaaS), platform-as-a-service (PaaS), or serverless.

This chapter covers the Google Cloud security model and the services that you can use to protect your applications in Google Cloud.

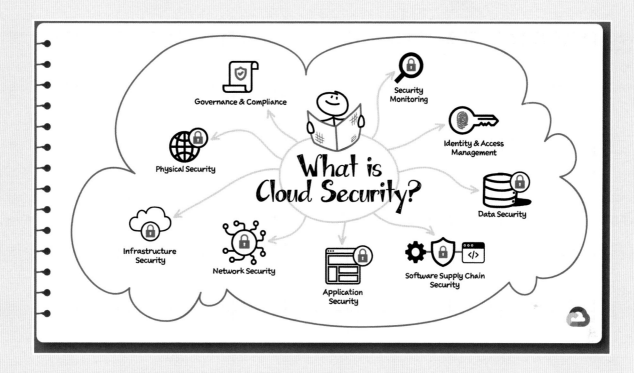

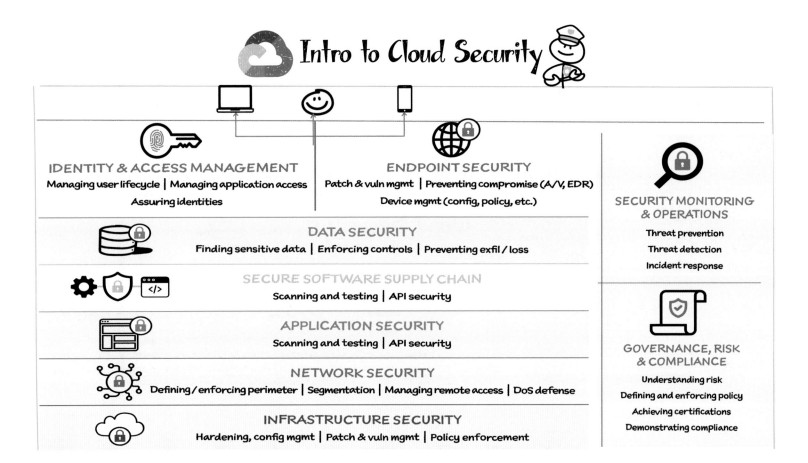

Intro to Cloud Security

IDENTITY & ACCESS MANAGEMENT
Managing user lifecycle | Managing application access
Assuring identities

ENDPOINT SECURITY
Patch & vuln mgmt | Preventing compromise (A/V, EDR)
Device mgmt (config, policy, etc.)

DATA SECURITY
Finding sensitive data | Enforcing controls | Preventing exfil / loss

SECURE SOFTWARE SUPPLY CHAIN
Scanning and testing | API security

APPLICATION SECURITY
Scanning and testing | API security

NETWORK SECURITY
Defining / enforcing perimeter | Segmentation | Managing remote access | DoS defense

INFRASTRUCTURE SECURITY
Hardening, config mgmt | Patch & vuln mgmt | Policy enforcement

SECURITY MONITORING & OPERATIONS
Threat prevention
Threat detection
Incident response

GOVERNANCE, RISK & COMPLIANCE
Understanding risk
Defining and enforcing policy
Achieving certifications
Demonstrating compliance

When you think about Cloud Security there are many areas of responsibility — securing infrastructure, securing the network, securing data, securing applications, managing identities and access, and securing endpoints. There are also ongoing processes for security operations and governance as well as risk and compliance management. But the best part of building your application on the cloud is that you share the security responsibility with the cloud provider.

Cloud Security Is Shared Fate

Cloud security requires collaboration and is usually operated on a "shared fate" model, where the cloud provider is responsible for the security of the underlying cloud infrastructure and you are responsible for securing the applications you deploy on the cloud. This gives you the flexibility and control you need to implement the required security controls for your application and business. Depending on your use case, you can restrict access to the sensitive data and projects or selectively deploy public applications. So keep the following in mind:

- Providers are responsible for securing infrastructure.
- You are responsible for securing your data.
- Providers help you with best practices, templates, products, and solutions.

Infrastructure Security

Cloud providers are responsible for providing infrastructure security, which includes security through the entire information processing life cycle, such as hardware infrastructure, service deployment, storage services, user identity, Internet communications, and operational and device security.

Network Security

Network security is partly the cloud provider's responsibility and partly yours. Providers make sure the traffic on their networking infrastructure is secure and encrypted at all times and that communication with other services on the public Internet are secure. Due to the scale, they also offer inherent denial-of-service (DoS) protection.

You are responsible for defining and enforcing your application perimeter, segmentation of your projects between teams and organizations, managing remote access for your employees, and implementing additional DoS defense.

Application Security

When building an application or API on the cloud, you are responsible for application security, including scanning and testing. Adopt practices such as the following:

- Allow and deny traffic based on authentication and authorization of the user.
- Use or implement services to block bot and fraudulent users from your website.

Secure Software Supply Chain Security

Securing your software requires establishing, verifying, and maintaining a chain of trust, to establish the provenance or origin trail of your code, via attestations, generated and checked throughout your software development and deployment process. Open source SLSA, or Supply-chain Levels for Software Artifacts, is an end-to-end framework for supply chain integrity that you can adopt incrementally to increase your security posture.

Data Security

Data security is a shared responsibility between you and the cloud provider. The cloud provider offers data encryption at rest and in transit, while you are responsible for your applications' data security. This includes secure key and secret management, finding sensitive data, enforcing controls, and preventing exfiltration and data loss.

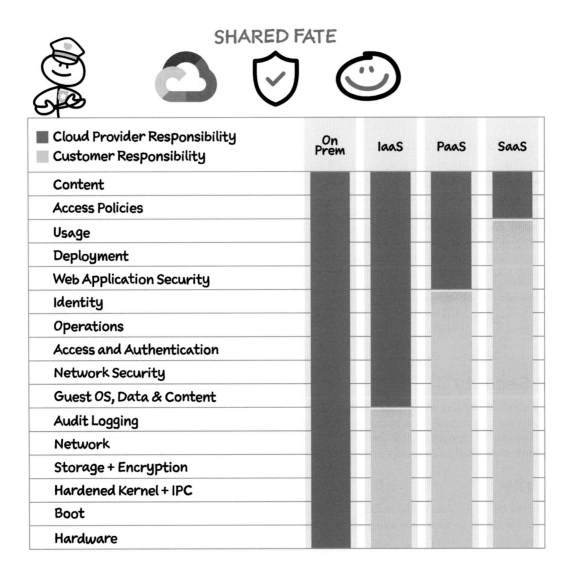

SHARED FATE

Identity and Access Management

Identity and access management (IAM) includes securely managing user life-cycle and application access. Identity security includes creating and managing user accounts, and protecting the user accounts with two-step verification. Access management also includes securely providing users with access to resources they need and making sure the access policies follow least privilege rules — nobody should have more access than they need.

Endpoint Security

Endpoint security is critical to defining access to your systems. You need to make sure you apply patches and vulnerability management, prevent compromises, and manage user devices, including assessing the policies that define which device has access to which resources in your application or projects.

Security Monitoring and Operations

From a security operations (SecOps) perspective, there are few core requirements that you need for effective security and risk management in the cloud. Detecting threats in the system, preventing them, and responding to them are some of the responsibilities of a SecOps team.

Governance, Risk, and Compliance

This area includes understanding security risk, defining and enforcing policy, and demonstrating compliance by achieving certifications.

Google provides capabilities across Google Cloud, Google Workspace, and connected devices that cover the whole stack. We'll cover those in this chapter.

Infrastructure Security

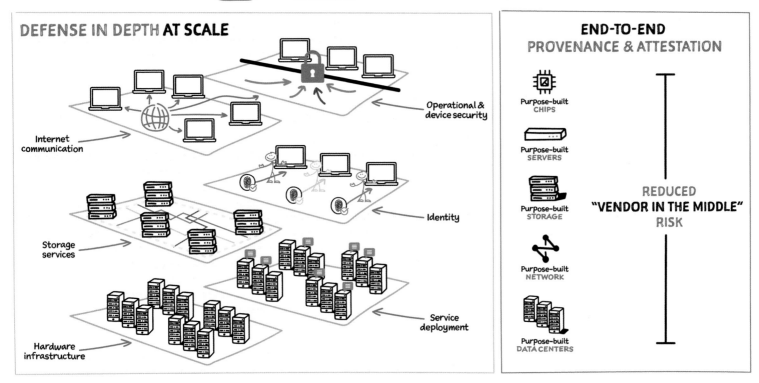

DEFENSE IN DEPTH AT SCALE

- Operational & device security
- Internet communication
- Identity
- Storage services
- Service deployment
- Hardware infrastructure

END-TO-END PROVENANCE & ATTESTATION

- Purpose-built CHIPS
- Purpose-built SERVERS
- Purpose-built STORAGE
- Purpose-built NETWORK
- Purpose-built DATA CENTERS

REDUCED "VENDOR IN THE MIDDLE" RISK

The security of the infrastructure that runs your applications is one of the most important considerations in choosing a cloud vendor. Google Cloud's approach to infrastructure security is unique. Google doesn't rely on any single technology to secure its infrastructure. Rather, it has built security through progressive layers that deliver defense in depth.

Defense in Depth at Scale

- **Data center physical security** — Google data centers feature layered security with custom-designed electronic access cards, alarms, vehicle access barriers, perimeter fencing, metal detectors, biometrics, and laser beam intrusion detection. They are monitored 24/7 by high-resolution cameras that can detect and track intruders. Only approved employees with specific roles may enter.

- **Hardware infrastructure** — From the physical premises to the purpose-built servers, networking equipment, and custom security chips to the low-level software stack running on every machine, the entire hardware infrastructure is controlled, secured, and hardened by Google.

- **Service deployment** — Any application binary that runs on Google infrastructure is deployed securely. No trust is assumed between services, and multiple mechanisms are used to establish and maintain trust. Google infrastructure was designed from the start to be multitenant.

- **Storage services** — Data stored on Google's infrastructure is automatically encrypted at rest and distributed for availability and reliability. This helps guard against unauthorized access and service interruptions.

- **User identity** — Identities, users, and services are strongly authenticated. Access to sensitive data is protected by advanced tools like phishing-resistant security keys.

- **Internet communications** — Communications over the Internet to Google cloud services are encrypted in transit. The scale of the infrastructure enables it to absorb many distributed denial-of-service (DDoS) attacks, and multiple layers of protection further reduce the risk of any DDoS impact.

- **Operational and device security** — Google operations teams develop and deploy infrastructure software using rigorous security practices. They work to detect threats and respond to incidents 24x7x365. Because Google runs on the same infrastructure that is made available to Google Cloud customers, all customers directly benefit from this security operations and expertise.

End-to-End Provenance and Attestation

Google's hardware infrastructure is custom-designed "from chip to chiller" to precisely meet specific requirements, including security. Google servers and software are designed for the sole purpose of providing Google services. These servers are custom built and don't include unnecessary components like video cards or peripheral interconnects that can introduce vulnerabilities. The same goes for software, including low-level software and the server OS, which is a stripped-down, hardened version of Linux.

Further, Google designed and included hardware specifically for security. Titan, for example, is a purpose-built chip intended to establish a hardware root of trust for both machines and peripherals in cloud infrastructure. Google also built custom network hardware and software to improve performance as well as security. This all rolls up to Google's custom data center designs, which includes multiple layers of physical and logical protection.

Tracking provenance from the bottom of this hardware stack to the top enables Google to control the underpinnings of its security posture. This helps Google greatly reduce the "vendor in the middle problem;" if a vulnerability is found, steps can be immediately taken to develop and roll out a fix. This level of control results in greatly reduced exposure for both Google Cloud and its customers.

Network & Application Security

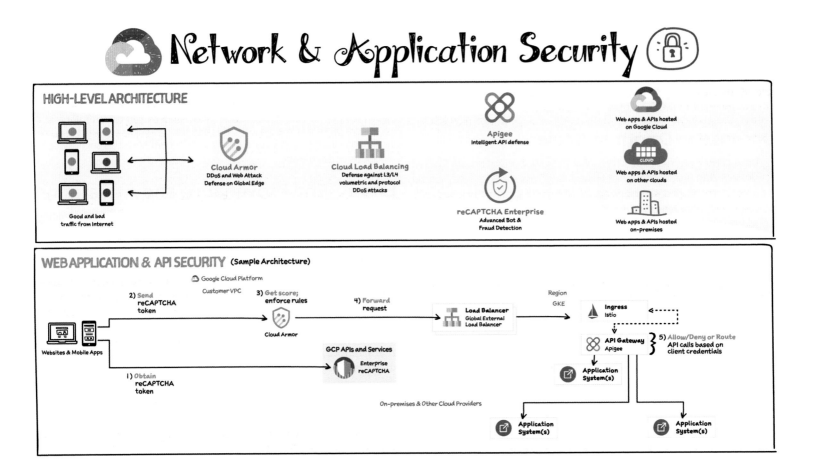

HIGH-LEVEL ARCHITECTURE

Good and bad traffic from Internet

Cloud Armor
DDoS and Web Attack Defense on Global Edge

Cloud Load Balancing
Defense against L3/L4 volumetric and protocol DDoS attacks

Apigee
Intelligent API defense

reCAPTCHA Enterprise
Advanced Bot & Fraud Detection

Web apps & APIs hosted on Google Cloud

Web apps & APIs hosted on other clouds

Web apps & APIs hosted on-premises

WEB APPLICATION & API SECURITY (Sample Architecture)

Google Cloud Platform

Customer VPC

Websites & Mobile Apps

2) Send reCAPTCHA token

1) Obtain reCAPTCHA token

3) Get score; enforce rules

Cloud Armor

GCP APIs and Services

Enterprise reCAPTCHA

4) Forward request

Load Balancer
Global External Load Balancer

Region

GKE

Ingress
Istio

API Gateway
Apigee

5) Allow/Deny or Route
API calls based on client credentials

Application System(s)

On-premises & Other Cloud Providers

Application System(s)

Application System(s)

Google owns and operates one of the largest backbone networks in the world to connect its data centers. When your traffic is on the Google network, it no longer transits the public Internet, making it less likely to be attacked, intercepted, or manipulated. Data is encrypted in transit, and the scale of the network provides robust denial-of-service protection. Along with this inherent network security, you have access to services that help protect your applications against network-based threats and attacks even further. Let's look at those services now.

Application Security

When you are building websites, web applications, or API-based services, you need to think about protecting them from different attacks such as the following:

- Bot Attacks — "Robot"/scripted attacks can be used to take down a site or used for fraud.
- Distributed Denial of Service (DDoS) Attacks — These attacks can cause unplanned application downtime.
- Credential Theft — This type of theft can take on many different forms, from phishing for people's usernames and passwords, to using leaked credentials to gain access to systems or accounts.
- Application Fraud — This can take on many forms, such as a bad actor using a stolen or fraudulent identity to make purchases (tickets, limited-release products) or to apply for credit cards or bank loans.
- API Attacks — These attacks can include DDoS attacks against an org's APIs or a bot or a bad actor attempting to utilize APIs to obtain sensitive information or to use the API for other malicious activities.

Cloud Load Balancing

When you use HTTP(S) Load Balancing, you are using a proxy-based Layer 7 load balancer that enables you to run and scale your services behind a single external IP address. The scale at which it operates provides automatic defense against Layer 3 and Layer 4 volumetric and protocol DDoS attacks. It also provides an SSL offload feature that enables you to centrally manage SSL certificates and decryption for the highest level of security between your load balancing and backend layers.

You can protect your Internet-facing applications against all these attacks by using Google Cloud's Web App and API protection (WAAP) solution. WAAP combines Cloud Armor, reCAPTCHA Enterprise, and Apigee to help you mitigate many common threats. Let's look at each of these in more detail.

DDoS Protection and Web Application Firewall: Cloud Armor

Cloud Armor works in conjunction with Cloud Load balancing and helps mitigate infrastructure DDoS attacks. It can filter incoming web requests by geography or by a host of L7 parameters such as request headers, cookies, or query strings. Each security policy in Cloud Armor is made up of a set of rules that filter traffic based on conditions such as an incoming request's IP address, IP range, region code, or request headers.

Cloud Armor is also a full-fledged web application firewall (WAF) and contains preconfigured rules from the ModSecurity Core Rule Set to prevent against the most common web attacks and vulnerability exploit attempts such as SQL injection and cross-site scripting. All decisions are logged to the Cloud Logging and Monitoring dashboard, which gives granular views of allowed, denied, or previewed traffic.

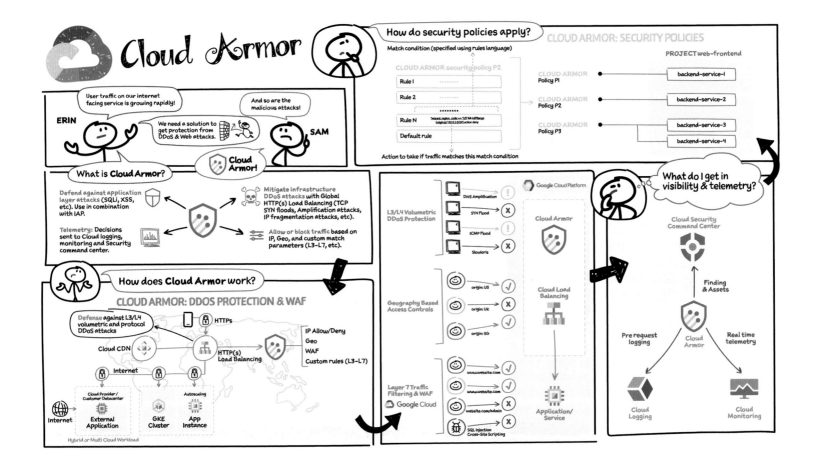

Cloud Armor

ERIN: User traffic on our internet facing service is growing rapidly!

We need a solution to get protection from DDoS & Web attacks.

And so are the malicious attacks!

SAM

Cloud Armor!

What is Cloud Armor?

Defend against application layer attacks (SQLi, XSS, etc). Use in combination with IAP.

Mitigate infrastructure DDoS attacks with Global HTTP(s) Load Balancing (TCP SYN floods, Amplification attacks, IP fragmentation attacks, etc).

Telemetry: Decisions sent to Cloud logging, monitoring and Security command center.

Allow or block traffic based on IP, Geo, and custom match parameters (L3-L7, etc).

How does Cloud Armor work?

CLOUD ARMOR: DDOS PROTECTION & WAF

Defense against L3/L4 volumetric and protocol DDoS attacks

Cloud CDN

HTTPs

HTTP(s) Load Balancing

IP Allow/Deny
Geo
WAF
Custom rules (L3-L7)

Internet

Internet — External Application — GKE Cluster — App Instance

Cloud Provider / Customer Datacenter

Autoscaling

Hybrid or Multi Cloud Workload

How do security policies apply?

Match condition (specified using rules language)

CLOUD ARMOR security policy P2

Rule 1	....
Rule 2	....
Rule N	"request_region_code == 'US' && ipRange (originip'192.0.2.0/24') action deny"
Default rule	

Action to take if traffic matches this match condition

CLOUD ARMOR: SECURITY POLICIES

PROJECT web-frontend

CLOUD ARMOR Policy P1 ●———— backend-service-1

CLOUD ARMOR Policy P2 ●———— backend-service-2

CLOUD ARMOR Policy P3 ●———— backend-service-3
backend-service-4

Google Cloud Platform

L3/L4 Volumetric DDoS Protection

DNS Amplification (!)
SYN Flood (X)
ICMP Flood (!)
Slowloris (X)

Cloud Armor

Geography Based Access Controls

origin: US (✓)
origin: UK (X)
origin: SG (✓)

Cloud Load Balancing

Layer 7 Traffic Filtering & WAF

Google Cloud

www.website.com (✓)
www.website.com (✓)
website.com/admin (X)
SQL Injection Cross-Site Scripting (X)

Application/ Service

What do I get in visibility & telemetry?

Cloud Security Command Center

Finding & Assets

Pre request logging

Real time telemetry

Cloud Armor

Cloud Logging

Cloud Monitoring

Bot and Fraud Protection with reCAPTCHA Enterprise

reCAPTCHA Enterprise is an Enterprise cloud service that provides fraud and bot protection. It leverages Google's learnings with the reCAPTCHA service that already protects millions of sites on the web. The system brings in many signals from a JavaScript client in a browser or SDK in an app and learns per site what is human versus bot activity. It is headless (which means it can work with any website backend) and does not require users to solve visual puzzles. The system provides a risk score, allowing for progressive action based on risk, such as requirement for a second factor, outright block or redirect, or letting humans in.

API Security with Apigee

The Apigee API management platform provides a single point of management for APIs through the entire life cycle from both a development and operations perspective. The platform inspects API requests to protect, scale, adapt, control, and monitor API traffic. Apigee's out-of-the-box policies enable you to augment APIs with features to control traffic, enhance performance, and enforce security without writing any code or modifying any backend services.

Building security for an API takes time and significant expertise, but Apigee security policies let developers control access to APIs with OAuth, API key validation, and other threat protection capabilities. Apigee provides a positive security model that understands the structure of API requests so that it can more accurately determine valid and invalid requests.

API traffic can be throttled by quotas to prevent misuse and to defend against DDoS attacks. For example, Apigee can rate-limit something like account signups or checkouts differently than search queries across a product catalog.

Sample Web Application and API Security Architecture

Here's a sample web application and API security architecture that could include these components:

1. When a user tries to log into the website or mobile app, the reCAPTCHA token is obtained.

2. reCAPTCHA Enterprise deciphers the token in the incoming request and enforces allow/deny decisions in Cloud Armor.

3. If Cloud Armor allows the request, then it is forwarded to Load Balancer.

4. Load Balancer then sends the request to the respective backend with Apigee API Gateway in the middle, which allows/denies or routes API calls based on client credentials and quotas.

Secure Software Development Lifecycle
ON GOOGLE CLOUD

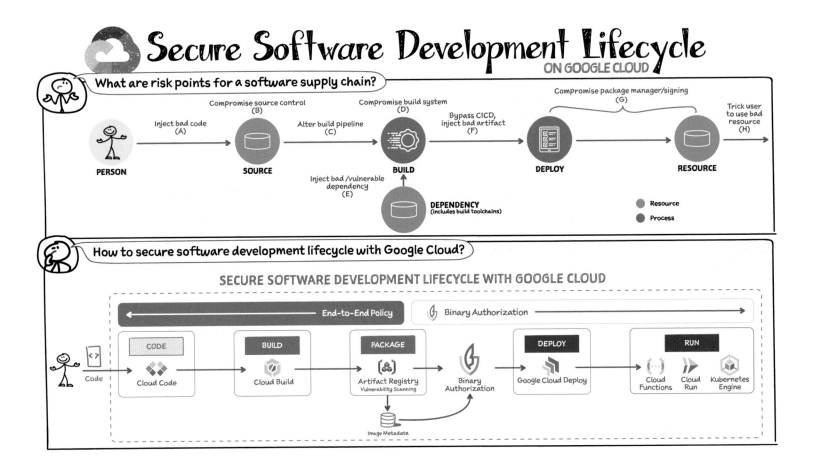

What are risk points for a software supply chain?

Inject bad code (A)

Compromise source control (B)

Alter build pipeline (C)

Compromise build system (D)

Inject bad /vulnerable dependency (E)

Bypass CICD, inject bad artifact (F)

Compromise package manager/signing (G)

Trick user to use bad resource (H)

PERSON · SOURCE · BUILD · DEPLOY · RESOURCE

DEPENDENCY (includes build toolchains)

Resource
Process

How to secure software development lifecycle with Google Cloud?

SECURE SOFTWARE DEVELOPMENT LIFECYCLE WITH GOOGLE CLOUD

End-to-End Policy

Binary Authorization

Code

CODE — Cloud Code

BUILD — Cloud Build

PACKAGE — Artifact Registry (Vulnerability Scanning)

Binary Authorization

DEPLOY — Google Cloud Deploy

RUN — Cloud Functions · Cloud Run · Kubernetes Engine

Image Metadata

Securing your software requires establishing, verifying, and maintaining a chain of trust. That chain establishes the provenance or origin trail of your code, via attestations, generated and checked throughout your software development and deployment process. At Google, the internal development process enables a level of ambient security, through code review, verified code provenance, and policy enforcement that minimizes software supply chain and related risks. These concepts go hand-in-hand with improved developer productivity. What are the security risk points in your software supply chain and how can you mitigate them with Google Cloud? Let's explore!

Risk Points for a Software Supply Chain

The software development and deployment supply chain is quite complicated, with numerous threats along the source code, build, and publish workflow. Here are some common threats that software development supply chains face:

- Submitting "bad" source code (includes compromising or coercing the developer)

- Compromising the source control platform, by gaining "admin" access, for example

- Injecting malicious behavior into the build pipeline, such as requesting a build from unsubmitted code or specifying build parameters that modify behavior

- Compromising the build platform to produce "bad" artifacts (in particular, many CI systems are not configured for "hostile multitenancy" within the same project, so an "owner" of a project can compromise their own builds without the team knowing)

- Injecting malicious behavior through a dependency (same attacks recursively)

- Deploying a "bad" artifact by bypassing CI/CD

- Compromising the package manager/signing platform

- Tricking users into using a "bad" resource instead of a legitimate one (for example, typosquatting)

- Modifying an artifact in transit or compromising the underlying infrastructure of any of development life-cycle systems

How Does Google Secure the Software Supply Chain Internally?

Google employs several practices to secure its software supply chain internally:

- Zero Trust (BeyondCorp) — the idea that implicit trust in any single component of a complex, interconnected system can create significant security risks

- Incidence and vulnerability response playbook — specifies actions, escalations, mitigation, resolution, and notification of any potential incidents impacting the confidentiality, integrity, or availability of customer data

- Binary Authorization on Borg — to reduce insider risk by ensuring that production software deployed at Google is properly reviewed and authorized, particularly if that code has the ability to access user data

What is SLSA?

Google Cloud is sharing these practices externally so that the whole community can benefit. SLSA (Supply-chain Levels for Software Artifacts) is an end-to-end framework for supply chain integrity. It is an OSS-friendly version of what Google has been doing internally. In its current state, SLSA is a set of incrementally adoptable security guidelines being established by industry consensus. In its final form, SLSA will differ from a list of best practices in its enforceability: it will support the automatic creation of auditable metadata that can be fed into policy engines to give "SLSA certification" to a particular package or build platform. SLSA is designed to be incremental and actionable, and to provide security benefits at every step. Once an artifact qualifies at the highest level, consumers can have confidence that it has not been tampered with and can be securely traced back to source—something that is difficult, if not impossible, to do with most software today. SLSA consists of four levels, with SLSA 4 representing the ideal end state. The lower levels represent incremental milestones with corresponding incremental integrity guarantees. The requirements are currently defined as follows:

	Requirement	Required at			
		SLSA 1	SLSA 2	SLSA 3	SLSA 4
Source	Version Controlled		✓	✓	✓
	Verified History			✓	✓
	Retained Indefinitely			18 mo.	✓
	Two-Person Reviewed				✓
Build	Scripted	✓	✓	✓	✓
	Build Service		✓	✓	✓
	Ephemeral Environment			✓	✓
	Isolated			✓	✓
	Parameterless				✓
	Hermetic				✓
	Reproducible				○
Provenance	Available	✓	✓	✓	✓
	Authenticated		✓	✓	✓
	Service Generated		✓	✓	✓
	Non-Falsifiable			✓	✓
	Dependencies Complete				✓
Common	Security				✓
	Access				✓
	Superusers				✓

○ = required unless there is a justification

How Does Google Cloud Help You Secure Your Software Supply Chain?

Securing your software supply chain involves defining, checking, and enforcing attestations across the software life cycle. Here is how it works.

Binary Authorization

A key element in software supply chain security is the Binary Authorization service, which establishes, verifies, and maintains a chain of trust via attestations and policy checks. Cryptographic signatures are generated as code or other artifacts move toward production. Before deployment, the attestations are checked based on policies.

Let's walk through the steps of how to achieve ambient security in your developer process through policies and provenance on Google Cloud. The first step is understanding your supply or what libraries and frameworks you use to write your code.

Code

Open source is heavily used in lots of software, and it can be challenging to determine the risk of open source dependencies. To help address this challenge, we recently launched Open Source Insights, an interactive visualization site for exploring open source software packages. Open Source Insights is unique in that it provides a transitive dependency graph, with continuously updated security advisory, license, and other data across multiple languages in one place. In conjunction with open source scorecards, which provide a risk score for open source projects, Open Source Insights can be used by developers to make better choices across millions of open source packages.

Build

Once your code is checked in, it is built by Cloud Build. Here, another set of attestations are captured, adding to your chain of trust. Examples include

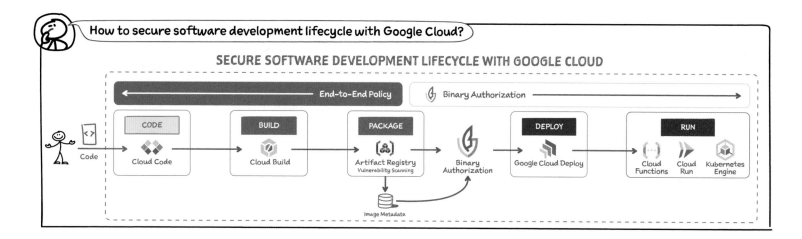

what tests were run and what build tools and processes were used. Cloud Build today helps with achieving a SLSA level 1, which denotes the level of security of your software supply chain. Cloud Build captures the source of the build configuration, which can be used to validate that the build was scripted (scripted builds are more secure than manual builds and this is a SLSA 1 requirement). Also as required, these provenance and other attestations can be looked up using the container image digest, which is a unique signature for an image.

Cloud Build is a fully managed cloud service. This means that in addition to developer agility, this service gives you a locked-down environment for securing builds, greatly reducing the risk of compromised build integrity or a compromised build system. You may also want to ensure you can enforce a security perimeter within your private network to keep data and access private. Cloud Build Private Pools adds support for VPC-SC and private IPs. You can take advantage of the locked-down serverless build environment within your own private network.

Test and Scan

Once the build is complete, it is stored in the Artifact Registry, where it is automatically scanned for vulnerabilities. This generates additional metadata, including an attestation for whether an artifact's vulnerability results meet certain security thresholds. This information is stored by Google's Container Analysis service, which structures and organizes an artifact's metadata, making it readily accessible to services like Binary Authorization.

Deploy and Run

Having built, stored, and scanned the images securely, you are ready to deploy. At this point attestations captured along the supply chain are verified for authenticity by Binary Authorization. In enforcement mode, the image is deployed only when the attestations meet your organization's policy. In audit mode, policy violations are logged and trigger alerts. Binary Authorization is available for GKE and Cloud Run (preview), ensuring that only properly reviewed and authorized code gets deployed. Verification doesn't stop at deployment. Binary Authorization also supports *continuous validation*, which ensures continued conformance to the defined policy even after deployment. If a running application falls out of conformance with an existing or newly added policy, an alert is triggered and logged.

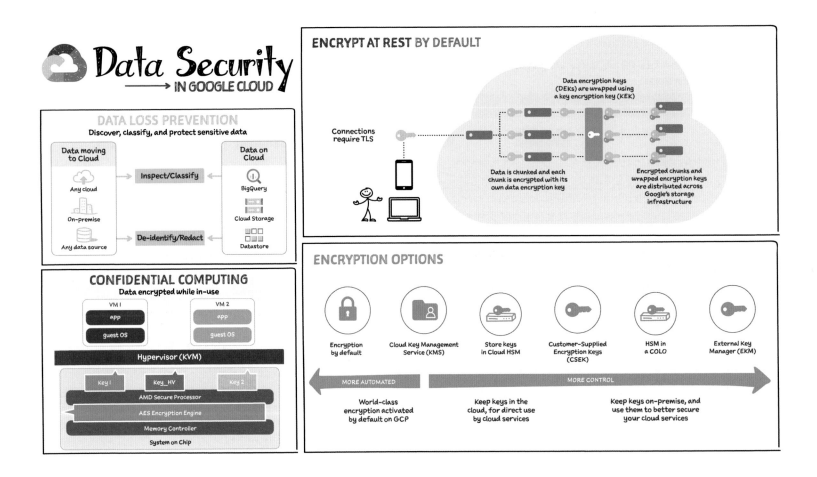

Data Security IN GOOGLE CLOUD

DATA LOSS PREVENTION
Discover, classify, and protect sensitive data

Data moving to Cloud
- Any cloud
- On-premise
- Any data source

Inspect/Classify

De-identify/Redact

Data on Cloud
- BigQuery
- Cloud Storage
- Datastore

CONFIDENTIAL COMPUTING
Data encrypted while in-use

VM 1
- app
- guest OS

VM 2
- app
- guest OS

Hypervisor (KVM)

Key 1 — Key_HV — Key 2

AMD Secure Processor

AES Encryption Engine

Memory Controller

System on Chip

ENCRYPT AT REST BY DEFAULT

Connections require TLS

Data encryption keys (DEKs) are wrapped using a key encryption key (KEK)

Data is chunked and each chunk is encrypted with its own data encryption key

Encrypted chunks and wrapped encryption keys are distributed across Google's storage infrastructure

ENCRYPTION OPTIONS

| Encryption by default | Cloud Key Management Service (KMS) | Store keys in Cloud HSM | Customer-Supplied Encryption Keys (CSEK) | HSM in a COLO | External Key Manager (EKM) |

MORE AUTOMATED ← → MORE CONTROL

World-class encryption activated by default on GCP

Keep keys in the cloud, for direct use by cloud services

Keep keys on-premise, and use them to better secure your cloud services

Data security is a huge part of an organization's security posture. Encryption is a core control for data security, and Google Cloud offers multiple encryption options for data at-rest, in-transit, and even in-use. Let's shed some light on each of these.

Encryption

Encryption at Rest by Default

To help protect your data, Google encrypts data at rest, ensuring that it can be accessed only by authorized roles and services, with audited access to the encryption keys. Data is encrypted prior to it being written to disk. Here's how:

- Data is first "chunked" — broken up into pieces — and each chunk is encrypted with its own data encryption key.
- Each data encryption key is wrapped using a key encryption key. The encrypted chunks and wrapped encryption keys are then distributed across Google's storage infrastructure.
- If a chunk of data is updated, it is encrypted with a new key, rather than by reusing the existing key.

When data needs to be retrieved, the process repeats in reverse. As a result, if an attacker were to compromise an individual key or gain physical access to storage, they would still be unable to read customer data, since they'd need to identify all the data chunks in an object, retrieve them, and retrieve the associated encryption keys.

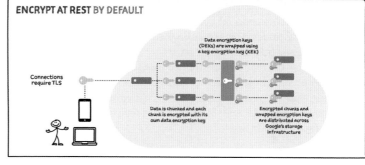

Encryption in Transit by Default

All communications over the Internet to Google Cloud require properly terminated Transport Layer Security (TLS) connections. Encryption in transit protects your data if communications are intercepted while data moves between your site and the cloud provider or between two services. This protection is achieved by encrypting the data before transmission; authenticating the endpoints; and decrypting and verifying the data on arrival. For example, TLS is often used to encrypt data in transit for transport security, and Secure/Multipurpose Internet Mail Extensions (S/MIME) is used often for email message security.

Encryption in Use: Confidential Computing

Confidential Computing adds a "third pillar" that protects your data in memory from compromise or exfiltration by encrypting data while it's being processed. You can encrypt your data in-use with Confidential VMs and Confidential GKE Nodes. This builds on the protections Shielded VMs offer against rootkit and bootkits.

Main memory encryption is performed using dedicated hardware within on-die memory controllers. Each controller includes a high-performance AES engine. The AES engine encrypts data as it is written to DRAM or shared between sockets, and decrypts it when data is read. Google does not have access to the encryption key.

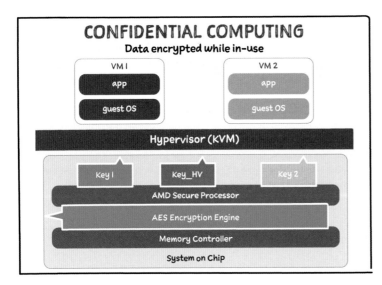

At-Rest Encryption Options

While in some cases the encryption by default might be all you need, Google Cloud provides other options for customers based on their trust level and business needs.

Customer-Supplied Encryption Keys (CSEKs)

If you need to operate with minimal trust, you can use customer-supplied encryption keys (CSEKs), which enable you to maintain your own separate root of trust and push keys at time of use to Google Cloud via an API. Those keys are stored in RAM during the time required to perform the specific operation.

With CSEKs, the burden and responsibility of protecting and not losing keys falls to you. Google has no way to recover your data if your keys are inadvertently deleted or lost. It is very easy to get this wrong. So, if you use CSEKs, then you need to be exceedingly careful and must also invest in your own key distribution system to push keys to Google to match the rate of use in your applications.

Key Management Service (Cloud KMS)

Another option is Cloud Key Management Service, which you can use to leverage Google's globally scalable key management system while maintaining control of key operations, including full audit logging of your keys. This solution alleviates the need for you to create your own key distribution system while still enabling you to control the visibility of your keys.

With KMS, keys created and maintained in Cloud KMS are used as the key-encryption keys in place of Google's default key-encryption keys.

Hardware Security Modules (HSMs)

You can also optionally store keys in a cloud-hosted hardware security module service that allows you to host encryption keys and perform cryptographic operations in a cluster of FIPS 140-2 Level 3 certified HSMs. Google manages the HSM cluster for you, so you don't need to worry about clustering, scaling, or patching. Because Cloud HSM uses Cloud KMS as its frontend, you can leverage all the conveniences and features that Cloud KMS provides.

Cloud External Key Manager (Cloud EKM)

With Cloud EKM, you can use encryption keys that you manage within a supported external key management partner to protect data within Google Cloud. Here's how it works:

1. First, you create or use an existing key in a supported external key management partner system. This key has a unique URI.
2. Next, you grant your Google Cloud project access to use the key in the external key management partner system.
3. In your Google Cloud project, you create a Cloud EKM key, using the URI for the externally managed key.

The Cloud EKM key and the external key management partner key work together to protect your data. The external key is never exposed to Google.

Other Data Security Services

Apart from data encryption, some other services that come in handy for data security in Google Cloud:

- VPC Service Controls, which mitigate data exfiltration risks by isolating multitenant services
- Data Loss Prevention, which helps discover, classify, and protect sensitive data.

For a more in-depth look into how encryption at rest and in transit works across Google's various services, check out the whitepapers.

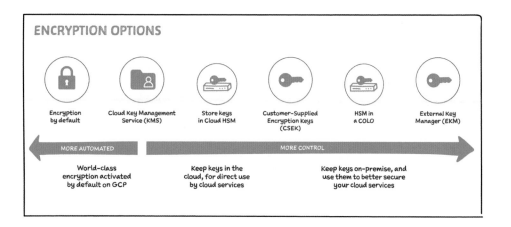

ENCRYPTION OPTIONS

| Encryption by default | Cloud Key Management Service (KMS) | Store keys in Cloud HSM | Customer-Supplied Encryption Keys (CSEK) | HSM in a COLO | External Key Manager (EKM) |

MORE AUTOMATED ← → MORE CONTROL

World-class encryption activated by default on GCP | Keep keys in the cloud, for direct use by cloud services | Keep keys on-premise, and use them to better secure your cloud services

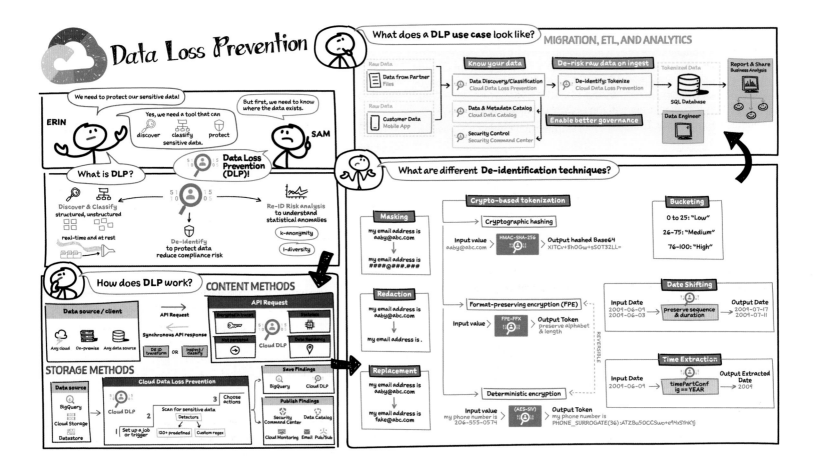

Sensitive data can show up in unexpected places — for example, customers might inadvertently send you sensitive data in a customer support chat or file upload. And if you're using data for analytics and machine learning, it's imperative that sensitive data be handled appropriately to protect users' privacy. It's important to take a holistic look at where your data resides and how it's being used, and then create processes to ensure it's being handled appropriately. That's where Cloud DLP comes in.

What Is DLP?

Cloud Data Loss Prevention (DLP) is a fully managed service designed to discover, classify, and protect your sensitive data in text-based content and images. It helps provide visibility and classify your sensitive data across your entire organization. It reduces data risk by inspecting and transforming structured and unstructured data using obfuscation and deidentification methods like masking and tokenization. You can run reidentification analyses to enhance your understanding of data privacy risk. Reidentification risk analysis is the process of analyzing data to find properties or demographics that might increase the risk of subjects being identified. Consider, for example, a marketing dataset that includes demographic properties like age, job title, and zip code. On the surface these demographics may not seem identifying, but some combination of age, job title, and zip code could uniquely map to a small group of individuals or a single person and thus increase the risk of that person being reidentified. This analysis includes measurement of statistical properties such as k-anonymity and l-diversity, expanding your ability to understand and protect data privacy.

How Does It Work?

Cloud DLP offers multiple interfaces, including an API for incorporating it into existing systems and a console UI for easy, code-free integration. Content API methods provide the ability for customers to inspect and transform data anywhere and allow for real-time interactions such as protecting live traffic. Storage methods for BigQuery, Cloud Storage, and Datastore have both UI and API interfaces for analysis and are good for scanning large amounts of data at rest. Automatic DLP for BigQuery from the UI, for example, can automate the discovery and classification of an entire GCP organization and runs continuously to give visibility into data risk.

Inspection and classification is powered by Google Cloud's Data Loss Prevention technology, which has detectors for over 150 built-in information types, provides a rich set of customization and detection rules, and supports a variety of formats, including structured tables, unstructured text, and image data using OCR.

A Variety of Deidentification Techniques

Cloud DLP offers several deidentification techniques that can help obscure sensitive information while preserving some utility:

- **Masking** — Masks a string either fully or partially by replacing a given number of characters with a specified fixed character. This technique can, for example, mask everything but the last four digits of an account number or Social Security number.

- **Redaction** — Redacts a value by removing it.

- **Replacement** — Replaces each input value with a given value.

- **Pseudonymization with secure hash** — Replaces input values with a secure one-way hash generated using a data encryption key.

- **Pseudonymization with format-preserving token** — Replaces an input value with a "token," or surrogate value, of the same character set and length using format-preserving encryption (FPE). Preserving the format can help ensure compatibility with legacy systems that have restricted schema or format requirements.

- **Generalization bucketing** — Masks input values by replacing them with "buckets," or ranges, within which the input value falls. For example, you can bucket specific ages into age ranges or distinct values into ranges like "low," "medium," and "high."

- **Date shifting** — Shifts dates by a random number of days per user or entity. This helps obfuscate actual dates while still preserving the sequence and duration of a series of events or transactions.

- **Time extraction** — Extracts or preserves a portion of Date, Timestamp, and TimeOfDay values.

Cloud DLP's deidentification methods can handle both structured and unstructured data obfuscation to help you add an additional layer of data protection and privacy to virtually any workload.

Identity and Access Management (Authentication)

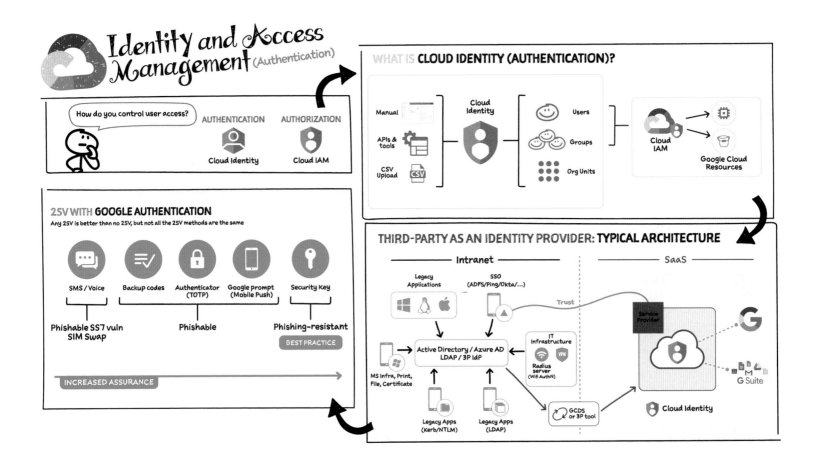

How do you control user access?

AUTHENTICATION — Cloud Identity

AUTHORIZATION — Cloud IAM

WHAT IS CLOUD IDENTITY (AUTHENTICATION)?

Manual

APIs & tools

CSV Upload — CSV

Cloud Identity

Users

Groups

Org Units

Cloud IAM

Google Cloud Resources

2SV WITH GOOGLE AUTHENTICATION

Any 2SV is better than no 2SV, but not all the 2SV methods are the same

SMS / Voice | Backup codes | Authenticator (TOTP) | Google prompt (Mobile Push) | Security Key

Phishable SS7 vuln SIM Swap — Phishable — Phishing-resistant

BEST PRACTICE

INCREASED ASSURANCE

THIRD-PARTY AS AN IDENTITY PROVIDER: TYPICAL ARCHITECTURE

Intranet | **SaaS**

Legacy Applications

SSO (ADFS/Ping/Okta/...)

Trust

Service Provider

MS Infra, Print, File, Certificate

Active Directory / Azure AD LDAP / 3P IdP

IT Infrastructure

Radius server (Wifi AuthN)

Legacy Apps (Kerb/NTLM)

Legacy Apps (LDAP)

GCDS or 3P tool

Cloud Identity

G Suite

In security, the three "A"s of controlling access are authentication (Who is the user?), authorization (What is the user allowed to do?), and auditing (What are they doing?) Going a bit deeper:

- **Authentication (AuthN):** Authentication is the process of identifying a user through a private form of verification (for example, a password, a certificate, a key, and so on). In Google Cloud, Cloud Identity performs authentication.

- **Authorization (AuthZ):** Authentication on its own provides no set of permissions; authorization is used to set permissions that a user is allocated after authentication. In Google Cloud, Cloud IAM is used for authorization (and Cloud Identity for assigning admin roles with broad default permissions).

- **Auditing:** Auditing is about monitoring the resources accessed or modified by a particular identity. In Google Cloud, Cloud Audit Logging helps with auditing resources and the Reports API helps auditing in Cloud Identity operations.

This section is focused on authentication.

What Is Cloud Identity?

Cloud Identity is the identity provider (IdP) for Google Cloud. It also is the identity-as-a-service (IDaaS) solution that powers Google Workspace. It stores and manages digital identities for Google Cloud users. When you migrate to or start using Cloud Identity, you create a free account for each of your users from the Google Admin console. Cloud Identity provides user life-cycle management, account security, and single sign-on (SSO) support.

Setting up Cloud Identity is a prerequisite to onboarding your organization onto Google Cloud. Here's how it works:

- Upon setting up your Cloud Identity instance, you will be asked to add a domain that you own (typically your company's main domain).

- You will be asked to validate that you own this domain; this is most typically done by adding a TXT record in your DNS records.

- Once this validation is complete, a Google Cloud organization will be created with the same name as your domain and you can begin using Google Cloud.

How Cloud Identity Connects with Google Cloud

There are a variety of ways in which identities can be imported into Cloud Identity: manually, through a CSV file/export, or using APIs and tools. Once set up, users and groups will be used by Cloud IAM to grant access to Google Cloud resources. It's important to understand that Cloud Identity roles are used for user/group management and are distinct from Google Cloud IAM roles, which manage permissions to cloud resources. This distinction is covered in the Cloud IAM section next.

Authentication Options

Aside from username and password, there are two frequently used authentication options:

2-Step Verification (2SV) with Google Authentication

2-Step Verification adds a second factor for authentication in addition to a username and password. Any 2SV is better than no 2SV, but not all the 2SV methods are the same. SMS, backup codes, one-time passwords (OTPs), and mobile push prompts provide additional protection but they are still phishable. FIDO Universal 2nd Factor (U2F) security keys are highly phishing-resistant. The U2F protocol uses cryptography to verify a user's identity and URLs of the website that is being accessed. Keys stay on the device so there are no server-side shared secrets to steal, which protects against phishing, man-in-the-middle, and replay attacks.

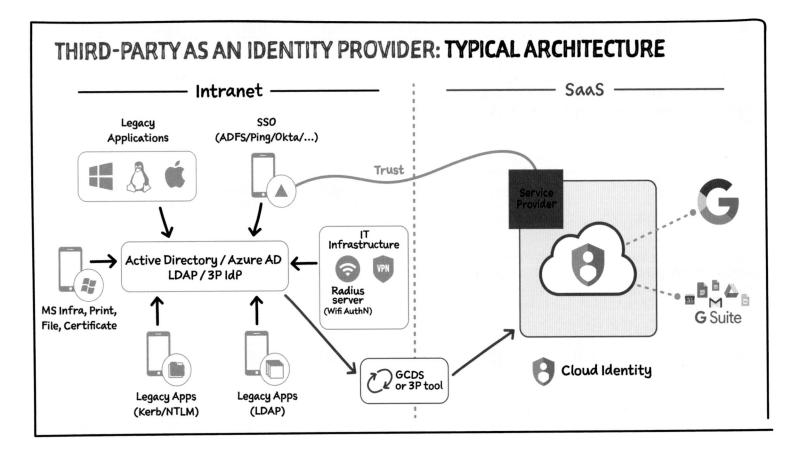

THIRD-PARTY AS AN IDENTITY PROVIDER: **TYPICAL ARCHITECTURE**

Google recommends security keys for best-in-class security. Further, security keys should be considered *mandatory* for admins for optimal security. Google offers the Titan Security Key, which includes special firmware engineered by Google to verify the key's integrity. Android and iOS devices can also be used as security keys (Bluetooth is required). With the Titan Security Key, the user experience is similar to signing on via the Google prompt but the protection is stronger, because the key uses the FIDO U2F protocol.

Cloud Identity also offers the possibility to require 2SV with a third-party IdP (e.g., Azure AD or Okta). For example, with this option a user will log in to Azure AD by entering their password, and after a successful SAML exchange between the IdP (Azure AD) and Google they will be challenged with the 2SV method set up in Google as an extra authentication step.

SSO Authentication with a Third-Party Identity Provider

You can also delegate authentication using SSO to a third-party SAML 2.0-compliant identity provider, such as Okta, Ping, Active Directory Federation Services (AD FS), or Azure AD. This method normally means faster Google Cloud onboarding and less disruption if you are already using a compatible IdP.

User experience

To an employee, the sign-on user experience looks like this:

- Upon requesting a protected resource, the employee is redirected to the Google Sign-In screen, which prompts them for their email address.

- Google Sign-In redirects you to the sign-in page of your IDaaS.

- You authenticate with your IDaaS. Depending on your IDaaS, this might require you to provide a second factor such as a code.

- After you are authenticated, you are redirected back to the protected resource.

Advantages

Using an external IDaaS as IdP and authoritative source has the following advantages:

- You enable a single sign-on experience for your employees that extends across Google services and other applications that are integrated with your IDaaS.

- If you configured your IDaaS to require multi-factor authentication, that configuration automatically applies to Google Cloud.

- You don't need to synchronize passwords or other credentials with Google.

- You can use the free version of Cloud Identity.

- When to use this architecture.

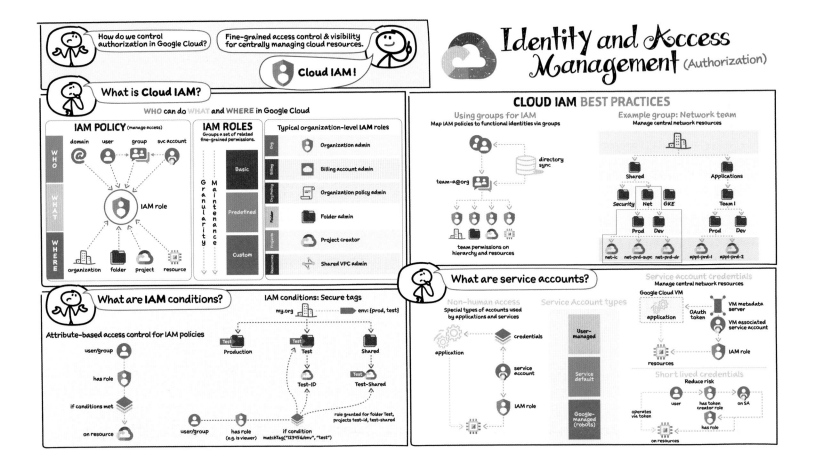

Once you have identified who a user is (authenticated them) using Cloud Identity, the next step is to define what they can do on Google Cloud (authorize them) so they can access the resources they are permitted to use. Access control for Google Cloud resources is managed by Cloud IAM policies for humans and by service accounts for applications and services. Let's take a closer look at Cloud IAM and service accounts.

What Is Cloud IAM?

Cloud IAM helps define *who* can do *what* and *where* on Google Cloud. It provides fine-grained access control and visibility for centrally managing cloud resources.

IAM policies manage access control for Google Cloud resources. They are collections of IAM bindings, each one "binding" together a principal, a role, and the resource to which the policy is attached. What is commonly thought of as an authorization group is an IAM binding on Google Cloud: the union of an identity group and a role, bound to a specific resource or hierarchy node. Binding principals can be:

- an org domain, granting the role to all org members
- a Workspace/Cloud Identity user
- a Workspace/Cloud Identity group
- a service account (described later)

IAM roles group a set of related fine-grained permissions. There are three types of roles:

- **Basic** roles are easy to understand and apply but include broad permissions and scope. For example, *owner* includes *editor* permissions.

- **Predefined** roles map well to the model of "which services users are allowed to use." They provide a narrower per-service permissions scope; they require a bit more effort but are safer than primitive basic roles.

- **Custom roles** enable you to define custom-defined permissions scopes at the organization, project, or service level. Although this is the most secure option, it requires substantial maintenance effort to manage dependencies and updates.

IAM Conditions: IAM policies can also be bound to conditions based on resource and request attributes. This allows for the following use cases:

- Time-limited access; for example: only allow access during working hours
- Access to a subset of resources; for example: grant access only to VMs prefixed with 'webapp-frontend-'
- Network address space; for example: only allow access from the corporate network

IAM Conditions also enable granular control on which roles can be assigned or revoked. In practice this means centrally controlling which services (via IAM roles) users can use in their projects, but still giving autonomy to the teams to manage permissions directly on their projects (as long as those permissions are for the approved services).

IAM Conditions also support secure tags. Tags are access-controlled key-value resources defined at the organization level, which can be associated with hierarchy nodes (organization, folders, projects). Once tags are associated with a node, they can be set in IAM Conditions to scope role assignment to relevant nodes.

CLOUD IAM BEST PRACTICES

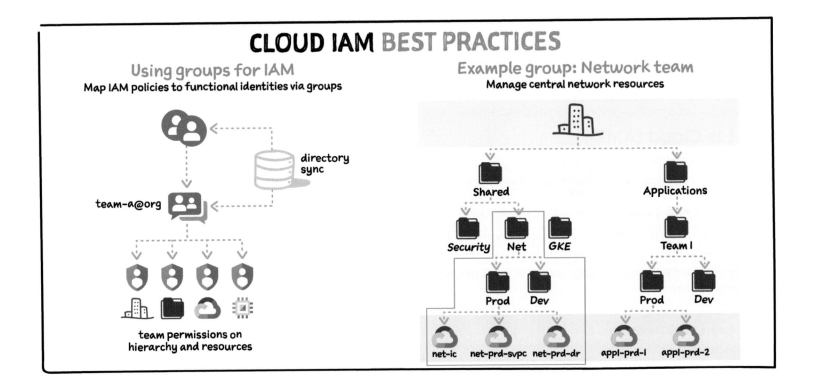

Using groups for IAM
Map IAM policies to functional identities via groups

directory sync

team-a@org

team permissions on hierarchy and resources

Example group: Network team
Manage central network resources

Shared

Applications

Security Net GKE

Team 1

Prod Dev

Prod Dev

net-ic net-prd-svpc net-prd-dr appl-prd-1 appl-prd-2

Cloud IAM best practices

When using Cloud IAM, you should map IAM policies to functional identities using groups:

- Use individual identity groups as recipients of functional sets of IAM roles, with clear permission scopes and boundaries (org, folder, project, resource).

- Use groups to mirror on-premises workflows (networking, DevOps, etc.) or map to new cloud-specific workflows.

- Sync groups from your source of truth so that its join/leave process is shared.

- Define and enforce a naming convention for group names.

- Minimize the points where IAM policies are applied by using folders.

- Optionally nest groups when specific cross-team functions are shared across different teams.

- Optionally enforce domain membership via the iam.allowedPolicyMemberDomains organizational policy.

What Are Service Accounts?

Service accounts are a special type of account used by applications and services. Nonhuman access to Google Cloud APIs and services is usually done through service accounts. They are created and managed within projects like most other resources. Because they are typically used by services, they don't have an associated password and cannot log in through a browser or cookies.

Authentication is done via private/public key pairs (either Google or customer-managed) or identity federation. They can be impersonated by either regular users or other service accounts (via IAM roles).

Service Account Types

Some types of service accounts are built into Google Cloud services:

- **User-managed:** Created by you and managed like all other resources. No IAM role is assigned by default. Can be used via key, VM association, or impersonation.

- **Service default:** Created at API activation. Used by default when no customer service account is selected. For example, Compute Engine has a default service account for VMs. They have a fixed naming convention, and an editor IAM role is assigned at creation.

- **Google-managed** (robots or service agents): Created at API activation. Used by Google Cloud services to perform actions on customer resources so that they are created with specific IAM roles assigned. The Compute Engine robot account is an example of a Google-managed service account.

Service Account Credentials

There are different ways of managing and accessing service account credentials:

Google-managed keys: Both the public and private portions of the key pair are stored in Google Cloud, auto-rotated, and secured. They can be used by associating a service account with a VM or other compute service, or by impersonation from a different identity.

User-managed keys: You (as the customer) own both public and private portions and are responsible for rotating and securing them. Key pairs can be created from Google Cloud, or created externally and the public portion uploaded to Google Cloud. Used via the customer-managed private key.

Key creation can be limited via organization policies.

It is a best practice to use short-lived credentials when you need to grant limited access to resources for trusted identities.

What are service accounts?

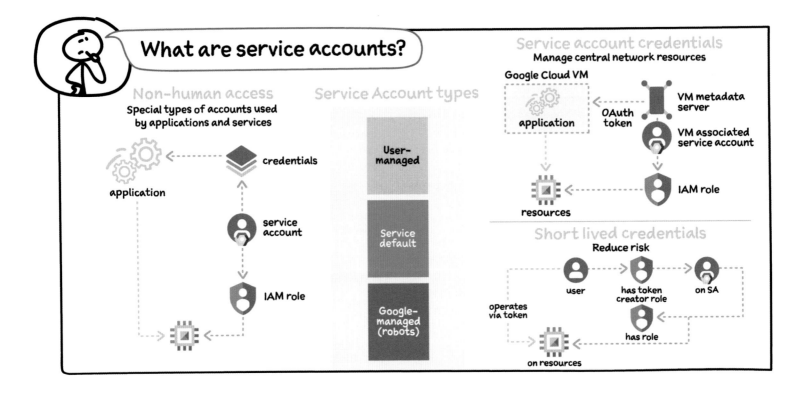

Non-human access

Special types of accounts used by applications and services

application → credentials

service account

IAM role

Service Account types

- User-managed
- Service default
- Google-managed (robots)

Service account credentials

Manage central network resources

Google Cloud VM

application ← OAuth token ← VM metadata server

VM associated service account

IAM role

resources

Short lived credentials

Reduce risk

user → has token creator role → on SA

operates via token

has role

on resources

Service Account Best Practices

- From a workflow perspective, the default service account is generous with permissions (i.e., Project Editor). It's a good idea to create app-specific accounts and only grant needed permissions.

- Service accounts can be used for selective applications to apply firewalls. For example: Open port 443 (HTTPS) for VMs for service account 'webapp-fe'.

- Create service accounts on dedicated projects for centralized management.

- A major security risk related to user-managed keys is keys being compromised, either maliciously or by mistakenly publishing keys by embedding them in code. To help mitigate this risk, rotate keys frequently.

- VPC Service Controls help limit who can access Google Cloud services (which is what service accounts are ultimately for). For example: Access only permitted from on-prem IP ranges (when interconnecting). This greatly minimizes your attack surface.

- Combine service accounts with a proactive approach by using Forseti to alert on old keys that need to be rotated.

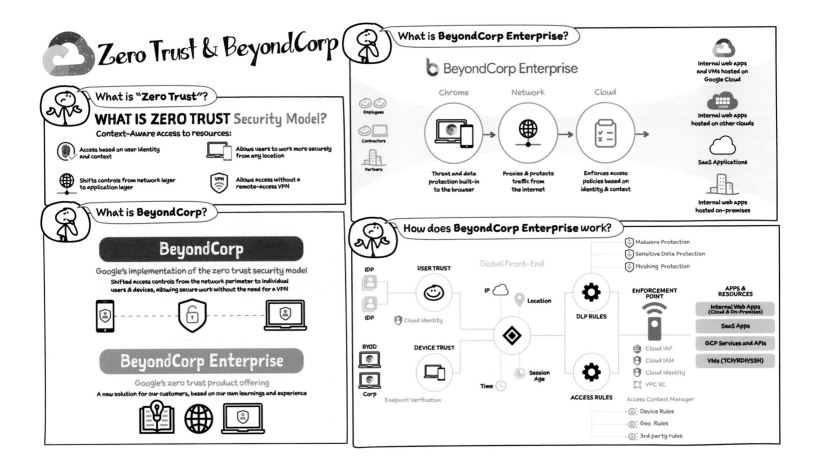

What Is BeyondCorp?

In 2011, Google came up with a new approach for enterprise access management: the BeyondCorp implementation of the zero trust security model. It started as an internal Google initiative to enable every employee to work from untrusted networks without the use of a VPN. BeyondCorp shifts access decisions from the network perimeter to individual users and devices, thereby enabling employees to work more securely from any location and transforming the way they work.

What Is BeyondCorp Enterprise?

BeyondCorp Enterprise is Google Cloud's commercial implementation of a zero trust access model. With this model, no one can access your resources unless they meet all the rules and conditions codified in per-resource access policies. Basically, Google wants to help your workforce access your applications and resources in a secure, yet simple way. How do they do that?

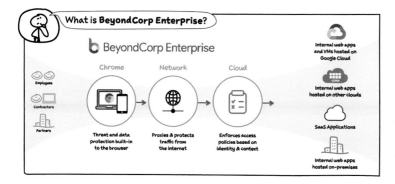

Employees use Chrome (or a Chromium-based browser) with built-in threat and data protection as they would normally to access applications and resources. The Google network protects and proxies traffic to resources and enables organizations to enforce context-aware policies (using factors such as identity, device information, location, time of day, the network the employee is using, and so on) to authorize access.

BeyondCorp Enterprise provides two essential capabilities:

- Richer access controls protect access to systems (applications, virtual machines, APIs, and so on) by using the context of an end user's request to ensure each request is authenticated, authorized, and as safe as possible.

- Threat and data protection brings security to your enterprise devices by working to protect users from exfiltration risks such as copy and paste, extending data loss prevention (DLP) into the browser, and helping to prevent malware from getting onto enterprise-managed devices.

How Does BeyondCorp Enterprise Work?

Identity Aware Proxy (IAP) is the core of BeyondCorp Enterprise, letting you grant access to your HTTPS apps and resources. Once you've set up your apps and resources behind IAP, your organization can craft granular access policies that IAP will enforce. BeyondCorp Enterprise can limit access based on properties like user device attributes, time of day, and request path.

BeyondCorp Enterprise works by building on four Google Cloud offerings:

- Identity-Aware Proxy (IAP): A Google offering that enables employees to access corporate apps and resources from untrusted networks without the use of a VPN

- Identity and Access Management (IAM): The identity management and authorization service for Google Cloud

- Access Context Manager: A rules engine that enables fine-grained access control through defined tiers of access

- Endpoint Verification: A Google Chrome extension that collects user device state and metadata

Gathering Device Information

Endpoint Verification gathers employee device information, including encryption status, OS, and user details. Once it's enabled through the Google Admin Console, you can deploy the Endpoint Verification Chrome extension to corporate devices. Employees can also install it on their managed

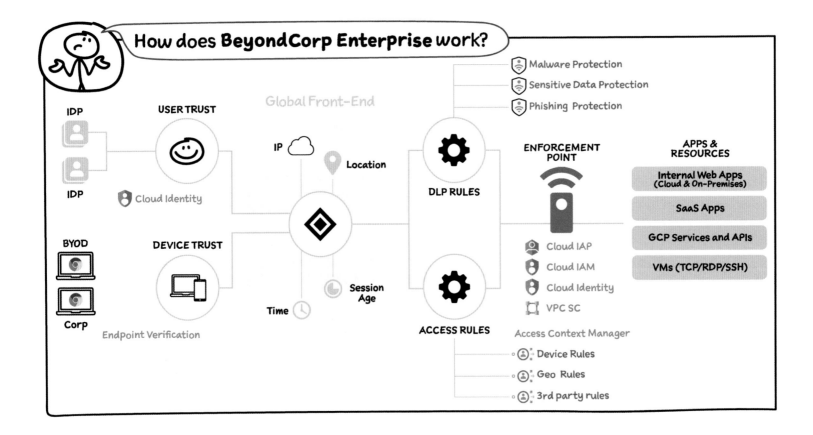

personal devices. This extension gathers and reports device information. The end result is an inventory of all the corporate and personal devices accessing your corporate resources.

Limiting Access

Through Access Context Manager, you create access levels to define access rules. Access levels applied on your resources with IAM Conditions enforce fine-grained access control based on a variety of attributes, including IP subnetwork, region, principal, and device attributes.

When you create a device-based access level, Access Context Manager references the inventory of devices created by Endpoint Verification. For example, an access level can restrict access to only employees who are using encrypted devices. Coupled with IAM Conditions, you could increase the granularity of this access level by allowing access only between 9:00 a.m. and 5:00 p.m.

Securing Resources with IAP

IAP ties everything together by letting you apply IAM Conditions on Google Cloud resources. IAP lets you establish a central authorization layer for your Google Cloud resources accessed by HTTPS and SSH/TCP traffic. With IAP, you can establish a resource-level access control model instead of relying on network-level firewalls. Once secured, your resources are accessible to any employee, from any device, on any network, as long as that employee, network, and device all meet the access rules and conditions.

Applying IAM Conditions

IAM Conditions enable you to define and enforce conditional, attribute-based access control for Google Cloud resources. With IAM Conditions, you can choose to grant permissions to principals only if configured conditions are met. IAM Conditions can limit access with a variety of attributes, including access levels. Conditions are specified in the IAP role bindings of a resource's IAM policy.

BeyondProd Since a user's credentials can be captured by bad actors, a security model that focuses on the perimeter is inadequate. Likewise, any software that interacts with the larger world needs protection on many levels. That's why it makes sense to apply a zero trust approach to how you operate your production environment, encompassing the way software is conceived, produced, managed, and interacts with other software. Google published a whitepaper on their BeyondProd model to explain how they protect their cloud-native architecture and to help organizations learn to apply zero trust security principles to this domain.

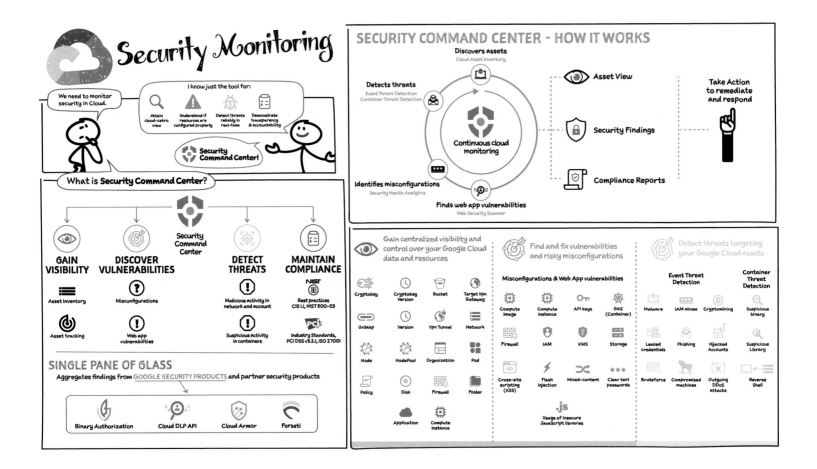

Moving to the cloud comes with the fundamental question of how to effectively manage security and risk posture. From a security operations (SecOps) perspective, there are few core requirements that you would need for effective security and risk management in the cloud. Here are four big ones that are essential for SecOps:

- Need a single, security-centric view of all the cloud resources and policies in your environment

- Know if resources and policies are configured as expected

- Detect threats reliably so your workloads are safe

- Demonstrate on an ongoing basis that you're maintaining compliance, transparency, and accountability

Security Command Center is focused on addressing these pillars.

What Is Security Command Center?

Security Command Center is a native security and risk management platform for Google Cloud. Security Command Center continuously monitors your Google Cloud environment, allowing you to:

- Gain visibility — You get real-time monitoring for all Google Cloud resources.

- Discover Vulnerabilities — It detects misconfigurations on your resources and vulnerabilities associated with your web apps (e.g., the OWASP Top 10).

- Detect Threats — It helps detect external threats that are targeted at your environment, such as malicious activity targeting your Google Cloud resources and unauthorized behavior across your organization.

- Maintain Compliance — It helps address industry benchmarks and standards with ongoing reports that tie key technical controls to the vulnerabilities and misconfigurations.

How Does Security Command Center work?

Security Command Center features various built-in services that roll up to a single pane of glass to allow oversight of your security in Google Cloud.

- It discovers assets in your Google Cloud environment using Cloud Asset Inventory. Cloud Asset Inventory is tightly integrated with Security Command Center, enabling you to discover, monitor, and analyze all your assets in one place.

- It identifies misconfigurations in your Google Cloud environment using a built-in service called Security Health Analytics. It also ties those findings to the industry standard and compliance benchmarks.

- It finds web app vulnerabilities using Web Security Scanner, which automatically detects web applications running in Google Cloud and starts scanning them for vulnerabilities.

- It detects threats using Event Threat Detection, a service that analyzes platform logs for identifying malicious activity, and the Container Threat Detection service to surface top suspicious activity in container deployments.

Security Command Center's continuous monitoring and analysis automatically provides you with these key deliverables for you to effectively manage security and risk:

- An **asset view** that provides a real-time view of your resources and policies, changes to your inventory, and the security findings associated with each of those assets.

- A consolidated set of **security findings** that span across misconfigurations, vulnerabilities, and threats to your Google Cloud environment. Security Command Center gives you a prioritized security findings view that helps you address potential security issues.

- A view from the **compliance** lens as to where you stand by correlating all its tracked misconfigurations and vulnerabilities to industry standards like CIS, PCI DSS, NIST 800-53, and ISO 27001. Security Command Center provides compliance reporting segmented by these standards that you can use to track how your environment compares with the technical controls of these industry-recommended benchmarks.

Security Command Center also gives you recommendations and remediation steps for you to take action. You can also send these findings to your security ecosystem such as the security orchestration, automation, and response (SOAR) or the security information and event management (SIEM) platform.

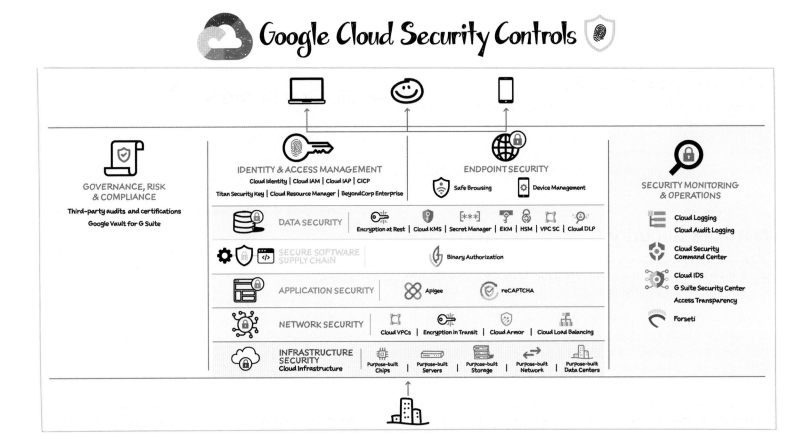

As you saw at the beginning of this chapter, security is a layered approach. Now, let's see how Google Cloud provides capabilities across the various layers of security.

Infrastructure Security

Google's stack builds security through progressive layers that deliver true defense in depth at scale. Google's hardware infrastructure is custom-designed "from chip to chiller" to precisely meet specific requirements. Its software and OS are stripped-down, hardened versions of Linux. Titan purpose-built chips help establish a hardware root of trust. This end-to-end provenance and attestation helps Google greatly reduce the "vendor in the middle" problem.

Network Security

Network security is partly the cloud provider's responsibility and partly yours. Providers work to make sure the traffic is secure and encrypted and that the communication with other services on the public Internet are secure. They also offer strong baseline protection against network attacks.

You are responsible for defining and enforcing your application perimeter, segmentation of your projects between teams and organizations, managing remote access for your employees, and implementing additional DoS defense.

- Google Cloud Virtual Private Cloud (VPC) offers private connectivity between multiple regions without communicating across the public Internet. You can use a single VPC for an entire organization, isolated within projects.

- VPC flow logs capture information about IP traffic to and from network interfaces and help with network monitoring, forensics, real-time security analysis, and expense optimization.

- Shared VPC helps configure a VPC network to be shared across several projects in your organization. Connectivity routes and firewalls are managed centrally. You can also segment your networks with a global distributed firewall to restrict access to instances.

- Firewall Rules Logging lets you audit, verify, and analyze the effects of your firewall rules.

- VPC Service Controls extend the perimeter security to manage Google Cloud services by preventing access from unauthorized networks.

Application Security

When building an application or API on the cloud, you are responsible for the application's security, including scanning and testing. Adopt practices such as these:

- Allow and deny traffic based on authentication and authorization of the user.

- Use or implement services to block bot and fraudulent users from your website.

You can protect your Internet-facing applications against attacks by using Web App and API protection (WAAP) solutions. This solution is a combination of:

- Cloud Load Balancing: Provides automatic defense against Layer 3 and Layer 4 DDoS attacks.

- Cloud Armor: Filter incoming web requests by geography or a host of L7 parameters like request headers, cookies, or query strings.

- reCAPTCHA Enterprise: Provides protection against bots and fraudulent users.

- Apigee API Gateway: Protects API backend by throttling API traffic against DDoS attack and controls access to APIs with OAuth, API key validation, and other threat-protection capabilities.

Software Supply Chain Security

Securing your software requires establishing, verifying, and maintaining a chain of trust, to establish the provenance or origin trail of your code, via attestations, generated and checked throughout your software development and deployment process. Open source SLSA (Supply Chain Levels for Software Artifacts) is an end-to-end framework for supply chain integrity that you can adopt incrementally to increase your security posture.

In Google, the Cloud Binary Authorization service establishes, verifies, and maintains a chain of trust through attestations and policy checks across different steps of the SDLC process.

- Code: Use Open Source Insights to identify dependencies, security advisory, and license across open source code.
- Build: Cloud Build captures another set of attestations (tests run, build tools used, etc.) that add to your chain of trust.
- Test and scan: Complete build when stored in Artifact Registry is automatically scanned for vulnerabilities.
- Deploy and run: Binary Authorization verified for authenticity and deploys when attestations meet organization policy. It even continuously validates conformance to the policy after deployment.

Data Security

Data security is a shared responsibility between you and the cloud provider. The cloud provider offers some capabilities built into the infrastructure such as data encryption at rest and in transit, whereas you are responsible for your applications' data security. This includes secure key and secret management, finding sensitive data, enforcing controls, preventing exfiltration, and preventing data loss.

Google Cloud offers data encryption at rest and in transit with the option to encrypt data in use using Confidential Computing. If you need the data to be encrypted via your own keys, you can bring your own key (CSEK), use Google's managed Key Management Service (KMS), use a hardware security module (HSM), or use an external key manager (EKM). Data Loss Prevention (Cloud DLP) helps discover, classify, and protect sensitive data.

Identity and Access Management (IAM)

IAM requires securely managing the user life cycle and application access, including authentication of the user and authorization of those users to appropriate services.

In Google Cloud, Cloud Identity is the IdP that provides the authentication options. It stores and manages digital identities for cloud uses, and it also provides two-step verification and SSO integration with third-party identity providers such as Okata, Ping, ADFS, and Azure AD.

Once authenticated, Cloud IAM provides the authorization (*who* can do *what* and *where* on Google Cloud) by providing fine-grained access control and visibility for centrally managing cloud resources. IAM policies manage access control for Google Cloud resources, and IAM Roles help set fine-grained permissions.

BeyondCorp Enterprise enacts a zero-trust model for access to your applications and resources. No one can access your resources unless they meet all the rules and conditions codified in per-resource access policies.

Endpoint Security

Endpoint security is critical for protecting users and access. You need to make sure you apply patches, prevent compromises, and manage user devices, including the policies that define which device has access to which resources in your application or projects.

Safe Browsing or Web Risk API: Lets client applications check URLs against Google's constantly updated lists of unsafe web resources. With Safe Browsing you can:

- Check pages against Google's Safe Browsing lists based on platform and threat types.
- Warn users before they click links in your site that may lead to infected pages.
- Prevent users from posting links to known infected pages from your site.

Device Management: To ensure corporate data is controlled, Device Management lets you administer mobile devices, such as smartphones, tablet computers, laptops, and desktop computers that are associated with your organization.

Security Monitoring and Operations

From a security operations (SecOps) perspective, you need to prevent, detect, respond to, and remediate threats in the cloud. In Google Cloud you can achieve this using these features:

- Security Command Center: Continuously monitors your Google Cloud environment for misconfigurations, detects threats and malicious activity, and helps maintain compliance. More on Security Command Center at https://cloud.google.com/security-command-center/docs/concepts-security-command-center-overview.
- Audit Logs: Cloud Logging offers audit logs that record administrative activities and accesses within your Google Cloud resources. Audit logs help you answer "who did what, where, and when?"

- Access Transparency: Logs record the actions that Google personnel take when accessing customer content.
- Cloud IDS: Cloud Intrusion Detection System provides managed, cloud-native network threat detection from malware, spyware, and command-and-control attacks.

Governance, Risk, and Compliance

Google Cloud is compliant with major security certifications such as PCI DSS, FedRAMP, HIPAA, and more. Google Cloud products regularly undergo independent verification of their security, privacy, and compliance controls, achieving certifications, attestations, and audit reports to demonstrate compliance.